Turkish Folk Music between Ghent and Turkey

Transcultural Music Studies

Series Editor: Britta Sweers, University of Bern

Founding Series Co-editor: Simone Krüger Bridge, Liverpool John Moores University

Transcultural Music Studies publishes monographs and edited collections on contemporaneous explanations surrounding the nature of music and human beings in a (post-)global world. Books in this series encompass a comprehensively wide selection of subject matters alongside a shared interest in fieldwork – physical, virtual, historical – and its complex challenges and fascinations in a postcolonial age. Topics include music's use in social, collective and psychological life; musical individuals; music in globalization and migration; music education; music, ethnicity and gender; and environmental issues.

Published

Bikutsi
A Beti Dance Music on the Rise, 1970–1990
Anja Brunner

Cultural Mapping and Musical Diversity
Edited by Britta Sweers and Sarah Ross

Provincial Headz
British Hip Hop and Critical Regionalism
Adam de Paor-Evans

The Lifetime Soundtrack
Music and Autobiographical Memory
Lauren Istvandity

Turkish Folk Music between Ghent and Turkey

Context, Performance, Function

Liselotte Sels

eQuinox

SHEFFIELD UK   BRISTOL CT

Published by Equinox Publishing Ltd.

UK: Office 415, The Workstation, 15 Paternoster Row, Sheffield,
      South Yorkshire, S1 2BX
USA: ISD, 70 Enterprise Drive, Bristol, CT 06010

www.equinoxpub.com

First published 2021

Published with the support of Ghent University and AP University College Antwerp.

GHENT UNIVERSITY   **Royal Conservatoire Antwerp**   **AP** | ARTESIS PLANTIJN HOGESCHOOL ANTWERPEN

British Library Cataloguing-in-Publication Data
A catalogue record for this book is available from the British Library.

ISBN-13 978 1 78179 948 2 (hardback)
         978 1 78179 949 9 (paperback)
         978 1 78179 950 5 (ePDF)
         978 1 80050 113 3 (ePub)

Library of Congress Cataloging-in-Publication Data
Names: Sels, Liselotte, author.
Title: Turkish folk music between Ghent and Turkey : context, performance, function / Liselotte Sels.
Description: Bristol : Equinox Publishing Ltd, 2021. | Series: Transcultural music studies | Includes bibliographical references and index. | Summary: "This book aims at exploring, describing, interpreting, and linking musical, contextual, and functional aspects of the manifestations of Turkish folk music in contemporary Turkey and the Turkish diaspora in the city of Ghent (Belgium)"-- Provided by publisher.
Identifiers: LCCN 2021005482 (print) | LCCN 2021005483 (ebook) | ISBN 9781781799482 (hardback) | ISBN 9781781799499 (paperback) | ISBN 9781781799505 (pdf) | ISBN 9781800501133 (epub)
Subjects: LCSH: Turks--Belgium--Ghent--Music--History and criticism. | Folk songs, Turkish--Belgium--Ghent--History and criticism. | Folk music--Belgium--Ghent--History and criticism. | Folk songs, Turkish--Turkey--History and criticism. | Folk music--Turkey--History and criticism.
Classification: LCC ML3615.8.G45 S45 2021 (print) | LCC ML3615.8.G45 (ebook) | DDC 782.42162/94350493142--dc23
LC record available at https://lccn.loc.gov/2021005482
LC ebook record available at https://lccn.loc.gov/2021005483

Typeset by S.J.I. Services, New Delhi, India

Dedicated to the Turkish people of Ghent

Contents

List of Figures and Tables   ix

Preface and Acknowledgements   xiii

Prologue   xv

Introduction: Turkish Folk Music in a Transnational Context   1

1   A Brief History of Turkish Music in Ghent   10

2   The Turkish Folk Music Network in Ghent   30

3   Turkish Folk Music in Theory and Practice   54

4   Turkish Folk Music Notation and the TRT Archive   80

5   Turkish Folk Music Events in Turkey and Ghent   96

6   Contextual and Musical Aspects of Performances in Turkey and Ghent   139

7   Case Study of a Song: 'Hüdayda'   169

8   Musical Functions in Turkey and Ghent   200

Conclusion: Looking Back and Forward   221

Notes   238

Bibliography   253

Appendix 1: Remarks on the Turkish Language 270

Appendix 2: Glossary of Turkish Terms 272

Appendix 3: Attended Events 277

Appendix 4: Visited Institutions and Consulted Informants in Turkey 280

Index 282

List of Figures and Tables

Figure 1.1: Main regions of origin of the Turks in Ghent   12

Figure 1.2: Turkish enclaves in Ghent (2011)   13

Figure 1.3: The Ibıdıklar in the 1990s   15

Figure 1.4: Turkish music and dance performances during the Gentse Feesten edition 1971   16

Figure 1.5: Celebration of 10 years De Poort–Beraber, 1993   19

Figure 1.6: Dr. Recai Özdil and his pupils in the venue of non-profit organization Özdil   21

Figure 3.1: *Tavırs* represented by Gazi Erdener Kaya (1995)   61–63

Figure 3.2: Location of the province Afyonkarahisar   72

Figure 3.3: Map of Emirdağ and its villages   72

Figure 3.4: Frequently used modes in Emirdağ   74

Figure 4.1: The first and last entry of the TRT archive in 2012, as kept in the Ankara Radyo House   82

Figure 4.2: Sample score of the TRT repertoire   83

Figure 4.3: The Ankara TRT Radio House, downtown Ankara   86

Figure 4.4: The Ankara TRT General Management, uphill Ankara   86

Figure 4.5: Accidentals used in the notation of Turkish classical and folk music   88

Figure 4.6: Sample of descriptive notation from the TRT repertoire   89

Figure 4.7: Sample of prescriptive notation from the TRT repertoire   89

Figure 4.8: Official TRT transcription of the song 'Uzun ince bir
yoldayım' by Aşık Veysel, with a regular 4/4 metre   93

Figure 4.9: Alternative transcription of the song 'Uzun ince bir
yoldayım' by Aşık Veysel, showing the greatly
versatile metre   94

Figure 5.1: Henna ceremony during wedding party in Nazareth   106

Figure 5.2: Circumcision party in Milas   109

Figure 5.3: Circumcision party in Rupelmonde   111

Figure 5.4: *Cem* in the newly opened Karabel *cemevi* in Beypınar   114

Figure 5.5: Collective *horon* dancing during the Lişer Yaylası
Soğuksu Şenlikleri   118

Figure 5.6: *Halay* dancing during the *seyran* in Wachtebeke   120

Figure 5.7: *Davul* dance accompanied by *davul* and *zurna* during
the Kaman *abdal* festival   123

Figure 5.8: *Mehterhane* during the cultural festival in Ghent   125

Figure 5.9: *Türkü* night in Türkü ve Şiir Evi Şafak Türküsü
(Bornova-Izmir)   127

Figure 5.10: Turkish evening in Muzikantenhuis (Ghent)   129

Figure 5.11: *Aşıks* in their association in Sivas   132

Figure 5.12: Suvermez night in Temse   135

Figure 5.13: Performance of the Ibıdıklar during the celebration of
50 years of Turkish migration to Belgium   136

Figure 6.1: Occurrence of the regional and transregional styles in
the attended events in Ghent   151

Figure 6.2: Occurrence of the Central Anatolian sub-styles in the
attended events in Ghent   152

Figure 6.3: Occurrence of instruments in Turkey and in Ghent   154

Figure 6.4: Example of ephemeral influence from Western classical
music (fragment)   160

Figure 6.5: Example of a jazzy interpretation of Turkish folk music
(fragment)   161

Figure 6.6: Example of a lightly popularized performance style
(fragment)   163

Figure 6.7: Example of a heavily popularized performance style
(fragment)   165

Figure 7.1: TRT score of 'Hüdayda'   171–175

Figure 7.2: Musical themes of 'Hüdayda'   176

Figure 7.3: Transcription of a performance of 'Hüdayda' on flute   177–178

Figure 7.4: Transcription of a performance of 'Hüdayda' with
acoustic bağlama and voice   179–183

Figure 7.5: Transcription of a heavily popularized version of
'Hüdayda' (Emirdağ)   184–187

Figure 7.6: Transcription of a heavily popularized version of
'Hüdayda' (Kırşehir)   189–194

Figure 8.1: Functions of Turkish folk music in Turkey   208

Figure 8.2: Functions of Turkish folk music (performances) in Ghent   218

Table 2.1: Turkish bands and artists performing at De Centrale
in 2013   47

Table 2.2: Muzikantenhuis's musical programming in 2013   49

Table 2.3: Mızrap's programming (March 2013–February 2014)   51

Table 4.1: Information on TRT scores   83

Table 6.1: Categorization by kind of event (use)   141

Table 6.2: Time-related aspects of the musical events   143

Table 6.3: Elements defining a performance style influenced by
Western classical music   159

Table 6.4: Elements defining a performance style influenced by
jazz music   162

Table 6.5:   Elements defining a lightly popularized performance style 163

Table 6.6:   Elements defining a heavily popularized performance style 164

Table 6.7:   Occurrence of the different performance styles   166

Table 7.1:   Pitch classes of Hüdayda-0   170

Table 7.2:   Musical form of Hüdayda-0   170

Table 7.3:   Pitch classes of Hüdayda-1   178

Table 7.4:   Musical form of Hüdayda-1   178

Table 7.5:   Pitch classes of Hüdayda-2   183

Table 7.6:   Musical form of Hüdayda-2   183

Table 7.7:   Pitch classes of Hüdayda-3   188

Table 7.8:   Musical form of Hüdayda-3   188

Table 7.9:   Pitch classes of Hüdayda-4   188

Table 7.10:   Musical form of Hüdayda-4   188

Table 7.11:   Intervallic structure of the different versions of
              'Hüdayda'   195

Table 7.12:   Formal structure of the different versions of 'Hüdayda'   197

Table 8.1:   Functions of Turkish folk music (performances) in
              Turkey and the diaspora   220

Preface and Acknowledgements

The idea of researching Turkish folk music in the diaspora in Belgium originated from a personal desire to understand, encounter, and engage with important but largely undisclosed parts of our everyday (inter-)cultural environment. This wish converged with a consciousness about the absence of academic and sociopolitical interest in the cultural production and consumption of (post-)migrant populations in Belgium. It is my hope that my research and this book in some way encourage or contribute to the debate inside and outside academia.

During the course of this project, I transformed from being a pianist and piano teacher with a background in "traditional" musicology to being an "ethnomusicologist". My in-depth study of a new music culture changed me as a musicologist, but also as a musician and a person. Studying Turkish – the gateway to my fieldwork – taught me new ways of thinking and communicating. In addition to the multifaceted academic outcomes and the rich aesthetic experiences that my work afforded me, this research project helped me forge a plethora of valuable relationships and sincere friendships. I consider this book a human account in the first place: it has been formed through contacts with people and articulates their genuine thoughts and actions. It is a tribute to the richness, diversity, and humanity of the culture of Turkey and its diaspora.

The idea of publishing this book was triggered by the launch of Equinox's new book series *Transcultural Music Studies* edited by Britta Sweers and Simone Krüger Bridge.[1] The collaboration with Britta and Simone was very agreeable and professional, and I wish to thank them and the two anonymous reviewers for their helpful and constructive feedback on my subsequent manuscripts. The proofreading of the last versions of my manuscript by Rachel Perfecto has been supported by the research office of my current employer, the Royal Conservatoire of Antwerp, and by the Ghent University Department of Art History, Musicology and Theatre Studies.

I am grateful for the assistance and guidance of numerous helpful and hospitable musicians, organizers, and other members of the thriving Turkish community in Ghent, as well as those in Antwerp and in Brussels. I was always warmly welcomed in the music cafés Muzikantenhuis, Beste, and Mızrap by their owners Mustafa Avşar, Fakı Edeer, and Metin Toplar, and their friends. Intercultural Centre De Centrale was another much-visited place where I was able to learn a lot about Turkish folk music.

In every village and city of Turkey that I visited, from the western to the eastern border, many people contributed to this project, each in their own way. I would like to explicitly thank a few people because of their great investment of time and energy. Martin Greve (Orient-Institut Istanbul) has given me warm and firm moral and academic support throughout the years. Abdürrahim Karademir (Ege University, Izmir) helped me plan a large part of my fieldwork trip. Kubilay Dökmetaş and the late Altan Demirel (Turkish Radio and Television) gave precious detailed insights in the way their institution worked. Other people providing extensive guidance and information during my fieldwork were Dursun Girgin (Dibekdere village), Mehmet Özkan (Suvermez village), Süleyman Can (City of Kırşehir), Halil Balcı (City of Rize), Ali Akyıldız (*Cem* Foundation of Sivas), Ferhat Uzunkaya (Ardahan University), Fatma Reyhan Altınay (Ege University), the Şatıroğlu family (Sivrialan), Zekeriya Kaptan (Sivas Cumhurriyet University), and many more. Numerous musician-informants helped me with insider information and musical performances: Doğan Karagöz and family (Aşağıpiribeyli), Ibrahim Ethem Yağcı (Muğla), Halil Rıfat Aydemir (Emirdağ), Yoksul Derviş and family (Karacalar), Adem Göçer and family (Kaman), Nazmi Köksal (Kırşehir), Ziya Aytekin (Şavşat), among many others. I have received countless gifts and experienced infinite hospitality. It would be impossible to name everyone who has supported me, but I have not forgotten them, and they are a part of this research.

Last but not least, I would like to thank my husband Sohrab Jabbari, without whom the fieldwork would have been much more difficult and less rewarding, and who has been my sounding board and biggest support throughout the whole research, writing, and publication process.

Sonsuz teşekkürlerimi arz ederim! Bedankt! Kheili mamnoun!

Prologue

We are in a tea house in a side street of the central square in Emirdağ, a small town in Central Anatolia, on a Wednesday afternoon in June. The building is surrounded by shops and cafés. One side of the venue is completely open towards the street, so that passengers are easily seduced into stepping in and having a sugared bitter Turkish tea. The decor and furniture are very sober, and the floor has gathered a thick patina over the years. Besides the basic equipment for preparing tea, the only notable object is Atatürk's portrait on the wall. A small group of men sit around a table. The centre of attention is music teacher Halil Rıfat Aydemir, playing the long-necked folk lute (*bağlama*). He performs a series of folk songs from the region, while his company – friends and acquaintances and regular customers – try to sing along. Although all attendees are very familiar with the repertoire, one of them stands out for his knowledge of the songs, and he takes the lead in singing with the others following him. Sometimes the *bağlama* player sings himself, but most of the time he leaves that task to his friends. They laugh when they make mistakes or forget the lyrics; they move and clap their hands, snap their fingers, and drum with their fingers on the table. Meanwhile, a lot of tea is consumed, and the headlines of the newspaper are consulted. Clearly, the joy of making music and their shared happiness are more important than the correctness or artistic quality of the performance. The playing may be a bit rudimentary, the singing out of tune, or the tempo unstable, but faces shine and everyone seizes the moment. It is a kind of rehearsal of the regional repertoire, both for the musician, who may soon perform the same music on more formal occasions, and for the attendees, who become more closely connected to the cultural heritage of their region.

A second scene takes place in the music café Muzikantenhuis ("Musicians' House") in the Belgian city of Ghent on a Friday evening in May. This heavily decorated, cosy venue is situated near a train station in a multicultural neighbourhood with many Turkish inhabitants. The café welcomes all kinds of musicians and music lovers, but any visitor will immediately notice the Turkish atmosphere. The furniture has a rustic character, and the walls and ceiling are covered with rural Anatolian utensils, kilims, wall paintings of Turkish poets and musicians, and shelves full of books. A small stage is installed and there is an open bar with some kitchen equipment. Friday evenings in Muzikantenhuis are reserved for Turkish music. Tonight, the stage is empty, but a small group seated around the table is playing music. The company consists of the owner of the café, Mustafa Avşar, and a few young male friends and acquaintances – regular visitors. Most of them are holding an instrument, forming an ensemble with two to three *bağlama*s, a guitar, a cajon, and a frame drum (*bendir*). All instruments belong to the café and are free to use. The line-up constantly changes, the ensemble grows and shrinks, and the role of lead singer is in turn taken on by different people. A bit later, three girls join the group and participate by moving along with the music, clapping their hands, and softly singing along. A few men sitting at another table also join in on the action by making requests for specific songs, which are subsequently sung by both tables in unison. The repertoire consists almost exclusively of Turkish folk music from the collection compiled and administered by Turkish Radio and Television, complemented by a few alternative protest songs in a similar style. While the succession of the pieces proceeds in an arbitrary manner, a voluminous folder with song lyrics provides some guidance. The setting appears to have an important social function: social ties are being strengthened. On another level, the sometimes insecure rendition of the songs and the attitudes of the active and passive participants in the performance strongly suggest that musical training is a major rationale underpinning this collective music-making session. Expansion of the repertoire, repetition of the lyrics, and practice of the performance styles and techniques are all elements of this training. On a deeper level, this shows the underlying value attached to the cultural patrimony of Turkish folk music, as a heritage to be cherished in the diaspora as much as – or perhaps even more than? – in Turkey.

Throughout my observation of these two informal social gatherings in different sociocultural contexts, one in Turkey and one in the diaspora, it becomes clear that both "musical events" share many similarities, while at the same time being very different. Similarities include the café setting, the presence of a small company gathered around a table, the familiarity, intimacy, and informality of the setting, the flexibility of the music-making group, the interaction and participation, the absence of competitiveness, the presence of a mild form of hierarchy between more and less experienced participants, and the innocent character of the social gathering (e.g., avoiding the consumption of alcohol). The most glaring difference between these settings is that they are taking place on different continents, 3000km from each other, implying that the first setting is embedded in the indigenous culture of the country while the second setting is bound to a diasporic minority community. However, several other differences can also be observed. While the musicians in Ghent relied on written cues, those in Emirdağ played entirely from memory; in Ghent, while the more distanced attendees vividly interacted with the players, in Emirdağ, no one away from the table showed any signs of interest in the action; while the entire active and passive presence in Emirdağ was exclusively male, girls and women were present in the music café in Ghent. A less tangible difference, possibly related to the different ages of the people involved, was the impression that the performers in the tea house in Emirdağ were more self-confident, more at ease, and more conscious (maybe even proud) of their role as representatives of their culture, while the performers in the café in Ghent gave the impression of being somewhat uneasy and inexperienced. Still more speculative but possibly meaningful is the feeling that the performers in Turkey welcomed me and my husband wholeheartedly, while the diasporic performers seemed rather introverted when I entered their intimate setting. Some of the observed differences are likely related to the peculiarities of the two settings; others will be accidental. The complexities of the ways in which Turkish folk music has manifested itself transnationally in the beginning of the twenty-first century will be explored and interpreted throughout this book.

Introduction: Turkish Folk Music in a Transnational Context

In our twenty-first-century world, shaped by transformative transnational processes (including migration, diasporization, and cosmopolitanization on different scales), conditions and contexts of musical performance are constantly changing, and musical forms are newly emerging and developing. Cultural and musical change, although sometimes radical and sudden, do not occur in a vacuum; factors influencing or shaping the processes and results of transformations can often be identified. Folk music provides an interesting case for the study of musical and contextual change. The development of Turkish[1] folk music is well-documented – at least since the establishment of the Turkish Republic – and provides rich material for study in the motherland as well as in the diaspora.

Folk music in the Turkish Republic has been subjected to strong transformative tendencies. A first tendency was an official, state-controlled, ideologically informed, top-down movement; a second, later tendency was a bottom-up, spontaneous, commercially motivated movement. The first involved a synthesis of the repertoire of rural (and urban) folk music with principles and procedures originating in the realm of Western classical music and its theoretical and practical framework. The second involved a synthesis of roughly the same repertoire with diverse elements and practices belonging to diverse "Eastern", "Western", and hybrid popular musics. While the first tendency was incorporated by various official state organizations, such as conservatoires and music schools, Turkish Radio and Television (TRT), and official music publishers and record companies, the second tendency manifested itself in the actions of private persons and companies.

The robust position of the genre of Turkish folk music (*Türk halk müziği*[2]) in contemporary Turkey, in public and official life as well as in private, depends in part on the legacy of Atatürk's cultural policy, which favoured the so-called "pure, unpolluted" music of the villages of Anatolia over the Ottoman cosmopolitan musical patrimony, which was strongly intertwined with Iranian, Arabic, and Byzantine musical traditions. The state-controlled collection of rural (and sometimes urban) folk songs and dances resulted in an official repertoire serving as a basis for the creation of a "modern" national Turkish music, following the aesthetic, educational, and institutional standards of Western Europe. Subsequently, many rural and urban institutions were created to disseminate the unified national repertoire on different levels. The state radio created models for the professional, contemporary performance of this repertoire, involving Western-derived ensemble playing and choral singing. The domesticated and standardized *bağlama* became an iconic instrument believed to represent the Turkish/Turkic soul.[3]

The result of these procedures was an ever-increasing standardization of musical content and style, and a continuously widening gap between the "modern", "official" concept of "Turkish folk music" and the living (or sometimes dying) traditions rooted in rural practice. In the 1970s, Turkish television joined the endeavours of the radio, and the TRT has ever retained its dominant position in the field of Turkish folk music, based on its combined efforts ranging from research and collection to performance and state media policy (Stokes 1992a: 40). In 1976, the first Turkish music conservatoire (Türk Musıkisi Devlet Konservatuvarı) was established in Istanbul. Ever since, it has been the most important training institution for professional Turkish folk musicians, subsequently employed in the TRT or various educational institutions (Stokes 1992a: 40; Markoff 1986: chs. 1–2, 7, 16; Stokes 1992a: chs. 1–3; Öztürkmen 1993: chs. 2, 4, 5; Tekelioğlu 1996; 2001; Balkılıç 2005; Değirmenci 2006; Karahasanoğlu and Skoog 2009: 62).

The circuit of commercial music, involving Arab- and Western-influenced genres, emerged in the 1960s and 70s, but could only start to flourish in the 1990s when the state monopoly on radio and television was abolished. Many of these popular songs employ elements from the traditional folk music repertoire and style (Tekelioğlu 1996: 206, 211–12; Karahasanoğlu and Skoog 2009: 62).

Since the 1960s, large numbers of Turks have been emigrating to Europe, establishing substantial diaspora communities in many European cities. The displacement and repositioning of the Turkish folk music repertoire (which was already transformed by the tendencies outlined above) in this different sociocultural environment entailed new musical and contextual changes. Of the more than 4.5 million Turkish citizens estimated to be living abroad, four-fifths reside in Europe. Germany accommodates by far the largest Turkish diaspora (approximately 3 million), followed by Bulgaria, France, and the Netherlands (Hecker 2006: 3; Küçükcan 2007: 87; Abadan-Unat 2011: xxii). Belgium accommodates approximately 240,000 people of Turkish descent (Noppe et al. 2018: 139). The city of Ghent, the province capital of East-Flanders with a population of ca. 250,000, accommodates a substantial Turkish population of at least 20,000 people (Verhaeghe, Van der Bracht, and Van de Putte 2012: 14). An estimated 8 to 10 per cent of the total city population has Turkish roots. This high percentage is not paralleled in any other urban environment in Belgium,[4] although it is surpassed by certain smaller mining towns in the Belgian province of Limburg (Heusden-Zolder 21%, Genk and Beringen 17%, Maasmechelen 13%) (Noppe and Lodewijckx 2012: 9).

Migration, in particular rural-urban and transnational migration, is a significant event with implications on different levels: personal, social, cultural, economic, and political. An individual or group is transplanted into a new context, which entails building up a fresh relationship both with the place of origin and the place of destination, and their respective sociocultural environment. A new web of social and cultural networks has to be constructed. Former identities, strongly intertwined with a specific sociocultural context embedded in a particular environment and locality, have to be reshaped in relation to the new, transnational context.

The specific conditions that have defined the present status and role of folk music in contemporary Turkey, and have created a parallel cultural context in the dense Turkish diaspora of Ghent, provide rich material for a transnationally oriented study of Turkish folk music in the early twenty-first century. This book aims to explore, describe, interpret, and link musical, contextual, and functional aspects of the manifestation of Turkish folk music in the defined transnational context.

State of the Art

Current musicology, ethnomusicology, cultural musicology, popular music studies, and related academic fields show a strong focus on themes such as migration, diaspora, minorities, urban music, popular music, transnationalism, globalization, and hybridization (Myers 1992: ch. 1; Nettl 2005: chs. 29–31; Rice 2010: 109–10; Pegg et al. n.d.). Migration-related musicological research became highly topical beginning in the 1990s and even more so after the millennium shift. While migration, diaspora, and transnationalism have been important topics in social sciences and economics for a few decades already, it has taken some time for the cultural repercussions of these phenomena to become the subject of study. The emergence of migration-related topics in (ethno-)musicology has run parallel with the development of the subfield of urban ethnomusicology, to which it has strong thematic ties: the forming of diasporic communities is a pre-eminently urban phenomenon, and diasporic music, like other urban musics, often shares the trait of hybridity (Kiwan and Meinhof 2011; Krüger and Trandafoiu 2014).

Although scholarly literature on music and migration/diaspora is quickly expanding, and several edited volumes have been entirely devoted to it,[5] there is still a vast domain of knowledge to be elicited and cases to be studied in detail. The music and musicking of (post-)migrants in Belgium is understudied, which sharply contrasts with the large academic interest in (post-)migrant – pre-eminently Turkish – music in neighbouring Germany.[6] The music and musicking of the Turks in Austria (Huber and Sigmund 2008; Sağlam 2008, 2009), Canada (Erol 2008; Markoff 2008), and the USA (Beken 2008; Heck 2011) are also the subjects of studies. In addition, Martin Greve has reviewed institutional aspects of Turkish music in Europe (Greve 2008, 2009).

Migration-related academic writings about the Belgian context are mostly historically, sociologically, demographically, medically-psychologically or politically oriented, addressing themes such as migration history, identity construction, integration and participation, the role of religion (Islam), educational or economic challenges and opportunities, marriage migration, migration policy, language use, and associations and non-profit organizations.[7] During the past 25 years, the subject of music and migration has been touched on in a handful of master's theses, focusing mainly on music education and, to a lesser extent, on media use.[8] More recently, Emma Bider (Ottawa) wrote an ethnographic master's thesis on tendé drumming by Tuareg women in Paris and Namur (Bider 2018), while Hélène Sechehaye (Saint-Étienne/ Brussels) completed her doctoral work *Des Gnawa à Bruxelles aux Gnawa de Bruxelles: analyse de pratiques musicales relocalisées* [From Gnawa in Brussels to Gnawa of Brussels: Analysis of Relocated Musical Practices] in 2020 (Hanáková, Dobbelaere, and Sechehaye 2016; Sechehaye and Weisser 2015).

Recent developments regarding Turkish folk music and its contextual aspects in Turkey have received relatively little, yet growing attention. Martin Greve discusses the different sorts of synthesis (*sentez*) that contemporary Turkish performers and composers developed, and provides analytical tools and categories. New instrumental and vocal timbres, novel instrumentations and ensembles, the use of harmony, and hybrids of different genres, including contemporary composition, are discussed in relation to the whole repertoire of Turkey's traditional musics (including folk music) (Greve 2017: ch. 4). Karahasanoğlu and Skoog (2009), Greve (2006: ch. 4), and Tekelioğlu (1996) identify and describe the mechanisms and results of musical hybridization (including popular arrangement) of folk music and other genres in Turkey. Usually, the approach is abstract, without detailed musical examples or analysis. Bryant (2005), Karahasanoğlu and Skoog (2009), and Üstüner, Ger, and Holt (2000) identify and describe new meanings and functions of folk music and being a folk musician in contemporary urban contexts in Turkey from the perspectives of identification, affiliation, and ritual. Kayhan (2014) analyses the implications of folk music performance in Istanbul's *türkü* bars (emerging in the 1990s) in relation to fields of tension between urban and provincial identities, popular-commercial culture and tradition, and party politics and bottom-up politics. Güran Aydin (2016) focuses on cultural memory in her exploration of the function and meaning of Turkish (folk) music as learned, performed, or consumed in specific spaces for different generations of Turkish migrants in Berlin.

Authors such as Martin Greve and Martin Stokes have identified gaps in the field of Turkish music studies. In *The Arabesk Debate* Stokes argues that "[t]he extent to which [the state] reforms have been absorbed, 'domesticated' and attained a degree of autonomy at local level is … an issue which has remained relatively unexplored" (1992a: 8–9). Twenty-eight years later, this statement is still valid to a great extent.[9] In *Makamsız*, Greve points to the lack of "serious debate in Turkey on [what he calls] an aesthetic crisis of Turkish music" (2017: 13), and to the need for unideological "research on musical styles and stylistic differences based on musical analysis" (2017: 255). He identifies several underdeveloped fields of study, such as "the perception and reception of music, music psychology, sociology of music, and … the didactic of music" (2017: 265).

This book addresses some aspects of these gaps, by means of a grounded, inductive approach, focusing on the ways in which Turkish folk music manifests itself musically, contextually, and functionally in contemporary Turkey and its diaspora. The multi-sited and transnationally oriented ethnographic outlook employed in this study allows for a richer and wider view on the subject, especially since it purposefully includes rural and small-town contexts to complement the urban perspective. The village and small town are inextricably tied to the transnational realities of Turkish-Belgian migration and diasporization, and they generate important narratives. Similar approaches are largely absent from the existing literature; a rare, early comparative attempt was made by Ursula Reinhard, who juxtaposed certain musical and contextual aspects in Turkey and Germany (Reinhard 1987). Like Alessandro Testa, I consider comparison and its "informative and, at times, even illuminating" power as "an irreplaceable methodological tool" besides and beyond the search for "commonalities and 'universals', allowing one to "theori[ze] about cultural differences and social transformations" (Testa 2019: 6).

Methodology

The study of a musical genre in a sociocultural context involves methods from diverse fields of knowledge and disciplines, such as music theory, the anthropology of music, and music sociology. The first two chapters of this book, on the history and network of Turkish folk music in Ghent, are the result of long-time immersion, participant observation, numerous informal conversations, semi-structured interviews with selected informants, internet searches, and a quest for scarce written documents, recordings, and pictures. Chapter 3, discussing aspects of the theory and practice of Turkish folk music, is written on the basis of Turkish- and English-language, specific and general, academic and non-academic books and articles,[10] complemented by ethnographic fieldwork including formal and informal interviews. Chapter 4 on Turkish Radio and Television is based on first-hand information obtained from interviews with TRT functionaries and employees, and official TRT documents, complemented by published sources. Chapter 7, on performance styles, involves musical transcription and analysis.

A major data collection method in Chapters 5, 6, and 8 consists of ethnographic fieldwork (more precisely: the ethnography of musical events), involving participant observation and interviews. The gathered data are interpreted through qualitative inductive (bottom-up) analysis, allowing the researcher to explore, describe, and interpret the subject in a thorough way.[11] The musical events studied in the mentioned chapters all qualify as "(non-educational) social events involving live performance of Turkish folk music". My definition of musical events, and their ethnography, is mainly based on Ruth Stone and J. H. Kwabena Nketia. Stone elaborates:

> The approach of studying music events … grounds ethnomusicological research in empiric reality. The basic unit of study is the music event, that interaction from which participants

derive meaning ... The approach attempts to account for meaning, through study of music process, approaching the sound
and behaviour components at corresponding levels of analysis.
(1982: 36)

For Nketia, a "musical event" is "any event that incorporates music. It
may be an artistic production or event such as drama or dance or a particular
form of cultural expression such as liturgy, ritual, a celebration, or a festival"
(1990: 84).

According to Stone, music(al) events engage performers as well as listeners, while the meanings and interpretations of both actors are equally
important. Like Stone, Nketia underlines the importance of contextuality in
ethnomusicological research:

> [T]he ultimate goal of the contextual approach is to facilitate the
> exploration of meaning in music beyond descriptive analysis ...
> Thus it is based on the assumption that ethnographic description,
> analysis, and interpretation of music events approached from the
> perspective of context should lead to a richer and more dynamic
> view of a music culture. (1990: 79)

I attended 46 musical events in two different research contexts: the Belgian
city of Ghent and its surroundings, and a range of rural, small-town, and urban
localities in Turkey.[12] An overview of the events can be found in Appendix 3.
The main period of fieldwork in Turkey was June and July 2011. The visited
regions were the Aegean Sea region (featuring the genre of *zeybek*), Emirdağ
(a town in the Central Anatolian province of Afyon, greatly represented in
Ghent), Kırşehir (a province in Central Anatolia), the Black Sea region, and
eastern Central and Eastern Anatolia (home to *aşık* music and Alevi music).
Following the first fieldwork period in Turkey, I transferred my methodology to the diaspora context, where I conducted fieldwork mainly between
August 2011 and June 2012 (and most intensively in April and May 2012). I
attended events in the city of Ghent and in its close vicinity (maximum 30km
distance) as well as events with commissioners and/or an audience living in
Ghent.[13] Participant observation of the musical events involved filling out
a structured observation form (specially designed for the purpose), making
video and audio recordings, taking pictures, and conducting semi-structured
interviews. Besides these core activities, I collected various kinds of relevant additional contextual information from private and public cultural and

educational institutions or informants. Appendix 4 provides a list of visited institutions and consulted informants in Turkey.

The Book's Structure

So far, I have aimed to provide some context and perspective in relation to the subsequent chapters by discussing the transformative top-down and bottom-up tendencies that Turkish folk music experienced throughout the twentieth century, pointing out the significance of migration for the chosen research field, reviewing related literature, and revealing the applied methods and concepts.

Our ethnographic journey starts with the historical context of Turkish labour migration to Belgium, and a brief history of Turkish music in Ghent, focusing on individual people and institutions, and identifying transnational or parallel evolutions. Chapter 2 makes a shift from the past to the present by zooming in on the current Turkish folk music network in Ghent and high-lighting its different roles (commissioner, performer, listener, educator) by defining them, explaining their modalities, and portraying their institutional and individual representatives. Furthermore, it describes central places that are essential to Turkish folk music performance and education in Ghent. The next chapter alters the perspective and sketches a (fragmentary) picture of what Turkish folk music in its modern, post-Atatürkian form entails, focusing on general musical characteristics, genres and forms, regional styles, traditional performers, and thematic content. Case studies include a description of the music of Emirdağ and an inquiry of the musical knowledge of the Turkish folk musicians in Ghent. Chapter 4 examines another facet of "modern" Turkish folk music in greater detail: the development, composition, and significance of the "official" Turkish folk music repertoire, collected and processed by state institutions. It provides insight into and a critical evaluation of the discourses and practices developed by Turkish Radio and Television, based on first-hand information.

The last four chapters of the book are thematically related to each other. They take a closer look at the 46 Turkish folk music events I attended during my systematic fieldwork in Turkey and Ghent. Chapter 5 starts with a brief overview of traditional occasions for folk music performance in Turkish society. Its second part consists of an ethnographic, comparative description and analysis of a meaningful selection of the attended Turkish folk music events, either common to both the homeland and the diaspora context, or inherent to only one of the two contexts. The contextual and musical aspects of the whole series of 46 events are examined in the next chapter in order to apprehend some of the properties, commonalities, and differences of the performance of Turkish folk music in the motherland and the diaspora in a systematized way. Chapter 7 further illustrates the traditional, academic, and popularized performance styles introduced in Chapter 6 by juxtaposing different manifestations of the popular dance song 'Hüdayda'. The song's TRT version is compared to four concrete renderings encountered during my fieldwork in Turkey. Chapter 8 reveals the functions of Turkish folk music (performances) in Turkey and Ghent as experienced and worded by performers, listeners, and commissioners. Additionally, it provides an outlook on the genre's status and value as articulated by the informants. The concluding chapter summarizes the contemporary meaning, contexts, actors, characteristics, and functions of Turkish folk music in the studied transnational context (also identifying some interrelations), before offering a view that goes beyond the concrete details and findings of the study to comment on the past, present, and future of this musical genre "between Ghent and Turkey".

Chapter 1

A Brief History of Turkish Music in Ghent

The city of Ghent accommodates an important Turkish presence with a vibrant cultural life. An estimated 8 to 10 per cent of Ghent's inhabitants have Turkish roots, a figure that remains unparalleled in any other major Belgian city. This particular context is also defined by strong historical and current ties with the West Anatolian town of Emirdağ.

Before venturing into the historical and present situation of Turkish (folk) music in Ghent (in this and the next chapter), a brief historical overview of Turkish labour migration to Belgium and Ghent sketches a more complete picture of the specific diasporic context at stake. The ensuing musical chronicle on the one hand makes clear which individuals and institutions played significant roles, and on the other hand points to tendencies with transnational traits.

Migration in Belgium, Flanders and Ghent

Twenty per cent of the population of the Flemish Region of Belgium (excluding Brussels) is of foreign origin – with or without the Belgian nationality. The Netherlands, Morocco, and Turkey are the main countries of origin, followed by Italy, Poland, France, Russia, Serbia and Montenegro, Spain, and Romania. Moroccans are concentrated in the Antwerp-Brussels axis; Turks in the mining cities of the province of Limburg, Antwerp, and Ghent. Limburg also accommodates large concentrations of Italians, while people with Eastern European roots are concentrated in Antwerp (Poles and former Yugoslavs) and Ghent (Bulgarians) (Noppe and Lodewijckx 2012: 1, 4–5, 8–9; Noppe et al. 2018: 135, 140).

This diverse picture originates in the particularities of Belgian migration history, involving bilateral agreements with a series of Mediterranean countries: Italy (1946), Spain (1956), Greece (1957), Morocco and Turkey (1964), Tunisia (1969), and Algeria and Yugoslavia (1970) (Martiniello and Rea 2003). These treaties facilitated official labour migration of workers to be employed in heavy sectors such as mining, textile factories, and the steel industry (Furniere 2014).

The first phase (1964–73) of the history of Turkish migration started with the bilateral agreement between Belgium and Turkey of 1964, allowing official labour migration. This agreement was reached during a period of economic growth (the "Golden Sixties"), during which the government and private companies were proactively recruiting foreign workers. This immigration "by invitation" was complemented by immigration on personal initiative, through chain migration by wives and children, other family members, friends, or fellow villagers, often using tourist visas, and through further migration from other cities in Belgium or Europe. In particular, the strong "ethnic network" of people from Emirdağ largely expanded in this way. Towards the end of the 1960s, economic growth stagnated and labour migration was discouraged by stricter and more extensive immigration procedures.

During the 1970s, due to the oil crisis in Western Europe, the Belgian economy declined substantially and the need for extra foreign workers ceased to exist. Subsequently, an immigration stop was proclaimed, which heralded the second phase of the migration history (after 1974). This measure subjected new labour migration to strict conditions, but at the same time the workers already present in Belgium were temporarily granted the opportunity to obtain a permanent residence and work permit, and illegally residing migrants were regularized.

Since the immigration stop, chain migration through family reunification (with the partner or minor children) became an ever more important way to enter Belgium. Family reunification was complemented by family formation, involving new weddings with partners from Turkey. Besides the channels of family reunification and formation, only students, trainees, researchers, or political refugees succeeded in getting a residence permit for Belgium. During this second phase, Turkish "ethnic enclaves"[1] developed out of the former looser "ethnic networks", in some cases involving the "transplantation" of almost complete Turkish villages or communities.

Since about 2000, the Turkish presence in Ghent has been transitioning from relatively closed ethnic enclaves towards a more interactive ethnic mosaic – characterized by less spatial segregation and fewer immigration marriages – while new migration flows have been taking place, originating from Middle and Eastern European countries, such as Poland, Slovakia, Romania, Bulgaria, and former Yugoslavia. A prognosis for the future is the further integration (or decreasing segregation) of the Turkish presence in the general urban fabric (Verhaeghe, Van der Bracht, and Van de Putte 2012: 126–29, 130–31).

Turkey, Bulgaria, and Morocco constitute the top three countries of origin of Ghent's (post-)migrant inhabitants. The most precise data on the number of people of Turkish origin are provided in the *Lokale Inburgerings-en Integratiemonitor, editie 2013: Gent.*[2] In 2013, the city accommodated 21,606 people with origins in EU candidate countries (approximately 99% of which concern Turkey[3]), equalling 8.63 per cent of the total population (Noppe 2014a; 2014d).

The largest part of the Turkish population in Ghent has origins in the province of Afyon (in particular, the town Emirdağ). Afyon's adjacent provinces in the north and east (Konya, Eskişehir, and Ankara) are also well represented. Besides this population originating in West and Central Anatolia, there is a significant presence from the Eastern Anatolian province of Elazığ, from the town Posof in the extreme northeastern province of Ardahan, and from Istanbul (mainly concerning former immigrants from the Balkans).[4] The regions of origin are shown in Figure 1.1.

Figure 1.1: Main regions of origin of the Turks in Ghent (Liselotte Sels)

The Turkish presence in Ghent is concentrated in a few neighbourhoods in the north and east of the inner city. The neighbourhoods Rabot, Tolhuis-Ham, Dampoort, and Ledeberg are indicated in Figure 1.2 (Verhaeghe, Van der Bracht, and Van de Putte 2012: 70).

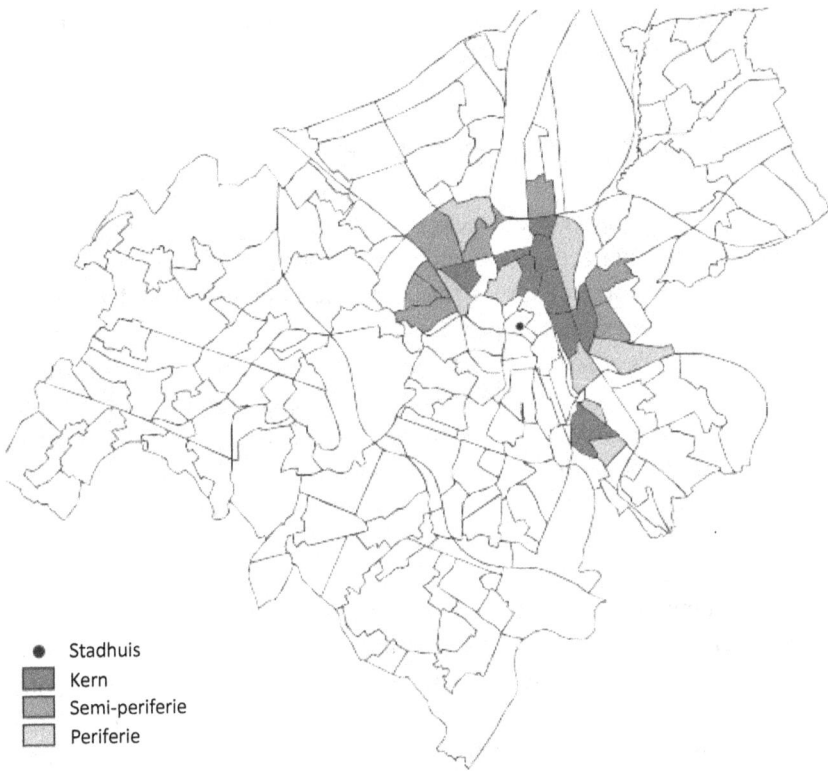

Stadhuis
Kern
Semi-periferie
Periferie

Figure 1.2: Turkish enclaves in Ghent (2011) (Verhaeghe et al. 2012: 70, reproduced with permission)

Klaartje Van Kerckem argues that there is an "ethnic boundary" between the Turkish and the Belgian (mainstream) population in Flanders and in Ghent. It has symbolic as well as social dimensions and is maintained by members of both groups (2014: 5). It "shape[s] Turkish Belgians' socio-cultural incorporation" and its "dynamics are central in understanding the … paths individuals take" (2014: 6). The ethnic boundaries are reflected in social boundaries, involving ethnic differentiation (residential segregation, enclave economy, institutional completeness, endogamy) and ethnic inequality (labour market inequalities, educational inequalities, political inequalities) (2014: 69). At the same time, the Turkish presence in Ghent possesses strong transnationalist traits, such as "reciprocity and solidarity within kinship networks", "political participation [in both countries]", "entrepreneurship … across borders", and "the transfer and re-transfer of cultural customs and practices" (Bauböck and Faist 2010: 11). The way in which Turkish music is incorporated into the sociocultural structure of Ghent is naturally related to these phenomena and tendencies.

The History of Turkish Music in Ghent[5]

The story of Turkish music in Ghent from its early beginnings until the present can be characterized as a complex development on different – sometimes seemingly contradictory – tracks. While throughout the decades and the successive generations, a progressing integration and growing connectedness with the host society has taken place, concurrently, a higher degree of self-sufficiency and a more independent position towards the same society can be observed, accompanied by an increasing and intensifying interaction with the country of origin. These trends connect to a general picture of gradual expansion, situated at diverse levels, and involving a rising quantity and quality of musicians, a growing variety of genres, styles, and sounds, and an overall increase in hybridity.

While some musicians have unfulfilled expectations towards the Turkish government, which provides little tangible support to musicians in the diaspora, it is common either to go knock on the doors of the local authorities in Ghent or the Flemish government, or to organize activities on their own initiative based on solidarity or sponsorship. Support from the City of Ghent only came about rather late, starting in the 1980s, usually in the form of direct subsidies to non-profit organizations[6] or to umbrella organizations uniting several (Turkish and non-Turkish) associations.

Pioneers[7]

The arrival of the Demirkaya-Çürükçü-Ateşli family, also known as "Ibıdıklar",[8] marked the beginnings of Turkish music in Ghent. Pater familias Isa Demirkaya (1930–2008) moved to Ghent in 1973 at the request of friends and fellow *Emirdağlılar* already living there. Although the Turkish community was still small, it needed musicians to play at the increasing number of wedding parties. Initially, these wedding parties were held in local cafés because of the lack of special halls catering to this type of event. Women usually celebrated at home. While initially tapes were played, the arrival of Isa Demirkaya and his family heralded the beginning of live music. The history of this musical family is both a success story and at times a bitter illustration of the ambiguous position of musicians in traditional Turkish society. On the one hand, they were needed to perform traditional regional folk music during celebrations and to offer an outlet during the weekends with their wide repertoire of Turkish light classical and folk music. On the other hand, they were considered as occupying a lower social position due to their association with the minority group of *abdals*[9] (see Chapter 3). After moving from Emirdağ to Ghent, the Ibıdıks' social role and position remained unchanged. Isa Demirkaya spent his first year abroad in unfavourable conditions. Nevertheless, he arranged for his family to travel to Belgium and since their arrival they have been steadily building a good reputation as a professional and reliable family of musicians (see Figure 1.3). The official invitation to play at the Gentse Feesten (Ghent's summer festival)[10] in 1984 was a step towards better living conditions and more recognition. For the first time in their career, the musicians were paid a decent wage for their performance. In 1988 and in 1994, the Ibıdıks were invited again to play at the same city festival (Audooren 1994: 50, 58, 80). This visibility in the public sphere and explicit recognition by a cultural organization opened doors to a positive reception and broader musical activity outside the restaurant and wedding circuit and beyond the Turkish community.

Figure 1.3: The Ibıdıklar in the 1990s (unknown photographer, permission granted by the family)

The 1970s and 1980s[11]

In the 1970s, opportunities to attend Turkish music performances in Ghent were limited. Tuning into international shortwave Turkish radio broadcasts was not always easy, and for most people a good radio was not afford-able. Live music could only be heard in some restaurants and cafés, first in Brussels, then in Ghent, and during weddings and later circumcision cele-brations. While Turkish concerts were sporadically organized in Brussels, in Ghent not much was happening at the time. An exception was the Day of the Migrant Worker organized during the Gentse Feesten in 1971 and in 1973, for which Turkish bands from Rotterdam[12] were invited at the initiative of Walter De Buck (see Figure 1.4).[13] During the 1980s, several Turkish bands from local communities as well as from Turkey were again included in the festival's programme.

Figure 1.4: Turkish music and dance performances during the Gentse Feesten edition 1971 (photograph © Julien Vandevelde, reproduced with permission)

In addition to the omnipresent Ibıdıklar, bands from Brussels or the Netherlands were regularly hired for parties and concerts. A band from Brussels named Ozanlar became very successful in the late 1970s and into the 1980s. The fact that at that time the scene was more lively in the cap-ital than in Ghent is witnessed by the existence of the Brussels recording studio "Stüdyo Gurbet" ("Studio Abroad"), where Ozanlar recorded many 45 rpm records. The band frequently performed in Ghent, not only for balls and wedding celebrations, but also in concert. Their repertoire was broad and included so-called *taverna müziği* – romantic, slow songs and dance music in Turkish and other languages. They had a typical eighties sound with a preference for electronic instruments (synthesizer, electronic drums, guitar and bass, with sometimes a violin added).[14] Vatan Orkestrası ("Homeland Orchestra") was a similar band based in Beringen, Limburg, at that time (the late 1970s).

In 1977, the first Turkish music lessons in Ghent were taught by Recep Çırık, a young teacher employed by the Turkish authorities in Belgium. His lessons mainly focused on Turkish language and culture, but they also included some music-making. The mandolin, initially used as a teaching instrument, was at that time thought to be better suited for children than the much more popular *bağlama*. In 1978 and 1979, Recep Çırık's choir of schoolchildren gave music and dance performances on the occasion of International Children's Day (23 April). Music lessons of a very different nature were offered at the Turkish mosque,[15] where children in the late 1970s were trained in azan singing and Quran recitation – even competitions were held.

In the early 1980s, the media slowly began to take more interest in Turkish music. Stekelbees, a children's theatre group, visited Recep Çırık's classes to record a Turkish song, which appeared – under the title "Turk Sarkisi" [sic] and without credits – on their 1981 LP *Ondersteboven* ("Upside Down") (*Stekelbees – Ondersteboven (4/4)* 2008; De Schepper 2011; "Stekelbees Ondersteboven" n.d.). Turkish music was broadcast during a television programme called *Paspoort* on the Dutch NOS channel and during *Nachbarn in Europa* on the German ZDF channel ("Paspoort (televisieprogramma)" 2014). In the 1980s, a few experiments with Turkish radio broadcasts occurred in Ghent, hosted in arts centre Vooruit and supported by Samenlevingsopbouw Gastarbeiders Oost-Vlaanderen (SGOV, Community Development for Immigrant Workers in East-Flanders) and Demokratik Halk Kültür Derneği (DHKD, Democratic People's Cultural Association). In the same period, music was becoming more accessible to the general public with the increased use of cassette tapes. Turkish music tapes from Turkey or Germany were brought into cafés and sold in local grocery or textile stores. Some musicians from Ghent would later record their own music tapes, usually in recording studios in Germany.

Aşıks *from Turkey*[16]

During the 1980s and early 1990s, *aşıks* or singer-poets (see Chapter 3) from Turkey visited the Turkish diaspora communities in Europe. They came to Europe on their own initiative almost every year. In a time without satellite television, a visit from an *aşık* was an excellent opportunity to hear interesting news and to spend an enjoyable evening. Big names visiting Ghent included the late Aşık Reyhani from Erzurum and the late Murat Çobanoğlu from Kars. Due to changing social conditions, the social role of *aşıks* in Turkey turned into a purely cultural role, with *aşıklık* cultivated as an art form. In 2009, the *aşık* tradition was added to the UNESCO List of Intangible Cultural Heritage ("Âşıklık (Minstrelsy) Tradition" 2009). Diaspora visits were recently revived by the Turkish Ministry of Cultural Affairs, but the socially critical element had disappeared completely. In 2010 and 2011, visiting *aşık* performances took place in Ghent once again, albeit in a highly officialized format, supported by Turkish (national) and Ghent (local) authorities ("Kültür-Sanat: Belçika'dan Aşıklar Geçti / 03/11/2010" 2010; Gök 2011).

De Poort–Beraber (1983–2002)[17]

Non-profit organization De Poort–Beraber,[18] founded in 1983, incorporated a local integration centre and a youth welfare centre (Kadanz) situated in the Sleepstraat, a Turkish neighbourhood. This pioneering organization, funded by the Flemish Community among others, and coordinated by Johan Devreese, launched numerous sociocultural initiatives and projects for a broad target group of migrants of different generations and genders. After having been active for almost 20 years, its activities, which focused on Dutch language lessons, welcoming newcomers, youth welfare work, training and employment projects, and integration activities, were transferred to the non-profit organizations Jong,[19] Kom-Pas,[20] and Intercultureel Netwerk Gent (Intercultural Network Ghent).

The musical activities of teacher Recep Çırık found a framework in De Poort–Beraber as well. One of the partnership projects was an event organized on International Children's Day (23 April) in 1985, involving a children's choir performing children's and folk songs, and traditional Turkish folk dances. For some years, the tradition of holding this event on 23 April was upheld, while other music and folk dancing events were organized and bands from Turkey were invited. In 1987, an anti-racism event was organized that included performances by Turkish and Moroccan bands (Amsab-ISG,

Sound and Image Collection n.d.b). An ambitious project took place in 1991, the year commemorating the 750th birthday of mystical Turkish poet Yunus Emre (Halman 1991). Again, a youth choir was established, named Seda,[21] which performed mystical songs based on poems by Yunus Emre, accompanied by a *bağlama* ensemble conducted by Recep Çırık. All this took place within the framework of a play depicting the life of the mystic. This project involved many musicians and singers who would later assume important roles in the Turkish music scene in Ghent, such as Metin Toplar, Fakı Edeer, and the young singers Melike Tarhan and Bülent Gök. In early 1992, the performance about Yunus Emre was also brought to the mining city of Genk, Limburg. Afterwards, several other performances took place at various locations in Ghent. Other memorable events include the tenth anniversary celebration of the association with a multicultural festival in 1993 (see Figure 1.5) and a benefit night for the victims of the earthquake in Izmit in 1999 (Amsab-ISG, Sound and Image Collection n.d.a). De Poort–Beraber was co-organizer of several Turkish concerts, organized a lecture series on Turkish music and culture, and encouraged young people to participate in other artistic projects (Devreese 1991: 36–37; 1992: 49–51; 1993: 69–70).

Figure 1.5: Celebration of 10 years De Poort–Beraber, 1993 (Amsab-ISG, Blijven Plakken, collection of Johan Devreese, reproduced with permission)

Dr. Recai Özdil[22]

Although music and *bağlama* lessons were sporadically organized in the 1980s, mainly at De Poort–Beraber and sometimes at Türk Ocağı ("Turkish Hearth")[23] in the Sleepstraat, only in the early 1990s were there indications of a greater dynamic that has continued until today. An important impetus was given by the months-long stay in Ghent of Dr. Recai Özdil (1927–2011), a neurologist from Ankara who had studied in Germany. He was also a researcher and collector of folk songs and a musical performer and lecturer at Turkish Radio and Television. In 1991, the retired doctor was invited by Metin Toplar to teach music to the local Turkish youth (see Figure 1.6). Like Recep Çırık, Recai Özdil also used the mandolin before switching to the *bağlama*. In 1992, non-profit organization Özdil–Turks Muziek- en Kultuurcentrum (Özdil–Turkish Music and Culture Centre) was founded. As was the case with De Poort–Beraber, the association engaged a number of Belgian people. Lucien Posman, a composer and teacher at the Royal Conservatoire of Ghent, conducted the association's women's choir, and the late Veerle Donceel took care of administrative duties. In addition to Metin Toplar, who was responsible for the organization's artistic and educational workings after the departure of Dr. Özdil, Tuğrul Yücesan and Mustafa Avşar were also involved. The choir Çıtı Pıtı included both Belgian and Turkish women and performed Turkish as well as Flemish folk songs, accompanied by an ensemble of young Turks playing the *bağlama*. The choir, and later also the instrumental ensemble, gave concerts at several locations throughout the city, including the large hall of the Conservatoire. In 1992 and 1993, they performed during the Gentse Feesten (Audooren 1994: 70–76). In 1994, the non-profit organization Özdil organized an ambitious concert together with the Stedelijk Migrantencentrum (Municipal Migrant Centre) and the Ghent chapter of Willemsfonds. The concert, which took place in the Lakenmetershuis (Vrijdagmarkt), featured important folk music stars Neşet Ertaş (1938–2012) and Talip Özkan (1939–2010).

After some organizational troubles, the association's activities eventually came to a halt. Intercultureel Ontmoetingscentrum (Intercultural Meeting Centre), established by the Ghent city council, took over many of Özdil's ideas and activities. Still, the founders and stakeholders of this small but influential association were to establish new bottom-up initiatives at a later stage, such as Mızrap and Tını. As a cultural centre, Özdil stimulated the Turkish music scene and associations in Ghent. An entire generation of young people learned to play the *bağlama* and experienced their first stage performances there. Quite a number of them are still (semi-)professionally involved with music. The Ghent-Turkish women's choir remains a unique phenomenon in Ghent's history to the present day.

Figure 1.6: Dr. Recai Özdil and his pupils in the venue of non-profit organization Özdil (photo by the late Hacı Halil Çekiç, belonging to Metin Toplar, reproduced with permission)

Intercultural Centre De Centrale[24]

The Municipal Migrant Centre (Stedelijk Migrantencentrum) (1991–2000), the forerunner of the current Municipal Integration Department (Stedelijke Integratiedienst), responded to many developments in the field and to the initiatives of Özdil, De Poort–Beraber, and other organizations. Although subsidies for non-profit organizations were rather limited, the city established its own sustainable project with support from the Flemish Community. In 1994, the Intercultural Meeting Centre (Intercultureel Ontmoetingscentrum) was opened in the former offices of an old power station centrally situated in one of the city's Turkish neighbourhoods. The official opening took place in March 1995. The centre began on a small scale, offering some rehearsal rooms, an office, and a café. Attila Bakıroğlu and Jos Lootens ran the place, also programming concerts and organizing courses (which they continue to do 25 years later). The centre was renamed De Centrale in 2000, when the upgraded "Basement room" and "Turbine hall" began to be used for concerts.

In the first years, most concerts were held either in the small cafeteria or in diverse external locations; focus was placed on Turkish concerts and more specifically on Turkish folk music. Later, this initial focus was complemented by North-African and crossover music as well as Turkish and other "world" pop and rock music. In the beginning, concert organizers frequently interacted with and sought input from migrant communities and Turkish non-profit organizations, such as Anadolu Kültür Derneği (AKD, Anatolian Cultural Association), Kardelen, and umbrella organization FZO-VL (Federatie van Zelforganisaties Vlaanderen: Federation of Self-Organizations in Flanders) (Vanparys 2002). In addition, a cross-border partnership was established with Külsan, a Turkish music organization from Amsterdam. Through shared efforts in programming and practical organizational matters, it became possible to take on more ambitious projects, such as organizing a concert by well-known Alevi artists Arif Sağ and Musa Eroğlu in October 1997 at De Bijloke music centre ("Kosten Concert Intercultureel Ontmoetingscentrum (19/01/1998)" 1997). Other big names featured in concerts during the early years are classical musician Kudsi Ergüner, Alevi folk musician Ali Ekber Çiçek (1935–2006), and folk singer Belkis Akkale (De Clerck 1999). From 2006 onwards, programming at De Centrale began to expand towards urban genres, Romani, and experimental music as part of the Istanbul Ekspres festival that was organized in 2006, 2009, 2010, and 2013 in cooperation with the Vooruit arts centre and annually in November since 2014 in partnership with the Handelsbeurs concert hall. In February 2016, De Centrale organized its first Bağlama Festival, followed by a second and third edition in 2017 and 2019 in collaboration with Istanbul Technical University–Turkish Music State Conservatory and Muzikantenhuis Gent.

In addition to programming concerts, De Centrale hosted many music-educational activities. The first *bağlama* lessons were given by Metin Toplar as an extension of his lessons taught at Özdil and by Mahir Tezerdi from Antwerp. Toplar succeeded for the first time in establishing a girls' ensemble. His successor, Iskender Arıcı, is the current *bağlama* teacher at De Centrale. In addition to *bağlama* lessons, *darbuka* (goblet drum) and Eastern music ensemble lessons were organized as well. Throughout the years, these lessons have reached a broad public, mainly consisting of children and young people of Turkish origin. However, these lessons also suffer much more than regular Western music lessons in music academies from a lack of continuity. Many Turkish pupils drop out fairly quickly without progressing to the advanced classes.

In addition to weekly lessons, workshops and masterclasses are held from time to time, taught by artists from abroad who are visiting for a concert or festival. Workshops and masterclasses for *bağlama* have been given by Deniz Güneş, Musa Kurt, Erhan Uslu, Çetin Akdeniz, Barış Güney, and Erdal Erzincan; for percussion by Mısırlı Ahmet and the Yarkın brothers; and for singers by Mercan Erzincan.

Throughout the years, De Centrale built a solid basis within the international Turkish music scene. Their regular and varied programming of Turkish music has been unique in Flanders. The audience reached by these musical offerings mainly consists of Turkish people and is not limited to Ghent. Certain events traditionally appeal to a mixed audience of Turkish and Belgian people, such as the Turkish *fasıl*[25] nights, offering light classical Turkish music and Turkish mezzes, and the Istanbul Ekspres festival. Turkish classical music concerts appeal more to a Belgian public.

Mızrap

In 1998, the non-profit organization Mızrap was founded by three veterans of Özdil: Metin Toplar, Tuğrul Yücesan, and Veerle Donceel. Official documents of the organization listed the following activities: 1) meeting place for musicians and bands, including two resident ensembles, 2) monthly programming of Turkish and other music, 3) meeting place for children and youth, 4) workshops for schools and clubs, 5) and lessons in *bağlama*, *darbuka*, and Turkish folk dance. The organization was partially supported by project subsidies from the Flemish government and by the Impulse Fund from the federal government. Much attention was paid to promoting the organization through performances at events attended by a Belgian audience, such as the Gentse Feesten and the Patershol Festival. Belgian musicians and interested parties regularly visited the nicely decorated venue – a kind of *türkü* bar – at Sluizeken (Vzw Mızrap 1999), and cross-cultural partnerships were forged. A number of young Turkish musicians had formative stage experiences at this place. Following the tradition of its precursors, De Poort–Beraber and Özdil, Mızrap founded a choir, again with the young soloists Melike Tarhan and Bülent Gök, this time conducted by Mehmet Kayık, a professional musician. After a hiatus of several years due to financial difficulties, during which many of those involved in Mızrap joined a similar initiative, Muzikantenhuis (Musicians' House) started by Mustafa Avşar, a new Mızrap non-profit was founded at the same location in 2013. From 2013 to 2015, performances were held several nights a week at this *türkü* bar, featuring mostly Turkish folk music and *özgün müzik*,[26] but also other styles and genres. In 2015, the venue faced definitive closure.[27]

Anka and Muzikantenhuis[28]

In 2002, Mustafa Avşar opened the first Turkish music store in the Benelux countries. Before then, people personally imported musical instruments, cassettes, and CDs from Turkey or Germany, or bought them in non-specialized stores. In his music store, named Anka ("phoenix"), Mustafa sold audio and video tapes, CDs, DVDs, Turkish instruments and their strings and plectrums, Turkish instrument methods, novels and poetry, traditional costumes and jewellery, movies, and more. His clientele consisted of both Turks and non-Turks, from Ghent and (far) beyond. Anka, easily accessible to Turkish customers thanks to its location in the centre of the Turkish neighbourhood and close to a railway station, was a catalyst for many young Turks to learn to play the *bağlama*. Partly due to the collapse of the CD market and problems emerging in the international trade of instruments (damaged instruments, high purchase prices, late deliveries, etc.), the business turned out to be no longer profitable and was closed in 2012.

Meanwhile, in 2007, Mustafa had initiated a second, parallel project in the adjoining venue. Because of the need for a meeting place for all musicians from Ghent – at that time a vacuum – he established a music café with the name Muzikantenhuis–Tını vzw (Musicians' House–Tını ("sound, timbre") non-profit organization). The rather conservative policy on alcohol – which differs from some other similar venues – was well received by a family-oriented Turkish audience, while a "Belgian" public was attracted by its broad programming and cross-border collaborations. Although certain Turkish customers may have preferred a somewhat more explicitly "Turkish" atmosphere, like that of Mızrap (see above) for instance, Mustafa Avşar's sociocultural project can be considered a successful example of cultural exchange. Thanks to relentless personal effort and despite minimal subsidies, Muzikantenhuis has grown into a true "musicians' house", where musicians and listeners with different cultural backgrounds meet. In addition, the music café proved to be a breeding ground for many young talented musicians, who later found professional success. Singers such as Bülent Gök and Kürşat Zengin, and *bağlama* players such as Bekir Gürbüz and Bülent Köken, basically grew up in the womb of Muzikantenhuis and are now established names in the Turkish folk and folk-pop music scene in Ghent, Flanders, and beyond.

Festivals and Other Events

The non-profit organization Posküder, an acronym for Posof Kültür Derneği (Posof Cultural Association), organized a major annual event for many years in the provincial domain of Puyenbroeck in Wachtebeke, a rural location approximately 20km from Ghent, supported by FZO-VL (Federation of Self-Organizations in Flanders) and sponsored by local Turkish retailers and firms. At this annual *seyran* (literally translated as "promenade" or "picnic"), described by Posküder as a "folkloric event" or "intercultural folk festival", people could attend live performances of traditional and popularized Turkish folk music, enjoy Turkish dishes, join in a tombola, and have their children entertained. Every year, hundreds of people from the Posof diaspora from Belgium and neighbouring countries attended the event ("Jeugdhuis Posküder: Gent Posof Culturele Vereniging" 2013). In 2014, the event celebrated its fifteenth and final edition.

Similar to this event, the Emirdağ diaspora has organized an *Emirdağ Kır Şenliği* (Emirdağ rural festival) at the same location. This event, which was organized four times between 2013 and 2017 by the Belçika Emirdağ Birliği (BEB, Belgium-Emirdağ Union) in cooperation with the Turkish Union of Belgium and sponsored by Turkish companies, featured live performances by a range of artists with roots in Emirdağ in addition to folk dance performances and a variety of regional dishes.

The cultural festival (*kültür şöleni*) at Ghent's Vrijdagmarkt in October 2011, supported by the Turkish Union of Belgium, the City of Ghent, and local Turkish retailers and firms, also fits in this festival tradition. Organizing major outdoor summer festivals is a cultural tradition directly derived from Turkey, where every self-respecting city or village hosts its own annual festival with live music from local or other artists, folk dances, and regional dishes, either in the centre of the city or in an open area in nature. Emirdağ organizes its own festival each year as well, aptly named *Gurbetçi Festivali* (Migrant Festival). In this way, migrants visiting their region of origin during the summer holidays get the opportunity to enjoy music from their region in a formal festive framework.

Charity happenings are a different type of event with the goal of raising money for a particular village. In April 2012, a "Suvermez night" was organized at a local hall in Temse (30km from Ghent) in benefit of the Suvermez village in Emirdağ. The live performances by musicians from Suvermez, Emirdağ, and beyond attracted *Suvermezliler* from Belgium and abroad.

Genres and Styles

The Turkish music scene in Ghent has gradually evolved into a true melting pot, with the "Turkish" genres situated on one side of the continuum and the "Western" genres on the other side, but where increasing flexibility and hybridity are paramount.

Turkish folk music has remained a constant in the Turkish diaspora in Ghent throughout the years and decades. Especially with regard to weddings and circumcision celebrations, strongly linked to tradition and rituals, this genre was and is considered an essential part by all people involved (both the organizing family and its guests). Turkish folk music is also indispensable during different types of festivals, particularly those rooted in ritual. The way of performing the Turkish folk music repertoire has evolved significantly throughout the last few decades. Today, in most (non-academic and non-rural) contexts, a strong influence from pop music is present. The semi-electric *bağlama* with a built-in pickup, or even the real *elektrosaz*, has become standard, rather than the acoustic instrument. The guitar, though fundamentally at odds with the "microtonal" intervals of Turkish music, has become omnipresent, as have Western and "world" percussion instruments. The most profound influence on the sound and performance modalities of Turkish folk music and other genres was exerted by the keyboard or synthesizer. It includes samples of all relevant instrument timbres, many more than the ones available live, and allows musicians to simultaneously perform melody instruments and rhythm sections. The expansion of the folk music repertoire is another trend to consider. While in the past musicians performed the repertoire of their own region, thereby meeting the expectations of the audience, nowadays they are expected to cover a broad repertoire that stretches across all regions of Turkey.

Turkish classical music is much less prevalent than Turkish folk music, and in Ghent, it is played only by the Ibıdıklar in a light classical form and by the *ud* (classical lute) player Hilmi Kaçar. In the late 1970s, international dance forms such as the bolero, tango, and waltz became popular. *Arabesk*, a hybrid melancholic-nostalgic genre with a strong influence from Arab music, was particularly popular in the 1980s, as was the so-called *taverna müzik* (a light genre including a mix of various international influences), and *aranjman* (Turkish arrangements of Western popular songs). In the 1990s, more collaborations emerged between Turkish and non-Turkish musicians from Ghent, which resulted in several crossover projects that could be categorized as "world" or "folk" music. An important development since 2000 is the strong rise of Turkish- and Dutch-language pop and rap music.

Transnational Evolutions[29]

As one looks back on more than four decades of Turkish music in Ghent, many evolutions or trends appear to align strongly with developments in Turkey. Social changes in the (transnationally connected) Belgian and Turkish contexts have resulted in musical changes. The processes of modernization and cosmopolitanization have led to greater sociocultural openness and an expansion of possibilities.

Increasing openness can be observed in relation to ethnic, cultural, linguistic, and religious minority groups, as well as the position of women in society. Turkey is a politically and ideologically divided nation, with sometimes sharp contrasts such as those between Turks and Kurds, ultra-nationalists and moderate tendencies, Sunnites and Shiites (Alevis), and secularists (Kemalists) and Islamists. The music of cultural minorities such as Kurds, Greeks, Armenians, and Roma was censored or manipulated for a long time. Since the 1990s, greater openness allowed these cultural expressions to gradually (re-)assume their rightful place in Turkey's cultural landscape. This evolution was also noticeable in the diaspora. Today, Kurdish dance music has been fully integrated into Turkish wedding repertoires. Intercultural Centre De Centrale has followed this evolution by programming Turkish bands such as Kardeş Türküler, or Marsis, singing in other languages, and presenting music from minorities. The same applies to Alevi music (see Chapter 3), which for a long time was only played at private Alevi religious ceremonies (*cems*). In the 1980s, emancipation of Alevi music outside the *cem* house was facilitated by the efforts of the successful band Muhabbet, in which five great musicians of Alevi origin played together (Greve 2006: 360). Since then, Alevi music has formed an essential part of the folk music repertoire. In Ghent, perhaps even more than in Turkish cities, Alevi music is heard everywhere. The persistent integration of Alevi and Kurdish music in diasporic musical life resonates with the greater emancipatory possibilities, compared to the more restricted and politicized situation in Turkey (especially until the 1990s).[30]

This greater openness also resulted in a changed attitude towards music and musicians in general. In traditional Turkish society, music-making and, in particular, playing an instrument were for a large part reserved for professionals belonging to specific social groups, such as Alevis, *abdals*, or Roma.

Amateur music-making, occurring in specific social settings for particular occasions (e.g., celebrations in a family context or gatherings of friends), was usually confined to a cappella singing. Playing an instrument was less common for ordinary people, although many shepherds played the *kaval* (flute). In the 1970s, music and music-making became more positively evaluated. The establishment of the Turkish Music State Conservatory at the Technical University of Istanbul in 1976 – the first conservatoire offering Turkish folk and classical music – was a milestone. Although a large share of (semi-)professional musicians to this day still appear to be of Alevi origin, it is now acceptable for most Sunnites, especially in the cities, to be involved in music, both at amateur and (semi-)professional levels. This trend is paralleled in the diaspora.

In the past, a rather strict separation was customary between men and women during family celebrations such as weddings. Music was often played for men only, and if women were present, the musicians were hidden from their sight by means of a curtain. This practice was abandoned in the 1970s. In traditional Turkish society, women faced severe restrictions on music-making, with more limitations on playing an instrument than on singing. Male and female musicking belonged to separated contexts.[31] Certain vocal musical genres, such as lamentations (*ağıt*), lullabies (*ninni*), and henna night songs, were traditionally performed by women. A typical "female" musical instrument is the *def* (frame drum), which was sometimes played by women in private settings to accompany singing (Picken 1975: 147). Even though the restrictions have eased, many women still hesitate to sing in the presence of men. In Ghent, some girls used to be discouraged from participating in musical activities. Musically educated women invariably belong to the younger generations, in Turkey as well as in the diaspora. In Ghent, Melike Tarhan and Damla Kırdaş are the only women presenting themselves as singers.

Many other changes in the Turkish music scene in Ghent are in line with developments in motherland Turkey. Technological advances in the field of mass media on the one hand, and developments in electronic instruments and recording options on the other hand, have been crucial. Mass media, especially television via satellite dishes and later the internet, allowed people to remain permanently in touch with their country of origin, which meant that all the latest trends in the field of music could be closely followed. At the same time, the musical trends of their new country of residence became ingrained through Belgian radio and television stations.

Concluding Thoughts: Turkish Music in Ghent

While the story of Turkish (post-)migration in Ghent is gradually evolving towards a more inclusive and diversified situation, the musical evolution is marked by gradual expansion at diverse levels, involving more musicians, stronger musicianship, a growing variety of genres, styles, and sounds, and an overall increase in hybridity. Nevertheless, "ethnic boundaries" remain persistent and consequential. On the other hand, the transnationalist traits of the Turkish presence in Ghent can be seen as a (alternative) lever towards emancipation.

The element of transnationality is present in various ways and degrees throughout personal, collective, and institutional initiatives and developments in the Turkish music scene in Ghent. From the very beginning, the scene in Ghent was shaped by contacts with Turkey on the one hand – the Ibıdıklar, for instance, were purposefully invited to Ghent as musicians – and with other Belgian and European immigrant cities on the other hand – recall the bands from the Netherlands and Brussels coming to Ghent for concerts or other performances. Communication and mobility were multidirectional. Musicians from Ghent travelled to Brussels in the early days to perform in restaurants due to lack of opportunities in Ghent. Contact greatly intensified in the following decades. Not only are bands from Turkey regularly invited by De Centrale to perform at formal concerts, but they also often visit smaller associations after their concerts to give informal performances or lessons. In case of a shortage of players for specific instruments, a solution is provided by inviting musicians from another city or even from a neighbouring country. However, a musician only really means something in the Turkish diaspora if he has performed in Turkey's big cities and if he has appeared on several Turkish television shows. In other words, musicians live with one foot in Belgium and one foot in Turkey.

Many of the personalities and institutions featured in this chapter still continue to exert an influence on, or play an active role in, the present situation. The next chapter offers a more systematic view on the Turkish music network in Ghent, its central places, and its institutional and individual protagonists.

Chapter 2

The Turkish Folk Music Network in Ghent

In the diaspora context of Ghent, the Turkish presence and its musical land-scape have been unfolding and taking shape for more than 50 years, since the arrival of the first Turks in 1964 and the first Turkish musician in 1973. Today, the Turkish cultural and musical life in the city presents itself as ani-mated, diversified, and colourful. The Turkish folk music network more spe-cifically represents an important, even central, part of it. Turkish folk music commissioners, performers, educators, and listeners all play their role, often coming together at central places functioning as crossroads and attracting high densities of activities.

I borrowed the "role" concept from Ulf Hannerz, because I consider it a useful tool for shedding light on the ways in which Turkish folk music functions in the city of Ghent, and how these functions are embedded in the city fabric and urban social life. Hannerz writes that "urban social life ... is made up of situations[, with] individuals participat[ing] in these situations". An individual's "purposive situational involvement" is termed a "role". "[W]hen different individuals' overt behaviour in a kind of situation is fundamentally comparable, taking on some approximately standardized form ..., they can be said to perform the same role" (1980: 100–101). The notion of "central place" is also from Hannerz, indicating a "point where relationships converge" as a result of "the presence of a person or a set of persons who are interdependent with a large number of others" (1980: 91).[1]

The actors constituting the Turkish folk music network in Ghent assume the roles of *commissioner*, *performer*, *educator*, and *listener* – in a non-mutually exclusive way. For example, a person who organizes a Turkish folk music performance one day, thereby also being an audience member, can be a musician himself, giving *bağlama* lessons in another location the next morning, and performing in yet another public setting the next evening. In many settings, there is no barrier between performers and audience; one person can assume both roles during one occasion, switching smoothly from listening to performing.[2]

The Turkish folk music network is by no means an isolated phenomenon. It is evidently connected to or overlapping with other content-related networks in the same city (e.g., the Turkish popular music network; the "general" folk music network; the world music network), to other social networks within the same city (e.g., the Bulgarian presence; the total migrant and post-migrant presence), and to broader translocal networks beyond the artificial boundaries delineating the city of Ghent.

In the years between the start of the fieldwork and the publication of this book, many changes have occurred, in accordance with the fluidity of roles, relationships, and the entire network, as mentioned by Hannerz (1980: 270). In a time span of 12 years, new actors have entered the scene; peripheral roles have been developing into central roles within the repertory of a certain individual; new roles have been entering the repertories of other individuals; formerly tight relationships have been cut and new relationships have been emerging; formerly important, central places have been disappearing while new ones have been developing, and so on. Despite this fluidity, certain structures and characteristics regarding the Turkish folk music network's actors and places could be identified, as presented in the following sections.

Commissioners

The role of commissioner can be performed in an informal or a formal way, by private persons or institutions, by individuals or a group. My term "commissioner" unifies several shades of meaning such as "organizer", "employer", and "patron".[3] How someone "commissions" a musician can take on different shapes and can possibly be very informal; a person persuading a befriended musician to play a tune on a *bağlama* hanging on the wall of the restaurant where they are having dinner can also be considered a commissioner. A private commissioner can be a man inviting some friends to bring their *bağlama* to a dinner at his home, or it can be a family employing (paying) a Turkish folk music ensemble to play at the wedding party of a young family member. An institutional commissioner can be the owner of a music café inviting befriended musicians to play and sing (pro bono) to entertain his guests or employing (paying) a more well-known ensemble of Turkish folk musicians to do the same. It can also be a larger concert organization where different people are employed, inviting the same Turkish folk music ensemble (pro bono, or more likely, for a remuneration). An informal way of commissioning a musician can be a spontaneous phone call or ad hoc oral invitation during an appropriate setting, without the need for special preparations or particular conditions. In general, informal commissions are not paid, although sometimes an informal kind of remuneration is involved (e.g., free food or drinks). Many informal commissions are given by private persons, although it is not impossible that an institution gives the impetus. A formal way of commissioning can be a written invitation by email, giving details about the specific conditions and expectations regarding the performance and the modalities of the payment. Although many formal commissions have an economic component, the performance can possibly be pro bono. The most formal way of employing musicians involves using a contract. In this case, institutions are usually involved, although it is also possible that a private person formally commissions a musician.

These different types of commissioners play specific roles in the Turkish folk music network in Ghent. Four types of institutional commissioners (local authorities, sociocultural organizations, translocal umbrella organizations, and other sociocultural institutions) emerge, as well as three kinds of non-institutional commissioners (community leaders, Turkish families, and other persons with an affinity for Turkish folk music).

Institutional Commissioners

Local authorities functioning as commissioners include the City of Ghent, municipalities of nearby cities and towns, and the province of East-Flanders. An example of a major engagement by the City of Ghent was the organization and support of a one-day cultural festival featuring Turkish artists and bands. The event took place on a central public square (the Vrijdagmarkt [Friday Market]) and was facilitated through the provision of large-scale infrastructure, such as a podium and stalls for information, food and drinks. The mayor of Ghent, in addition to some city councillors, participated in the event by giving an introductory speech, thereby granting an official character to the event. Elsewhere in East-Flanders, a multicultural festival called Loka Tierra organized biennially by the City of Lokeren[4] also invites Turkish (folk) musicians at times. In 2008, Tuğrul Yücesan was programmed at the festival; in 2012, the Ibıdıklar and Kürşat Zengin performed; in 2014, Mustafa Avşar played; and in 2016, Melike Tarhan was featured – all Turkish musicians residing in Ghent. In 2009, the City of Ghent and the province of East-Flanders, supported by Ghent University, organized a fair with a focus on Turkey and the region of Izmir. In this context, different events involving Turkish music and dance took place in the Flanders Expo exhibition hall and various other locations in the city ("Izmir, Turkije: Fascinerend Veelzijdig" 2009). In celebration of 50 years of Turkish migration to Belgium in 2014, the number of events supported by the local authorities increased exponentially. Turkish folk music-related activities included a kick-off event involving a performance of a Turkish singer from Ghent, a big concert of Turkish star Şevval Sam, a spring festival called *Hıdırellez*[5] in Wachtebeke, an intercultural musical puppet-play about Turkish migration to Ghent, a CD launch of an intercultural Turkish-Belgian ensemble, a concert of a Turkish folk music choir composed of Turkish singers from the motherland and the diaspora, and a project in which musicians from Flanders travelled to Istanbul to set up a concert with Turkish musicians.

A wide variety of sociocultural organizations constitutes the second type of institution, emphasizing either the social or the cultural aspect. The largest institutional actor in the Turkish folk music network is Intercultural Centre De Centrale, which depends on the City of Ghent. In addition to this large player, there are also various smaller organizations that are in many cases subsidized or at least officially recognized by the City. Muzikantenhuis, a non-profit organization in the form of a music café, has been functioning as an important actor in the Turkish folk music network for many consecutive years. A particular example of a musically active non-profit organization is Posküder, which has organized an annual *seyran* in Wachtebeke for several years (see Chapter 1), in addition to other activities regularly involving Turkish folk music such as a girls' evening or *türkü* evenings. Their activities are primarily oriented towards young people with roots in the northeastern Anatolian town of Posof. Student clubs constitute another category of institutional actors in the Turkish folk music-related network in Ghent. In contrast to the aforementioned organizations, their activities are not specifically music- or culture-oriented. Turkish student clubs Ozon and Flux have both (separately) organized a kind of Turkish karaoke evening, which also involved live performances of Turkish folk music.

A third type of sociocultural organization are translocal umbrella organizations such as UTV (Unie van Turkse Verenigingen: Union of Turkish Associations), TUB (Turkse Unie van België: Turkish Union of Belgium), FZO-VL (Federatie van Zelforganisaties Vlaanderen: Federation of Self-Organizations in Flanders), and CDF (Çağdaş Dernekler Federasyonu: Federation of Progressive Associations). All of them unite different associations oriented towards the Turkish community and have offices in Ghent.

These umbrella organizations or their member associations regularly organize or support the organization of events related to Turkish folk music. Subsidized by the Flemish Community, UTV is based in Antwerp and solely accommodates organizations oriented towards a Turkish public. Their radius of action is oriented towards Antwerp and Brussels and towards social and historical activities. The headquarters of TUB is situated in Beringen (one of the former mining towns in Limburg). According to their website, the organization is supported by different ministries. They unite diverse Turkish associations and develop activities in diverse fields. In 2020, they adopted the new name of UAV (Unie van Actieve Verenigingen: Union of Active Associations). FZO-VL is subsidized by the Flemish Community and based in Ghent and Brussels. Its member organizations are ethnoculturally diverse. Subsidized by the Flemish Community, CDF went bankrupt in 2018 but was based in Ghent and accommodated about 70 member organizations, not only Turkish but multifarious, ethnocultural minority associations.

Turkish folk music sporadically figures in the programming of a variety of other sociocultural institutions. Arts centres or concert halls such as Vooruit or Handelsbeurs sometimes give room to Turkish folk music performances, but in a rather peripheral way. The genre is integrated into the programming of certain festivals organized by non-profit organizations. Examples are the large-scale annual Gentse Feesten organized by many separate cultural associations and supported by the City of Ghent, and the deanery festivities[6] associated with the different neighbourhoods of the city. In particular, the deaneries of the Turkish neighbourhoods (e.g., Sleepstraat, Oudburg, and Patershol) are active in programming Turkish music.

Non-institutional Commissioners

I consider the role of community leaders as based on intellectual, political, or religious abilities or functions. Their role can be informal (not formally recognized by the community and only implicitly performed) or more formalized (explicitly established by the community and as such performed by the person involved). One example of a formal leader of a sub-segment of Ghent's Turkish population is the *muhtar* (elected head) of Suvermez, a village belonging to the town of Emirdağ. He represents the community of fellow villagers from Suvermez in Turkey as well as in the diaspora. The *muhtar*, together with a few associated persons from the Turkish community in Ghent, organized a large party for all *Suvermezliler* in Western Europe in 2012 to raise funds to support the inhabitants of Suvermez in Turkey. Different local, supra-local, and international Turkish folk musicians and ensembles performed on this "Suvermez night". A second example is the *dede* (socio-religious leader) of the Alevi community in Ghent. The Alevi *dede* typically asks an Alevi *bağlama* player to accompany the *cem* ceremonies. The organization and celebration of the *cem* takes place in a non-institutionalized manner, since the Alevi community is not sufficiently organized to be called an institution. However, if the Alevi community would take on a more defined and officialized form in the future, it would be appropriate to consider them as an institution.

Turkish families also play an important role as non-institutional commissioners. All families celebrate certain important changes in the social status of family members. In particular, circumcision and marriage are major events for which it is appropriate to organize a big party to which the whole family and many family friends are invited, to commemorate this ritual "passage". Particularly on these two occasions, Turkish folk music continues to play a crucial role. During such events, local, supra-local, or even international bands and musicians perform – depending on the financial means of the family.

Besides community leaders and Turkish families, many (usually informal) Turkish folk music performances in Ghent are simply commissioned by music lovers, people with a special appreciation for the patrimony of Turkey's folk music. They invite mostly local befriended or acquainted folk musicians to private gatherings or parties in their home or other (semi-)private locations.

Performers

A typical – though not unambiguous – way of characterizing performers is by distinguishing between "professional" and "amateur" musicians. In the literature, most authors converge on acknowledging that there are different degrees and forms of professionalism. Two criteria emerge as decisive in determining whether a musician is professional: (1) the performance of music as a main activity and means of earning a living and (2) recognition by the society or community of that performer as a musical specialist (Merriam 1964: 124–5; Bohlman 1988: 85–6). Hutchison and Feist (1991) discern several parameters for determining a particular musician's position on a continuum between amateur and professional musicianship. The following parameters are identified: income, education, artistic ambitions, time spent, societal status of the art form concerned, experience, content and style, and general attitude (Hutchison and Feist 1991, as cited in Vanherwegen 2008: 35). "Semi-professionals" are those performers who financially partially depend on their musical activities, and/or are partially recognized by their social environment as a specialist, and/or are positioned in the middle of the amateur-professional continuum of Hutchison and Feist. Education is an important factor.

Conservatoire-trained musicians can be considered professionals by definition, but except for Codarts in Rotterdam, Hochschule für Musik Freiburg, and Popakademie Baden-Württemberg in Mannheim, no other officially recognized conservatoire in Europe offers Turkish music or *bağlama* courses, and alumni from those institutions do not reach Belgium, neither do they attract musicians from Belgium yet. Hitherto, only one actively performing musician from Ghent has attended the conservatoire of Ghent, however, without completing the study. Some musicians from Ghent have attended formal music courses, such as solfège lessons or in some cases also instrumental training (piano or guitar). Some musicians have acquired some proficiency in reading and writing music. In this situation, music education is not an adequate factor in defining professionalism; a more viable factor is the judgement of the Turkish population in Ghent. If a junior (aspirant) musician is allowed to perform in public settings welcoming or requiring Turkish folk music, and if he/she accomplishes this task in a satisfactory way, he/she has the potential to become a new (semi-)"professional". Generally, an aspirant gradually progresses from being considered an amateur to being considered a young (semi-)professional, possibly even rising (usually only after many years of successful musician- and teachership) to the respected status of "master" (*hoca*[7]).

Another relevant marker of performers is their geographical location or distance to Ghent. Not all musicians performing Turkish folk music in Ghent are residents of the city. (Semi-)professional musicians tend to keep close relations with their colleagues in other Belgian cities, like Antwerp and Brussels, but also in cities in more distant provinces, or in smaller cities in the regions surrounding Ghent (e.g., Sint-Niklaas[8] and Lokeren). Those fellow musicians are regularly invited to join Turkish folk music performances in Ghent. Colleagues from neighbouring countries (in particular, the Netherlands or Germany) are also engaged from time to time to accompany or lead the local musicians. Finally, on some occasions, musicians from Turkey are purposely invited to give concerts in Ghent, or they are engaged to join (usually more or less informal) Turkish folk music performances while they are in Belgium for other purposes.

Making a living as a musician is not easy and, in many cases, a major challenge – the field of Turkish folk music is no exception to that rule. Compared to the motherland, the small scale of the potential "market" in the diaspora complicates this endeavour even more. Job opportunities for Turkish folk musicians are limited to performance in (mostly small-scale) concerts and festivals, performance at different kinds of family parties and celebrations, and some teaching. The majority of publicly performing, (semi-)professional-oriented Turkish folk musicians in Ghent are forced to combine their musical activities with other, more financially rewarding or stable jobs.[9] Commissioners and performers have told me that fees paid for musical commissions in Ghent and its environs vary between 250 to 500 euros per person and 900 to 3000 euros for an ensemble, depending on the kind of event, the length of the performance, and the size of the ensemble. Performing at family celebrations such as weddings and circumcision parties is considered one of the most lucrative musical jobs. Yet artistic satisfaction is limited, and musicians with higher artistic aspirations disdain this way of earning money. An international career could be a way out, but it is not for everyone.

Individual Musicians: Mustafa Avşar and Fakı Edeer[10]

The juxtaposition of the life stories of two musicians can provide greater insight into the different ways people respond to their displacement in the same diaspora context. Both Mustafa Avşar and Fakı Edeer were born in Emirdağ but they came to Belgium at different ages. While Mustafa migrated as a child, Fakı was already 30 years old when he came to Brussels and 35 when he moved to Ghent. Mustafa started to learn music at the relatively advanced age of 20, while Fakı had been performing music since his early childhood. Comparing the ways in which the musical careers of these two actors in the Turkish folk music network have developed, illustrates the complex combination of factors determining the position of Turkish musicians in Ghent. The given examples could be complemented by manifold other accounts, adding different nuances to the emerging general picture.

The concrete development of diasporic artistic personalities depends on many factors. Each diasporic population has its own particular migration history, and diasporas can be divided into different types: old or young, established or developing, large or small, concentrated or dispersed, open or closed. Subsequently, diasporic musicians and their public can occupy various starting positions within the different types of diaspora, partly determining artistic production and consumption (Sels 2017: 39). While Mustafa was raised in a still developing diaspora (migrating in 1975 at the age of seven in an exponentially expanding Turkish diaspora in Ghent), Fakı was a newcomer in an established diaspora (migrating in 1990 to Ghent at the age of 35). Furthermore, diasporic musicians make their way in a multidimensional field of tension defined by two distinct tendencies (axes of continua): the intracultural versus the transcultural[11] and the local versus the translocal. While Mustafa's musical activities have a transcultural orientation and local resonance, Fakı's musical activities are characterized by an intracultural orientation and translocal resonance.[12] Knowledge of language emerges as a determining factor in the shaping of diasporic careers. Sufficient knowledge of Dutch (even within limitations) is the key to many possibilities for transcultural career development.

Mustafa Avşar is a versatile entrepreneur, engaging with various culturally oriented activities on different levels. He succeeded in managing a Turkish music shop and an intercultural music café (Muzikantenhuis), which doubled as a non-profit sociocultural organization, where he engaged with the organization of small concerts, other artistic performances, and workshops. A factor of importance has been his broad network and strong contacts with Belgian people, in part constituted through his work in his shop. Mustafa's musical activities were initially limited to his personal, intimate circle of friends and family, although he had taken *bağlama* lessons. Unlike many of his peers, he has never engaged with the wedding party circuit. Mustafa had adopted the artistic identity of a poet rather than a musician. His musical activities organically grew out of his engagement with poetry – a logical development in the light of the close relationship between folk poetry and music in Turkish culture. In the course of his activities related to the music café, Mustafa gradually came to profile himself more and more as a musician, especially with folky Turkish-Dutch songs of his own invention and through collaborations with well-known Flemish musicians such as Walter De Buck, Wouter Vandenabeele, and Willem Vermandere. Without denying his Turkish origin and cultural background, Mustafa gradually expanded his broad network of Belgian musicians, artists, commissioners, and producers, which allowed him to develop his musical activities on relatively high echelons of the Belgian/Flemish cultural sector, financed by subsidies at different levels, personal investment, or artistic fees, and to build a wide – mainly non-Turkish and folk or world music minded – audience. A few examples of his accomplishments are the production of two CDs on the folk label Wild Boar Music, a performance in one of the largest concert halls in Flanders featuring him as a guest musician alongside an established Flemish artist (*Nekka-Nacht 2012/Mustafa Avsar & Willem Vermandere* 2012), and the organization of a broad series of folk and world music related workshops culminating in a large public music and dance performance (Van Herreweghe 2014).

The musical background and career development of Fakı Edeer differ greatly from those of Mustafa Avşar. Fakı grew up in the musicians' district in Emirdağ, where he had been a neighbour of the "Ibıdıklar" (see Chapter 1). He had been educated in the repertoire, instruments, and style of the traditional music of Emirdağ by this and other families of musicians, and perhaps also by Alevi family members from his mother's side. Folk music and poetry would never leave him, and after moving to Belgium, he continued his musical and literary activities without interruption and with great intensity, even if in a more limited environment. Fakı engaged in a broad range of musical activities, including performances at weddings and circumcision celebrations, in cafés, in his own restaurant (now closed), at poetry nights, at formal and informal social gatherings, in concerts, and at festivals. He writes his own songs, makes recordings, publishes anthologies of folk tales, poems and proverbs, is a teacher, performs in radio and television programmes, and is invited as a specialist in Emirdağ culture and music on many official occasions, both in Ghent and in Turkey. Thanks to the success of his restaurant, his reputation as a musician reached beyond the Turkish communities. From 2000 to 2012, Fakı ran a music café/*türkü* bar where various activities took place, including informal classes in Emirdağ music practice, poetry nights, jam sessions, and performances, all oriented towards a Turkish public.

Fakı regards himself as a cultural ambassador of Turkey in the diaspora. This role is reflected at four levels: (1) the practising, safeguarding, and passing on of traditional music and poetry of Emirdağ; (2) the further expansion of the existing poetic and musical repertoire in a similar idiom; (3) the practising of the art of *aşıklık* (see Chapter 3) along the lines of its stylistic, structural, content-related, creative, and technical requirements; (4) the creation of new music irrespective of traditional idioms. In his homeland Turkey, he is recognized as a folk music specialist and representative of the Emirdağ tradition as well.

Folk Music Ensembles

Turkish folk music ensembles in Ghent by definition possess a fluid nature – perhaps this fluidity is an inherent characteristic of folk music performance. Since the start of my research, existing formations have fallen apart, lost old members, incorporated new members, or transformed into other ensembles. New ensembles have arisen, uniting young musicians newly emerging into the scene, bringing new constellations of experienced musicians together, or constituting a mix of established and new musicians. A typical phenomenon are ensembles affiliated with a particular association, in practice often a music café. Grup Tını, the residential ensemble of music café Muzikantenhuis, has theoretically existed for many years, but its membership has been changing constantly. Its size also varies considerably: during performances in Muzikantenhuis, it usually consists of two or three musicians, while during its larger, external concert held annually in De Centrale, ten or more people are involved. Another example is the student ensemble of the world music school of De Centrale, led by its teachers. Its composition changes every year according to the students enrolled for the courses.

Regarding line-up, ubiquitous and central in every Turkish folk music ensemble are a singer and a *bağlama* player, often unified in one person. This smallest nucleus is sometimes expanded to include other Turkish or non-Turkish instruments. "Oriental" models of synthesizers are often combined with the *bağlama*. Another regularly appearing instrument is the guitar, sometimes becoming a substitute for the *bağlama*. The percussion instruments of *davul* (large double-headed drum), *bendir*, and *darbuka* can also join the ensemble. It is significant that the combination of *davul* and *zurna* (shawm), which is so common in Turkey, is seldom heard in Ghent. *Zurna* players are often from other provinces in Belgium. Recently, the use of the *zurna* has become more common in Ghent, with a few musicians developing their *zurna* skills.

Turkish folk music ensembles in Ghent are usually assembled for a specific occasion. Their line-up depends on the setting, the kind of event, the occasion, the budget of the commissioner, and other contextual factors. In many cases, the singer or the most experienced musician selects the other ensemble members, which implies a certain kind of hierarchy between the musicians. A few accomplished singers present themselves as purely vocal soloists, not playing an instrument but concentrating on the act of singing. Their ensembles can be considered as accompanying bands at their service.

Educators

I use the term educator in the broad sense of a person who teaches other people in certain aspects of the field of Turkish folk music, on the practical or theoretical level, irrespective of the methods or modalities, in a formal or non-formal setting. Practice-oriented education is concentrated on performance and can involve playing or singing techniques, tuning systems, style and interpretation, improvisational or variational skills, repertoire development, and so on. Theoretical education can cover intra-musical (music-theoretical) topics such as music notation, tonal and rhythmic-metrical organization, and regional styles or genres, or extra-musical (contextual) topics, for example, historical, societal (political, social, cultural, religious) or philosophical perspectives on the genre of Turkish folk music.

A formal educational setting is structured and institutionalized. It takes place in a public or semi-public setting and not in a private context, and it is organized at a fixed moment and place to a regular time schedule. Formal education involves intentional learning, is goal-oriented, and follows certain pre-defined rules and patterns, while non-formal education, although still intentional and goal-oriented, proceeds in a more spontaneous way, with less rigid preparation in advance. It can take place at irregular moments and in changing places. Formal education involves a fixed remuneration for the (professional) teachers and a fixed fee for the students, while non-formal education can involve different kinds of financial arrangements, including a fixed fee, a negotiated fee, or alternative forms of compensation. Informal education is to be situated at the other end of the continuum, involving unintentional, even accidental learning. It is the kind of permanent learning continuously taking place throughout daily activities and conversations apart from an educational context. Informal learning can possibly involve a person who could be labelled as "educator", but this is not necessarily the case. Informal learning does not involve a remuneration.[13]

Formal Educational Contexts

Formal Turkish folk music education in the strictest sense of officially recognized courses taught by accredited teachers and leading to a certificate, as is the case in the official "part-time arts education" (DKO: Deeltijds Kunstonderwijs), does not yet exist in Belgium. The most formalized educational context regarding Turkish folk music in Ghent is the world music school in De Centrale. The lessons take place at fixed moments every week and are suspended during the holidays. There are no obligatory solfège courses. No examinations or other formal evaluations are organized. The teachers are employed on the basis of relevant experience (acquired competencies). Generally, at least twice a year, an opportunity to perform on stage is offered, during the annual open house and student festival. As already mentioned in the previous chapter, Turkish folk music courses in this institution concentrate primarily on *baǧlama*, complemented by Turkish music ensemble lessons and *darbuka* and *bendir* lessons. The latter are not oriented towards Turkish music, but towards a general Middle Eastern (Arab and Turkish) repertoire and style. The didactics of all three courses are based on collective lessons, roughly divided into levels (small children, children, beginners, and advanced students).

The *baǧlama* lessons are taught by Iskender Arıcı and loosely involve note reading, but in practice, they appeal to the aural and kinetic memory of the students. A syllabus with general information about the *baǧlama*, elementary exercises in note reading, and a collection of scores or Turkish folk songs and dances is provided by the teacher. The lessons typically proceed in a semi-collective way, usually involving an equal onset for all students with moments of collective attention to a particular learning content or problem, but gradually evolving towards a greater differentiation of learning trajectories in the course of the session. In this situation, all students are simultaneously occupied with their own repertoire or specific technical or stylistic issues, while the teacher focuses his attention on each student separately. Although this approach has certain benefits (such as reaching a larger amount of students at the same time, which reduces costs and time investment, and the opportunity to learn from one another), drawbacks of this system are the chaos that sometimes occurs when all the students are playing different things at the same moment and the fact that the students cannot be constantly served by the teacher.[14] The *darbuka* and *bendir* lessons are taught by a Flemish teacher, Hilde De Clercq. Turkish rhythmic-metrical patterns are a part of the learning content, as well as Arab ones. The patterns are mostly taught by ear, although a basis for rhythmic notation is provided. The collective way of teaching allows the group to be divided into several subgroups to perform variants of the same rhythmic-metrical pattern or to perform polyrhythmic patterns. The Turkish music ensemble lessons are taught by both teachers together. The separate *baǧlama* and percussion classes function as a sort of preparation for this joint course; the repertoire performed in the ensemble courses is separately prepared in advance in Hilde De Clercq and Iskender Arıcı's classes. Instrumental pieces as well as songs are performed;

the songs are sung by the teachers or by the students (De Clercq, email to author, 3 June 2014).

Non-Formal Educational Contexts

Unlike formal education, there are many contexts for non-formal Turkish folk music education in Ghent. The *bağlama* is at the centre, being the most typical, iconic Turkish folk music instrument.

One type of non-formal lessons are more or less structured and regular *bağlama* courses. These kinds of lessons have been (or are currently) organized in various music cafés and other sociocultural non-profit associations, such as Mızrap (Sluizeken), Muzikantenhuis (Dampoortstraat), Türk Ocağı (Sleepstraat), De Poort–Beraber (Sleepstraat), Kardelen (Meerhem), AKD (Banierstraat, Sint-Amandsberg), DHKD (Hundelgemsesteenweg, Ledeberg), and Özburun (Opgeëistenlaan). All these venues are situated in Turkish neighbourhoods of the city. These kinds of courses are usually regularly organized at a fixed time in the week and involve collective teaching. Unlike the lessons in De Centrale, this non-formal education does not involve written scores. Nevertheless, both Bekir Gürbüz, in his lessons at Muzikantenhuis, and Tuğrul Yücesan, in his lessons at the non-profit organization Özburun,[15] made use of note names to teach new melodies of folk songs and dances. Gürbüz instructed his students to write down the notes by means of solmization (e.g., "do re mi"). In this way, the students could rely upon their written "scores" instead of memorizing everything. Rhythmic patterns were referred to by both Gürbüz and Yücesan using more or less standardized expressions stemming from Ottoman music theory and practice (e.g., "düm tek tek", "düm tekka").

Individual lessons by appointment, often on an irregular basis, are another form of non-formal education. This kind of education can take place in private locations, for example, at the teacher's home, but often finds a place in semi-public central locations such as the aforementioned music cafés or even venues belonging to sociocultural associations. These kinds of lessons are often more efficient than the collective lessons discussed above, since all the attention is directed to one student, and the content of the lessons can be tailored to the specific needs or interests of the student. Learning proceeds in a more profound way, and more attention can be given to stylistic and technical details (e.g., plectrum techniques, ornamentations, and texture – described as *tavır*), sound quality, and interpretation (*yorum*). The student's repertoire develops more quickly and towards more diversity. Similar to the collective lessons, note names and musical notation are used in a loose way, as a guidance or mnemonic device.[16]

A third form, consisting of jam sessions and "TLSs" ("tune learning sessions"[17]), is again collective and leans towards the informal ways of learning which will be discussed in the next section. It involves a small group of apprentice musicians sitting in a circle or around a table, training in the performance of new repertoire, genres, or styles. The difference with purely informal learning is the intentionality: the conscious intention of the participants in such a session is to learn. Jam sessions are often not planned in advance and occur spontaneously. Typical locations are music cafés such as Muzikantenhuis and Mızrap.

Experienced and knowledgeable musicians implicitly perform the role of educator by being a "medium" or "model" that provides the desired musical content. Metin Toplar has been a central musician functioning as a non-formal educator in such settings. TLSs, on the other hand, are usually planned in advance and are often oriented towards a broader target audience, including non-Turkish musicians. TLSs focusing on Turkish folk music and taking place in Muzikantenhuis are usually led by the owner of the café, Mustafa Avşar.

One last type of non-formal education, comparable to the previous type, involves an ad hoc, one-to-one relationship between teacher and student. In brief, spontaneous, and unstructured moments of Turkish folk music education, an experienced and knowledgeable musician teaches particular, defined musical content. Metin Toplar, a *bağlama* player and singer who owned the music café Mızrap until its closure in 2015, and Fakı Edeer, a *bağlama* player, singer, *ozan*, and expert in the folk music of Emirdağ, are known to have educated many current Turkish folk music performers in Ghent. Although Toplar has also taught regular, formalized courses in De Centrale, much of this teaching has taken place in a non-formal and ad hoc manner.

A similar kind of learning occurs in families of musicians, for example the *abdals* (see Chapter 3) from Emirdağ. Central figures in this familial music education are the deceased Isa Demirkaya – the pater familias – and the second generation: his children and children-in-law (Muharrem Ateşli, Mehmet and Hasan Çürükçü, and others). Although the heredity of the profession of musicianship is losing its importance in contemporary Turkey and even more in the diaspora, the younger generations of the *abdal* families are still musically gifted and active.

Informal Learning

Informal, non-intentional learning about the theory and practice of Turkish folk music can take place in many different settings and contexts. Turkish folk music performances of various kinds provide excellent learning opportunities. Attending a live performance, be it in a concert hall, a music café, or during a family or community celebration, gives the chance to assimilate a lot of implicit knowledge about, for example, repertoire and style, musical content and meaning, and instruments and playing techniques. The same is true for informal conversations with musicians; a lot of musical knowledge is transferred in an unintentional way. This kind of learning plays an important role in how music enthusiasts and apprentice musicians build their musical knowledge. Experienced or knowledgeable musicians or other persons with authority in the field of Turkish folk music can be considered informal "educators". This role becomes clearer if these persons possess the ability and inclination to communicate their knowledge and experience. Metin Toplar and Fakı Edeer, who were already mentioned as examples of ad hoc non-formal educators, also belong to this category.

Listeners

People who are in the (temporary) position of listening to musicians can be seen as "audience" or "attendees". The former term more strongly connotes formality and intentionality of the listening act than the latter. In the context of live musical performances, an "audience" is generally considered to be a group of people, purposely gathered to listen to the performance, usually not taking part in the performance, and maintaining a certain distance from the performers. The most typical setting involving a real "audience" is a formal concert. With respect to Turkish folk music performances, in many cases neither such a distance nor this division of roles is maintained. The people present at the musical setting may have come together for another purpose than to listen to music (e.g., for specific or unspecific social occasions) and may also be accidental witnesses of the musical performance. In those cases, it is more appropriate to use the term "attendees". The term "listener" is more neutral and applies to both categories.

Groups of listeners can be categorized according to criteria such as audience size, specificity (general versus specific audiences), and composition (exclusively Turkish, mainly Turkish, or mixed Turkish and non-Turkish). I consider an audience as specific if its members belong to a particular group (e.g., a religious movement), or if they are familiar or associated with the location or with the other actors (performers, commissioners) involved.

Specific audiences of Turkish folk music performances involve regular customers of the venue where the performance takes place (such as the music café Muzikantenhuis, or the intercultural centre De Centrale); friends or relatives of the celebrating family in the case of wedding or circumcision parties; friends or relatives of the performers during events such as an open house or a student festival at De Centrale or during certain *türkü* nights; members of the association organizing the event (such as the Ozon student club organizing a karaoke evening); former inhabitants of a particular village, town, or region and their descendants, in the case of activities oriented to this kind of audience (such as a benefit evening to raise funds for the village of Suvermez, a *seyran* organized by a sociocultural association of people from Posof, or an Emirdağ rural festival); and members of a religious group, such as the Alevis in the case of a *cem*.

In many cases, these specific audiences are mixed with a general audience. This is the case in events such as Turkish evenings, *türkü* nights and café concerts, De Centrale's open house and student festival, and the *seyran*. Entirely general audiences come to events such as a cultural festival organized in the city centre or a benefit concert in De Centrale for the victims of the mine disaster in Soma.

Events attracting a mixed Turkish and non-Turkish audience include the cultural festival in the city centre, De Centrale's open house and student festival, and certain café concerts. Exclusively or chiefly Turkish audiences attend events such as Turkish evenings or *türkü* evenings, circumcision and wedding parties, activities organized by Turkish student clubs, benefit concerts such as the Suvermez night, the *seyran*, the *cem*, and jam sessions in Turkish music cafés. However, these jam sessions can also involve the mixed interest and participation of non-Turkish people eager to learn to play or sing Turkish music. Wedding parties (more than circumcision parties, which are more rooted in tradition and ritual) also sometimes involve non-Turkish attendees, when, for example, the colleagues of the bride or groom are invited.

Central Places

Intercultural Centre

The Intercultural Centre De Centrale[18] (see Chapter 1) is a large institution supported by the municipality of Ghent. It offers a broad programming mainly consisting of different kinds of world music, folk music, and non-Western classical music. Turkish music, and in particular Turkish folk music, constitutes an important pillar in the venue's programming, most commonly in the form of concerts of renowned bands or singers from the popular folk music scene in Turkey. The centre has three concert spaces at its disposal: a large hall on the first floor (276 seats), a smaller hall in the basement (150 seats), and a reading café on the ground floor (max. 50 seats). In addition to these concert venues, different types of rooms can be hired by organizations for various cultural or social activities such as courses, workshops, and rehearsals. These opportunities are utilized by a great diversity of sociocultural associations, which grants a multi- and sometimes intercultural aura to this centre. A list of the Turkish bands and artists performing at De Centrale in 2013 (see Table 2.1) gives an impression of the focus and range of its programming, and the position of Turkish folk music in the larger whole.

Table 2.1: Turkish bands and artists performing at De Centrale in 2013

Name of the band or artist	Genre
Devrim Kaya, Deniz Güneş & Nurettin Rençber (TR)	Turkish folk music
Grup Tını (BE)	
Cengiz Özkan & Ismail Altunsaray (TR)	
Bülent Köken & Damla Kırdaş (BE) – external concert	
Selda Bağcan (TR) – external concert in Vooruit	Turkish folk music + other genres (*özgün müzik*, jazz, blues, pop, light classical, cross-over)
Yeni Türkü (TR)	
Kürşat Zengin (BE)	
Bülent Otaçgil & Erkan Oğur (TR)	
Mustafa Aydın, Nikolaj Delchev & Sattar Khan (BE) – free café concert	
Model (TR)	Rock, avant-garde rock, *fasıl*-rock and folk rock
Replikas (TR) – external concert in Vooruit	
Nev (TR)	
Pinhani (TR)	
Göksel (TR)	Pop
Baba Zula (TR)	Experimental (oriental dub, oriental blues, electro, psychedelic, free jazz)
Seni Görmem Imkansız (TR) – external concert in Vooruit	
Konstrukt (TR) – external concert in Vooruit	
Luxus (TR) – external concert in Vooruit	
Burhan Öçal & Trakya All Stars (TR & CH) – external concert in Vooruit	

Kudsi Ergüner (TR)	Cross-over
Levantijns Orkest (BE) – free café concert	Ottoman classical
Karsu Dönmez (NL) – external concert in Vooruit	Jazz
Sema Moritz (TR & DE)	Tango
Ibıdıklar (BE)	Light Turkish classical

Key: BE= Belgium; CH = Switzerland; DE = Germany; NL = Netherlands; TR= Turkey.

Self-organizations: Turkish Music Cafés

Beste, Muzikantenhuis, and Mızrap are variants of the typical Turkish folk music-related venue of the *türkü evi* (*türkü* house) or *türkü* bar, emerging in the 1990s in Istanbul and other major cities in Turkey, and being copied in smaller towns and the diaspora. In this type of music café, Turkish folk music is often supplemented by *özgün müzik* (Turkish protest music), in a setting abundantly filled with attributes from and references to traditional Turkish rural life. Alcohol, such as *rakı* (Turkish aniseed spirit), is not foreign to the concept of contemporary *türkü* bars, and mezzes are often served as well.[19] Within this general concept of the *türkü* bar, different aspects are highlighted by the three examples in Ghent.

Beste,[20] a music café run by Fakı Edeer, opened in 2000 and closed in 2012. It never enjoyed regular activity nor purposeful programming, but it functioned as a private space, uniting befriended musicians or culturally interested people at the invitation of the owner. More "official", public programmes were organized only sporadically, for example during the 2009 edition of the annual festival Les Goûts de Gand, during which De Centrale programmed performances in different external venues in Ghent. The focus was on acoustic or modestly amplified performance of Turkish folk music, and on recitation of folk poetry – in particular, music and poetry from Emirdağ – in addition to the creation of new songs and new poems. These performances and creations were accompanied by conversations about cultural subjects, often related to Emirdağ's particular heritage. Listeners and performers intermingled freely. The music café had a clear social and cultural function, but it closed due to problems of accessibility (parking space) and profitability (lack of publicity and customer-oriented management).

Muzikantenhuis,[21] a music café owned by Mustafa Avşar (see Chapter 1), opened in 2007. From the beginning, it actively attracted a broad audience. This public was reached by means of posters and printed monthly programmes, a website, and later a Facebook page. Another difference between

Muzikantenhuis and Beste is the fact that Muzikantenhuis has applied several times for subsidies on different levels. In addition, the programming has always been very broad, certainly not limited to Turkish music. At present, Turkish folk music has a more or less fixed place in the programming: on Friday evening and night, the residential Tını ensemble or another Turkish formation can be found on stage. After performances of other bands as well, the stage is often occupied by young and/or more experienced musicians of Turkish origin. Again, the boundaries between audience and musicians are flexible and continuously blurred. In addition to Turkish folk music, which is often rendered in a popularized and amplified version, making use of guitars and other non-Turkish instruments, many other music genres and other artistic disciplines are included in the venue's programming. An analysis of the musical programming in 2013 shows its broad offerings and the position of Turkish folk music within it (see Table 2.2).

Table 2.2: Muzikantenhuis's musical programming in 2013

Performer(s)/project	Genre	Frequency
Grup Tını	Turkish folk	42
Bülent Gök & Group Tarz		2
Mustafa Tekir, Bülent Köken & Ceylan Demirkaya		1
3 M & 2 B		1
Mustafa Avşar & friends	Folk/World music (including Turkish folk)	4
Hilde De Clercq & Aykut Durşen	World music (including Turkish folk)	1
Group Özgün	*Özgün müzik*	1
TLS (Tune Learning Session)	Folk	8
Querida		1
Broes		1
Midrid		1
Son of a Gun		1
Lien Kooijman		1
Strograss		1
The Silly Endings		2
Dirty Habits		1
Ghent Folk Violin Project		2
Aurélia & Tom		1
Elllis		1
April and June	Folk/World music	1

Andrew Mill	Folk/Singer-songwriter	2
James Cottriall (Austria)	Folk/Pop	1
Folgazan		1
Agustin Ribero (Argentina)		1
Tchayok	Russian folk	1
Surpluz	Dutch-language folk	1
Kadril		1
Walter De Buck & Wim Claeys		1
Irish session	Irish folk	6
Green Jacket		1
Amalia Vermandere	Singer-songwriter	1
Daithi Rua		4
Rufus Kain & Chuck Paisley		1
Peter Boone		2
Paul Russell		1
Moakley		1
Kameraad		1
Lavan		1
RedCoat		1
Oliver Pigott (Canada)		1
Kieran Halpin (Ireland)		1
Niall Connolly (USA)		1
Homelands	Singer-songwriter/Pop	2
Charliefields		1
Medes	Jazz	1
Laughing Bastards		1
JC Trio	Experimental jazz	1
Zulema	Punk-pop	1
New Bossa from Brasil	Bossa nova	1
André Cruyt	French chanson	1
Bones of Saint James	Pop/Soul	1
Joni Sheil	Pop	1
Les Busiciens	World music/Balkan	1
Vintage Blues Groovers	Blues	1
Hot Carl	Funk	1
Laura Castro	Flamenco	1
Mi Tierra	Latin	1
Flamingo Sisters	Music theatre	1

The music café Mızrap was active from 2013 to 2015 after having been closed for several years. The non-profit organization was revived by its former president, Metin Toplar. The programming expanded from an initial focus on Turkish folk music and *özgün müzik* towards a broader range of musical genres. The conception of the music café heavily resembled the functioning and appearance of Muzikantenhuis. An interesting fact is that the interior design of Mızrap, Muzikantenhuis, and Beste was realized by the same person: Metin Toplar. The three venues display rustic furniture, wall paintings of important figures from Turkish (and Ottoman) history, literary and music-related books on shelves, and multifarious utensils and decorative elements from Anatolian rural life. An analysis of the musical events displayed on the Facebook page[22] of Mızrap between March 2013 and February 2014 indicates the range of its programming and the position of Turkish folk music (see Table 2.3). Similar to Muzikantenhuis, this "official", planned programming was complemented by spontaneous jam sessions on stage or around the table. Within this complementary musical activity, Turkish folk music occupied a prominent place.

Table 2.3: Mızrap's programming (March 2013–February 2014)

Performer(s)/project	Genre	Frequency
Group Mızrap		13
Bülent Gök		3
Ferhat	Turkish folk	1
Melike Tarhan & Metin Toplar		1
Aytekin Kılıç & Barış Ercoş		1
Metin Toplar		1
Kürşat Zengin & Radi Kazakov	Turkish folk/ Balkan	1
Istanbul Trio		1
Ferhat Elma & Barış Ercoş		5
Barış Ercoş, Ferhat Elma, Nizamettin Kılıç & Tamer Akkuyu	*Özgün müzik*	1
Barış Ercoş & Nizamettin Kılıç		2
Ramazan Barış & Rüştü		1
Louis Márquez, Renato Márquez, Bruno Deneckere, H.T. Roberts, Daithi Rua, Fernant Zeste, & Joe Baele (different constellations)		10
Redcoat	Singer-songwriter	2
Dirk De Vriendt		1
Gabriela Arnon		1

Marie-Paule Franke and her Dreamband	Jazz	3
Kari Antila ft. Jouni Isoherranen		1
Paloma Samper & Jouni Isoherranen		1
Marina De Letter & Luis lopez Vega	Latin	1
Ann Vancoillie ft. Juan Pablo López		2
Mi Terra		1
Radi Kazakov	Romani music	5
Kürşat Zengin	Pop	1
Hip hop	Hip hop	1
Juan Carlos Sampe	Flamenco	1
Moufadhel Adhoum	Moroccan classical music	1
Songhunter	Folk/Jazz	1
Ethno-jazz	Jazz/World music	1
Trio Osama Abdulrasol	World music	1
Daniel Pettersson (Sweden)	Folk	1

Conclusion: The Turkish Folk Music Network in Ghent

Today's Turkish folk music scene in Ghent consists of a fluid yet structurally relatively stable network of individual and institutional commissioners, performers, listeners, and educators. The roles assumed by the actors are combinable and interchangeable. Places which are central for the network include the city's Intercultural Centre, a stable constituent since 1995, and several Turkish music cafés, which are self-organizations and likely more vulnerable.

Institutional commissioners playing an important role are local authorities such as the City of Ghent, and certain sociocultural organizations, most prominently the city's intercultural centre De Centrale as well as music café Muzikantenhuis. Influential non-institutional commissioners include community leaders (e.g., Alevi *dedeler*) and Turkish families (notably with regard to family celebrations). Turkish folk music in Ghent is performed by individuals and loosely-knit ensembles, from within and outside the city, and on many occasions without rigid or clear barriers between amateur and semi- or pre-professional players (although hierarchical relations prevail). The musicians operate in a field of tension consisting of intracultural versus transcultural, and local versus translocal tendencies. Their stance is influenced by voluntary and involuntary factors. Formal education in Turkish folk music is provided in De Centrale's world music school, while less formal or non-formal lessons are given in the framework of various organizations, including music cafés, and in some cases, in family contexts. Parallel to the other roles, listening to Turkish folk music can take on many gradations of (in)formality. Audiences can be specific or general, and Turkish or mixed, depending on several contextual and musical parameters.

The roles and their modalities return in Chapters 5, 6, and 8 in relation to the detailed description and analysis of a series of musical events attended in Ghent and Turkey. However, first, Chapters 3 and 4 shift focus from the context of migration and diaspora to the motherland context, to get a clearer view on the musical characteristics, genres and forms, regional styles, traditional performers and occasions, thematic content, and recent modification and notation of Turkish folk music, in its current manifestations, with reference to the past, and with attention to the different and changing ways in which it is performed, conceptualized, studied, and used or appropriated.

Chapter 3

Turkish Folk Music in Theory and Practice

A general picture of what "Turkish folk music" in its modern, post-Atatürkian form entails, can be constituted by looking into its general musical characteristics, genres and forms, regional styles, traditional performers, and thematic content. Unavoidably, this picture will remain fragmentary and sketchy, considering its vast size and the relatively limited availability of scholarly and English-language sources. Turkish-language sources are in some cases ideologically or politically biased, and contradictions are an inherent part of the literature. Until now, no comprehensive and detailed academic volume has been published about the musicological aspects of the folk music of Turkey – also of what serves as the reference point of diasporic performers, for example, in Ghent. The closest attempt, Atınç Emnalar's book *Tüm Yönleriyle Türk Halk Müziği ve Nazariyatı* (1998) does not seem to be well disseminated, nor upheld as a standard work.

The establishment of the Turkish Republic out of the relicts of the Ottoman Empire, and the concomitant radical political, social, and cultural changes, have effected fundamental and enduring changes in the field of folk music in Turkey. The political establishment and the existing cultural order were drastically turned around. Folk music had a significant role to play at the core of this cultural revolution. The meanings, functions, and positions of different types of music shifted greatly. "Turkish folk music", as it has been understood since the foundation of the Republic, is in many regards a political construction. Atatürk and his ideologues (most eminently Ziya Gökalp) have left a strong mark on the forms, essence, and sociopolitical embeddedness of this musical repertoire.

A conceptual framework was set up during the first decades of the Turkish Republic by musicologists associated with state institutions. The umbrella term "Turkish folk music" and several related concepts are constructions scarcely or not at all grounded in historical folk (or even elite) practices and conceptualizations. Even today, these terms are seldom used by performers, but by scholars and musicians who are part of the official artistic and educational cultural state project. Most performers employ specific terms transmitted throughout the generations, if they verbalize about their practices at all. In what follows, a general outlook on Turkish folk music is provided, bearing the (organic as well as imposed) changes of the past century in mind.

General Characteristics

Tone and Time System

Traditionally, folk music in Turkey is based on a non-tempered tone system, close to the natural harmonic system based on overtones. The unequal division of the octave limits transposition possibilities to closely related modes. Intervals of approximately 3/4 and 5/4 tone are common. Modern Turkish music theory generally agrees on the Pythagorean comma-system as its basis, dividing each whole tone into nine commas.

Middle Eastern music can be characterized as "modal". It should be kept in mind that "modality" is a Western concept and thus should be approached critically (Beyhom 2011: 101). It has been defined by Tran Van Khê on the basis of "fundamental" and "secondary" characteristics, the fundamental characteristics being: (1) a modal scale determined by a specific structure; (2) hierarchy between scale degrees; (3) a specific formula; (4) a modal feeling (ethos) linked to each concept of mode; and the secondary characteristics being: (1) specific ornaments; (2) length of notes and silences; (3) importance of ranges; (4) tempo (Tran Van Khê, as cited by Beyhom 2011: 101–2). Amine Beyhom makes a distinction between characteristics of intervallic structure and of melodic structure, partly based on Tran Van Khê and Powers et al. (n.d.):

> Intervallic structure:
> 1. composition and cutting of the intervals that structure the scale;
> 2. tonic and range being used;
> 3. mode ambitus;
> 4. modulations.
> Melodic structure (…):
> 1. hierarchy between notes;
> 2. proportions between notes (length of notes and silences);

3. existence of rules for notes or formulas of the beginning and the end of the modes as well as for their chronological order (modal progression);
4. characteristic melodic forms, if they exist. (Beyhom 2011: 101–3)

A state-of-the-art conceptualization of modality is provided by Powers et al.:

> Taking the term in the modern, twofold sense, mode can be defined as either a "particularized scale" or a "generalized tune", or both, depending on the particular musical and cultural context. If one thinks of scale and tune as representing the poles of a continuum of melodic predetermination, then most of the area between can be designated one way or another as being in the domain of mode ...
> This polarity of scale and tune is an instance of the familiar opposition of general to specific, which in music is often thought of as a contrasting of theory with practice. When modes (or their equivalents) are construed as primarily scalar, they tend to be used for classifying, for grouping musical entities into ideal categories. When the melodic aspects of modality are its predominant features, then modes are seen as guides and norms for composition or improvisation. (Powers et al. n.d.: para. 1)

Melody is central to the traditional Turkish musical system, related to a "horizontal" conceptualization of music. The music is essentially monophonic, sometimes performed as heterophony. Harmony manifests itself in parallel, non-tonal chords or drones in a modal context.

The time system of Turkish folk music allows for a large variety of metres: regular and irregular (changing) metres, symmetric and asymmetric metres, and mixed metres. Asymmetric metres consist of units of unequal length (e.g., 2+3 or 2+3+3). Mixed metres are combinations of asymmetric metres (e.g., 3+2+2+3 or 2+2+3+2+2). The time system of Middle Eastern art music is usually conceptualized as cyclical (based on short or long rhythmic-metrical cycles). An "additive" conception of musical time prevails, characterized by a flexible metre following the prosody of the poetry. This conception is tied to the centrality of vocal music in the Middle East.

Comparison with Turkish Classical Music

The tone system of Turkish folk music is closely related to that of Turkish classical music and is rooted in the same tuning system, but while the classical tone system has been heavily theorized (historically and recently), the folk tone system has not been underpinned by theories (except from some recent endeavours). It is less complex, less defined, and more flexible than the classical tone system. The movable frets of the *bağlama* are exemplary in this respect. The pitches and intervals to be played on the *bağlama* vary according to regional styles and genres, and personal preferences. While the classical system is based on the division of one tone into nine commas, allowing for a note to be raised or lowered by one, four, five, or eight commas, the folk system involves the raising or lowering of tones by two or three commas, as such approaching a quarter-tone system. The classical music theory is still subject to intense debate, and the rigid 0-1-4-5-8-9 comma system is not universally agreed upon.[1]

The remarks regarding the tone system are equally applicable to the time system. Complex conceptualizations of the metre and rhythm of Turkish classical music, concentrated around the concept of *usul* (rhythmic-metrical mode, cycle, or pattern), make way for a simpler and freer approach in Turkish folk music. Long rhythmic-metrical cycles do not occur in folk music, but irregular (changing), asymmetric, and mixed metres are common. A large part of folk music (categorized as *uzun hava*, in contrast to the metrical *kırık hava*) is non-metrical in the musical sense.

The texture of Turkish folk music is often richer than the texture of Turkish classical music. Classical music can be purely monophonic (allowing parallel movement at a distance of one or two octaves), heterophonic (involving a free approach of monophony whereby different variants of the same melody are performed simultaneously or in an imitative, quasi-canonic manner) or sometimes antiphonic (involving monophonic alternation between voice and instruments). Folk music is often performed heterophonically if involving several instruments/voices or a combination of instrument(s) and voice(s), but also often displays a kind of polyphony in the form of drones (of one tone or a dyad) or melodies in parallel fourths, produced on one instrument (diaphony).

Turkish classical music performance has developed around two large pillars: improvisation on the basis of a concrete mode (*makam*) (or more correctly: the instant crystallization of a specific manifestation of the general structure and development of a certain *makam*), and performance of an existing composition on the basis of a certain *makam*. Classical improvisation most often occurs in the free-metrical *taksim* (instrumental introduction of a certain *makam*). Turkish folk music performance always possesses certain improvisational traits, as it concerns either the re-creation of existing pieces involving (textual, melodic, rhythmic, ornamental) variation and personal interpretation, or the creation of new pieces on the basis of content-related, stylistic, and formal implicit guidelines, derived from the knowledge of the existing repertoire belonging to the specific context. Both closely related practices can be conceptualized as belonging to a continuum and can be regarded as parallel to the practices prevailing in the classical domain.

Modality in the context of Turkish folk music discursively develops around the concept of *ayak* (literally, "foot, base"), the folk music counterpart to the classical *makam* concept, developed in the context of Republican scholarly folk music research. While Turkish classical music is clearly modal and can be fitted without reservation into the conceptualizations of modality discussed in the previous section, the situation is somewhat more ambiguous with regard to folk music. A lesser degree of complexity and an absence of theoretical underpinning characterize the modal nature of Turkish folk music. Although several modal characteristics can be found across Turkish folk music, no explicit rules or principles for the hierarchy between tones or melodic progression are involved, and no modulations occur.

Recent studies by Okan Murat Öztürk and other scholars apply an integrated perspective, considering the folk and classical music from Turkey as a whole, which should be conceptualized and analysed within a single framework. Öztürk matches historical descriptions of typical melodic development of *makams* with examples from the folk repertoire, showing their full applicability. His contribution opens the way to new useful methods of folk music analysis in communication with classical music analysis, thereby overcoming long-lasting ideological, scholarly, and artistic divisions (Öztürk 2016).

Genres and Forms

Turkish folk music is usually classified according to the categorizations developed by Turkish music scholars Muzaffer Sarısözen[2] (1899–1963) and Mahmut Ragıp Gazimihal[3] (1900–61), distinguishing between *uzun hava* (non-metrical songs) and *kırık hava* (metrical songs) as the main bifurcation. This method of classification is maintained, for example, in Irene Markoff and Ursula Reinhard's contributions on Turkish music to the Garland

Encyclopedia of World Music (Markoff 2002b; Reinhard 2002), and partly in Kurt Reinhard and Martin Stokes' contributions to Grove Music Online (Reinhard, Stokes, and Reinhard n.d.). Many Turkish authors also maintain the basic distinction between *uzun hava* and *kırık hava*. Although the distinction between metrical and non-metrical folk music is valid[4] and should indeed be made, in my opinion, it should not be treated as the first-level dichotomy. It would be preferable to categorize Turkish folk music on the basis of other primary distinctions in order to gain meaningfulness and consistency. A review of the literature (Akdoğu 1996; Emnalar 1998; Demir 2013; Sabuncu n.d.) did not provide an adequate alternative; the propositions by other authors remain incomplete or unbalanced.

A meaningful basic distinction could be a division of the repertoire into secular and religious music, with a third ambivalent category added: *aşık* music. Further division into subcategories can take on different forms depending on the peculiarities of each category. An exhaustive classification – if ever achievable – falls outside the scope of this book and would involve countless categories based on, for example, literary genre divisions or regionally defined musical subgenres or dance forms.

I propose the following basic categorization:

A) Secular music:
   - Songs:
     - Metrical songs (*kırık hava*) – e.g., *türkü, mani, koşma*, lullabies (*ninni*), ballads (*destan*)
     - Non-metrical songs (*uzun hava*) – e.g., *hoyrat, barak, maya, bozlak, gurbet, garip, kerem, yol havası* (regionally defined genres); lamentations (*ağıt*)
   - Dances (*oyun havaları*):
     - Purely instrumental dances – e.g., *halay, horon, zeybek, hora, karşılama, bar, teke zotlatması*, spoon dances (*kaşık oyunları*) (regionally defined genres)
     - Vocal-instrumental dances (dance songs)
   - Solo instrumental music and instrumental preludes/interludes
B) Religious music (liturgical Alevi music):
   - Prayers – e.g., *ilahi, nefes, deyiş/deme, duvaz/duvazdeh imam, mersiye*
   - Sacred dances (*semah*)
C) Aşık music – e.g., *koşma, varsağı, semai*, epics (*destan*), *türkü, mani*.

Regional Styles

Stylistically describing the characteristics of the folk music repertoire of different regions and transregional genres is an intricate task. In the literature, no such endeavour is found. Attempts to describe the different regional styles are mostly limited to the enumeration of the genres, metres, dances, instruments, and so on occurring in that region. The reasons for this academic vacuum are manifold. Fatma Reyhan Altınay[5] mentions insufficiency of the fieldwork: on the one hand, not all the regions have been thoroughly studied, and, on the other hand, the academic output is fragmented into smaller studies of specific regions, lacking a general, overarching view. If general overviews are written, they are not grounded in the necessary fieldwork. Secondly, Altınay points out that it does not lead to good results when the geographical regions (*bölgeler*) and the "cultural" regions of Turkey are considered overlapping. The sole scientifically sound and effective approach is to focus on the local (*yerel*) level (the level of *yöre* instead of *bölge*), defined as "not only a geographical region, but also a cultural area on which people live"[6] (email to author, 27 January 2013).

A central concept in the analysis of Turkey's regional styles is *tavır* ("manner, style"). *Tavır* is defined by Irene Markoff as "the techniques used to produce sound on instruments, and the instrument-specific musical grammar that results" in a broad sense (1986: 119), and as "right-hand techniques, or various regional and genre-specific plectrum configurations" if specifically applied to *bağlama* playing (1986: 120). Martin Stokes defines *tavır* in the context of *bağlama* playing as "patterns of ornamentation and plectrum movement"; if applied to singing (*ağız*), the concept encompasses "correct attention to details of dialect, ornamentation, or vocal production" (1992a: 76).

The academic and professional approach of Turkish folk music conservation, study, and education as a part of the cultural policy of the Turkish Republic has left a strong mark on the ways in which *tavır* is used and conceptualized. The stylistic richness and flexibility grounded in the concrete performances of amateur and professional folk musicians has been crystallized into a limited number of fixed and standardized regional *tavır*s, propagated by state or state-associated institutions at various levels. A critical evaluation of the development and position of the *tavır* concept in official and academic Turkish folk music discourse and practice is provided by Stokes:

> *Tavır* and *düzen* [(tuning)] are two of the principal ways through
> which academics and ideologues associated with state-endorsed

folk music provide the music with intellectual credentials to rival the *makam* tradition and propagate the notion of a nation-state unified through its rural, as opposed to urban, culture.

These *tavır* are not entirely divorced from Anatolian rural techniques, and, as the conservatories disseminate students with knowledge of *tavır*, the "reformed" style has fed back into regional rural practice. This situation is deeply problematic from the point of view of the urban researcher's quest for authenticity. (1992b: 93)

For the sake of clarification, I reproduce the regional *tavır* categorization applied in Gazi Erdener Kaya's *bağlama* method, as found on the website www.turkuler.com (see Figure 3.1).

Tavır of the *zeybek*[7] dances (Aegean Sea region):

(Temel)

Tavır of Konya (Central Anatolia):

→ Üst Tel (sol)

Tavır of Silifke (Mediterranean region):

Azeri *tavır*:

Tavır of Yozgat (Central Anatolia):

Tavır of Kayseri (Central Anatolia):

Black Sea and Balkan *tavır*:

Aşık tavır:

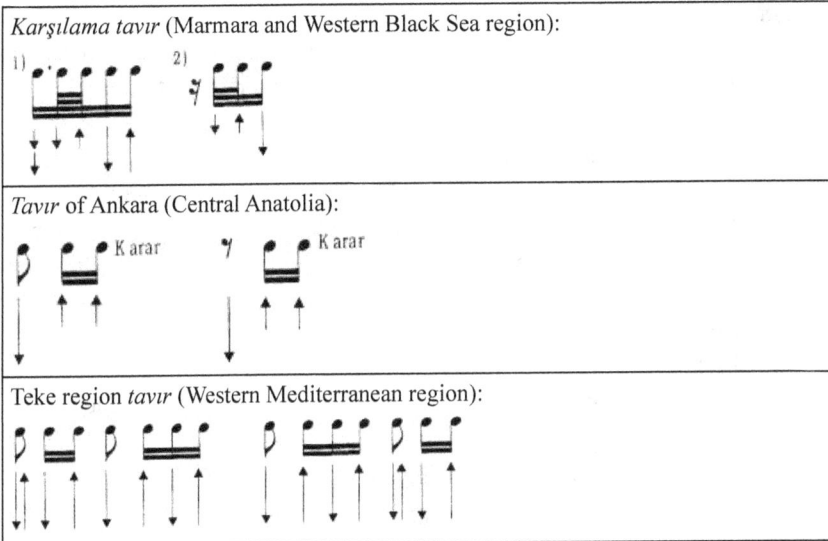

Karşılama tavır (Marmara and Western Black Sea region):

Tavır of Ankara (Central Anatolia):

Teke region *tavır* (Western Mediterranean region):

Figure 3.1: *Tavırs* represented by Gazi Erdener Kaya (1995)

Traditional Musician-types: *Aşıks, Abdals,* Roma

Aşıks

Aşıklık is a shared but diversified cultural heritage belonging to territories extending from Central Asia to the Middle East and the Balkans. Iran, Syria, parts of Russia, Georgia, Armenia, Azerbaijan, and Turkey display different forms of the phenomenon. The origins of the Anatolian version of the tradition can be traced back to *ozanlık* in ancient Central Asia, related to pre-Islamic spiritual poet-singers (shamans) ("Nomination for Inscription on the Representative List in 2009 (Reference No. 00179)" 2009: 2). The use of the title *aşık* (literally, "lover") dates from around 1500, and refers to bards mostly associated with Islamic Sufism or the military (Yang 2018: 18, 22).

Central to the *aşık* tradition is the moral content of its music and lyrics, and the ability of its representatives to create their own music and poems, often on the spot. Most of them accompany their singing on plucked instruments. *Aşıks* are often associated with Sufi or Bektashi orders, and sometimes perform the duty of *zakirlik* during Alevi *cem* ceremonies. *Ozans* (or *halk ozanları*) are less strongly associated with this religious, mystical background (Reinhard and de Oliveira Pinto 1989: 12, 23; Emnalar 1998: 221, 223; Büyükyıldız 2009: 136).

Aşıks perform an ancient corpus of love stories and heroic tales as well as report on recent events, often with a satirical or socially critical undertone. They are masters in improvisation; within the forms of certain poetic and musical genres, they respond to the circumstances and audience of their performances, sometimes even in the form of musical duels with the intention of defeating their opponents with words. They are professional musicians, expecting a remuneration for their musical services performed in *aşık* cafés, at social gatherings, during wedding parties, and in other contexts. Their repertoire consists of newly created personal songs as well as existing (older) songs written by other *aşıks* (Emnalar 1998: 219).

Büyükyıldız discerns two types of *aşıks*: (1) *badeli aşıks*, who have had a specific dream in which they drink wine offered by a *pir* (wise elderly man or master), and (2) *halk şairleri* or *saz şairleri*, who have not had this dream and in fact are not regarded as belonging to the class of real *aşıks*. *Badeli aşıks* adopt a pseudonym which they use in the form of a signature in the last stanza of their poems (Büyükyıldız 2009: 137). Another *aşık* typology, proposed by Artun, has three criteria for categorization: (a) *sazlı* and *sazsız aşıks* ("with *saz*" versus "without *saz*"); (b) improvising *aşıks* and *aşıks* performing pre-composed poems (Artun 2009: 1); (c) village *aşıks*, nomadic *aşıks*, town and city *aşıks*, military *aşıks* (*yeniçeri*), and Sufi *aşıks* (2009: 41). The composing *aşıks* (*kalem şairleri* or "pen poets") are characterized by Emnalar as belonging to the higher class with their classical poems, while the improvising *aşıks* (*meydan şairleri* or "public square poets") are considered as belonging to the class of common people (1998: 221). The distinction between urban and village *aşıks* is also made by Emnalar, who considers the *aşık tarzı* (*aşık* style) above all as an urban product.[8] Bates distinguishes wandering or itinerant *aşıks* from "coffeehouse" or settled *aşıks* (2011: 6–7).

The iconic example of a twentieth-century *aşık* is Aşık Veysel Şatıroğlu (1897–1973), who was born in the village of Sivrialan in the town of Şarkışla (province of Sivas) and became blind at the age of seven. He became famous as a wandering minstrel accompanying himself on the *saz* and was subsequently invited to perform on national radio and to teach in the village institutes. The subjects of his poems include love, nature, mystical beliefs, and events from social reality (Emnalar 1998: 219). Historical *aşıks* are sixteenth-century Pir Sultan Abdal, Köroğlu (singing about injustice), Aşık Garip (singing about exile), and Aşık Kerem (singing about love), seventeenth-century Karacaoğlan, and nineteenth-century Dadaloğlu and Ercişli Emrah. Additional twentieth-century examples are Aşık Mahsuni Şerif, Davut Sulari, Aşık Murat Çobanoğlu, and Aşık Yaşar Reyhani (Emnalar

1998: 211–19, 229; "Nomination for Inscription on the Representative List in 2009 (Reference No. 00179)" 2009: 3). In the past, no distinction was made between *abdals* (see below) and *aşıks*. Even today, important Alevi or *abdal* musicians (e.g., Neşet Ertaş or Ali Ekber Çiçek) are sometimes considered *aşıks*.

Nowadays, *aşıks* have lost their original social functions, but their art is still maintained. Although almost extinct, *aşık* cafés can still be found in certain cities, and state- or authority-supported *aşık* festivals are organized in many regions of Turkey.

Abdals

The historical *abdals* belonged to the Oğuz or early Turkmen people and formed a group characterized by a mystical (Sufi) belief. The term *abdal* approximates the "dervish" concept and indicates a modest way of life. During the twelfth century, the group ("tribe") of *abdals* settled in Anatolia, fleeing from Khorasan, a region belonging to present-day Iran, Afghanistan, and Turkmenistan. Later, they became associated with the Alevi-Bektashi form of Shiism.

Historically as well as currently, *abdals* have fulfilled the social role of professional musicians, particularly instrumentalists. In earlier times they were known as *ozans* or *halk ozanları* (see above). In addition to musicianship, *abdals* performed other jobs, often involving craftwork such as tent-making or metallurgy. Recently, they have adopted many other occupations and often combine musicianship with other sources of income. Their social role is to perform regional music on social occasions such as wedding or circumcision parties. *Abdals* often travel to different regions to perform their musical activities, assimilating to the musical style of the place where they are performing. The most common instruments are the *bağlama* and the *davul* and *zurna*, although in certain regions, other instruments are played as well. The Kırşehir province can be considered as the core of the *abdal* culture,[9] but communities can be found throughout the whole of Turkey, with a high concentration in the centre and the south. The only region without *abdal* presence is the Black Sea region. The *abdals* of the different regions of Turkey still consider themselves as related by family ties. In the middle of the twentieth century a large-scale movement from the villages to the cities occurred, when the nomadic *abdals* were obliged to settle down.

The subordinate position of Shiite Alevis throughout five centuries of Sunni Ottoman rule and the dubious status of music in orthodox Islam have contributed to the lower social position of the *abdal* musicians (Ágoston and Bruce 2009: 548–49). *Abdals* are often erroneously confused with Roma (see below), with whom they share diverse traits: they have a similar role and position in society, they have similar occupations, and they probably also intermarry. Although the history of both ethnocultural groups is intricate and mutually interrelated, the two groups should be distinguished from each other, since they belong to different migrant waves with a different background and history.

The difference between *abdal* and *aşık* concerns the way in which their respective artistry is acquired and transmitted: while *abdallık* is transferred from father to son and *abdals* are thought to possess musical talent by definition, *aşıklık* involves the discovery and training of a special talent, independent of hereditary traits. While *abdals* are trained in a family context, *aşıks* are educated by a chosen master (*usta*). *Abdals* generally do not improvise but perform existing poems and music, while the ability to improvise on the spot is a central feature of *aşıklık*. In Kırşehir, however, *abdals* do perform an active role in the creation of new musical pieces.

As was the case for *aşıks*, the social role of *abdals* is currently changing. In Kırşehir and Kaman, *abdals* have been recovered by the authorities and acquired the title of *devlet sanatçısı* ("state artist"). They take part in general and specific festivals and are broadcasted on the national radio (Picken 1975: ch. 2; Özdemir 2008; Başaran, i/v, 27 July 2012; Göçer, i/v, 27 July 2012; Karademir, i/v, 31 July 2012).

The most famous representatives of the *abdal* tradition of Kırşehir are Muharrem Ertaş (1913–84) and his son Neşet Ertaş (1938–2012), who were born in small Turkmen villages near Kırşehir. Both are considered unsurpassed masters of the *bozlak* genre, albeit in different stylistic idioms. The *bozlak*, performed in the typical *abdal* singing style (*abdal ağzı*) and accompanied by the *bağlama*, is a strongly emotional lamentation about impossible love or other unfortunate events happening to an individual or a people. Both the father and the son were extremely productive.

While Muharrem's music was very much a continuation of existing traditions, Neşet's music is the product of a different time. He modernized the tradition by creating a new authentic and emotional idiom, based on an amplified *saz* sound. Neşet's life and work have a strong transnational component, engaging diasporic and indigenous audiences and contexts. He lived in Cologne, Germany, for more than two decades, and produced numerous songs and albums in the diaspora, often related to the theme of *gurbet* (exile, living abroad). After his return to Turkey in 2000, he acquired official recognition, and grew to become the most beloved Turkish folk singer (*halk ozanı*) of his time. In his senior years, he received diverse awards and acknowledgements in Turkey as well as internationally. By refusing to accept the title of "state artist", he profiled himself as a singer of the people and took a critical position regarding the Turkish authorities, who have left many less well-known *abdal* musicians and other artists of the lower class to their fate.

Roma

Roma musicians, as mentioned above, share many common traits with *abdal* musicians. They belong to the same social class and have similar occupations and social functions. Like the nomadic *abdals*, the Roma were obliged to settle by the Turkish authorities, but, at the same time, they dispersed over different regions of Turkey (Girgin, i/v, 30 July 2012). Nowadays, they can be found in almost every Turkish province. The Roma communities in Turkey, which belong to the general branch of "Western Roma", are heterogeneous in language and origin (Duygulu 2006b: 19). They are migrants from Central Asian and Arab areas (Duygulu 2006b: 21). Melih Duygulu discerns three categories of Roma in Turkey: nomads, semi-nomads, and settled groups (2006b: 22). At present, between 500,000 and 2,500,000 Roma are living in Turkey (2006b: 27). Unlike the *abdals* who adhere to Alevism, many Turkish Roma have adopted the mainstream Turkish religion of Sunnism.

The musical repertoire performed by Roma in Turkey consists of Turkish music (local folk music, classical music and *fasıl*, *arabesk*, and other popular music genres) and a specific Roma repertoire (Duygulu 2006b: 37), mainly maintained by the Roma in the Marmara and Aegean regions (Duygulu 2006b: 37, 40).

Aşık Music

Aşık music occupies an ambivalent position in the domain of Turkish folk music, being an authored art form with ties to urban and high art as well as rural and folk art. While certain *aşık* genres are grounded in classical music and poetry, the strong embeddedness of the *aşık* repertoire in particular regional idioms renders its categorization as regional folk music justifiable. The artist name (*mahlas*) of the poet is always mentioned in the last stanza.

Emnalar structures the *aşık* repertoire by discerning different poetical forms on the basis of content or poetical form:

A) Prose:
- Folk story (*halk hikayesi*).

B) Poetry:
- Epos (*destan*): orally transmitted old epics narrating the history of the Turkic/Turkish people
- Ballad (*koşma*): widespread genre iconic for the art of *aşıklık*, consisting of quatrains with verses of mostly 11 syllables
- *Semai*: quatrains with verses of 4+4 syllables with or without a pause in the middle, displaying content related to love, nature, or separation
- Riddle (*muamma*). (1998: 206, 207, 210)

Regarding musical form, Emnalar discerns the following genres: *koşma, mani, semai, türkü, varsağı, atışma* (in which two *aşıks* alternate to create poems with a fixed end rhyme), *leb değmez* (which involves the insertion of a pin between the lips, limiting the number of consonants to be used), and *muamma* (1998: 226–27).

Aşık music can deal with diverse themes and subjects: death (*ağıt*), love, curse, legends and sagas (*destan*), displacement or migration (*gurbet*), praise (*güzelleme*), advice, social subjects, nature, religious-mystical themes, and satire (Emnalar 1998: 225–27). A typical feature is that historical and contemporary themes are mixed. The telling of the heroic deeds of a historical figure often conveys a political message relating to current events (Bates 2011: 7–8).

Alevi Music

"Alevi" means "follower of Ali", the cousin and son-in-law of the prophet Mohammad. Alevism as a denomination unites different but related forms of mystical Shiism. It is chiefly based on the teachings of thirteenth-century Haji Bektash Veli from Khorasan, but is enriched by pre-Islamic and other references. In practice, Alevism-Bektashism is closer to a philosophical-moral system than to a strictly religious system.[10] Alevis constitute 10 to 25 per cent of the Turkish population (Erol 2009: 166); the imprecise estimation is due to the persistent reticence to openly display Alevi identity, as a consequence of long-time oppression in the Ottoman Empire as well as the Turkish Republic.

Music is extremely important for many Alevis, their spiritual gatherings (*cem*) being a sequence of instrumental, vocal, and mixed musical expressions performed by the spiritual leader (*dede*), by a specialized musical assistant called *zakir* (or *aşık*), and by the entire community. The *bağlama*, which functions as a token of Alevi identity,[11] is often referred to as a "stringed Quran" (*telli Kuran*), and its parts are said to symbolize different figures and objects defining Alevism (Markoff 2002a).

Like the *aşık* repertoire, Alevi music occupies an ambivalent position. The broad and diversified repertoire is not unambiguously considered folk music, but neither is it considered art music (Bates 2011: 13). Emnalar and other authors do classify Alevi music as (religious or mystical) folk music, on the basis of similarities regarding scale, melody, rhythm and metre characteristics, and the instruments used (Emnalar 1998: 396). Ayışıt Onatça discerns two kinds of Alevi-Bektashi music: an urban repertoire with lyrics belonging to the classical *divan* literature and music influenced by Ottoman classical music, and a folk repertoire with lyrics belonging to folk Sufi literature (2007: 45). Only a part of the repertoire (with its authored lyrics) is included in the official TRT folk music archive, where it is not specified as Alevi music (Erol 2009: 168; Özdemir 2018: 181).

Emnalar discerns the following forms and genres of Alevi music:

- Hymn or anthem (*ilahi*): musical-poetic form shared between folk and classical, and between mosque and lodge repertoires:
  - *Nefes* (literally "breath"): general name for *ilahi* in the Alevi-Bektashi belief
  - *Savt* (literally "voice"): *ilahi* belonging to other Alevi orders, characterized by many repeats
  - *Gülbang*: Bektashi form of *savt*, non-metrical.
- *Kalenderi*: form close to the classical *gazel* (sonnet)
- *Semah*: accompaniment of the ritual Alevi-Bektashi dance
- *Mevlid*: remembrance of the birth of Ali. (Emnalar 1998: 397–408)

Ayışıt Onatça proposes another categorization on the basis of content:

- *Deyiş* (literally "saying"): didactic genre recounting the basic rules of Alevi belief and philosophy, also occurring outside a religious context
- *Nefes*: didactic genre recounting the basic rules of *Bektaşilik*, mostly occurring in a religious context
- *Duvaz imam* ("twelve imams"): song about the 12 successors of Mohammad recognized by the Alevis
- *Miraçlama*: song with epic character about the ascension of Mohammad
- *Mersiye*: epic mourning song (*ağıt*) about the battle in Karbala in which imam Hussein was killed
- *Semah*. (Ayışıt Onatça 2007: 46–55)

The *semah* or ritual dance is defined in an UNESCO document as a "set of mystical and aesthetic body movements in rhythmic harmony performed by … *semah* dancers, accompanied by *zakirs* playing *saz*" ("Nomination File No. 00384" 2010: 3). Performing (*dönmek* or "turning") the *semah* is a way to reach God. Unity with God is symbolized by the cyclical movements of the dance. Typically, *semah* involves mixed dancing of men and women together. There is no fixed form of *semah*: regional variations in music and dance exist throughout Turkey, for example, involving different melodies on certain texts or different texts on certain melodies (Ayışıt Onatça 2007: 48; "Nomination File No. 00384" 2010: 4). A *semah* generally consists of two or three gradually accelerating parts: *ağırlama* (slow prologue), *yürütme* (increasing tempo), and *yeldirme* (fast tempo). Throughout the course of the three parts, the mode, metre, and rhythm change as well (Ayışıt Onatça 2007: 181; "Nomination File No. 00384" 2010). The most common metres are 2/4, 4/4, and 9/8 (Ayışıt Onatça 2007: 186).

Topics and Themes in Turkish Folk Music

Turkish folk songs express an infinite number of concrete subjects in their lyrics. Several authors have attempted to channel this multiplicity and abundance into a discrete series of categories. Zeki Büyükyıldız justly remarks that it is "in fact impossible to categorize Turkish folk songs according to their subjects" since many folk songs deal with different subjects at the same time (2009: 151).

Doğan Kaya proposes the most detailed categorization: songs about nature, love songs, songs about bravery and songs with a historical subject, ceremonial songs (wedding songs: henna songs, veil songs, songs accompanying the fetching of the bride, songs to greet the bride, groom songs, dance songs; songs related to the *cem* ceremony; songs related to a children's ritual about shepherding; songs accompanying social gatherings), soldiers' songs, songs about food, songs about animals, songs related to concrete events, songs about plants and flowers, vendors' songs, sowing songs, songs related to the Ramadan *davul* players, songs about concrete persons, songs about sorrow, pain, and sickness, songs about displacement, migration, or nostalgia, occupation and work songs, songs about bandits, death songs (lamentations), lullabies and children's songs, songs about imprisonment, humorous songs, satirical songs, and educational and advisory songs (Kaya n.d.a; n.d.b).

The following important themes and topics emerge from a comparison of several authors' contributions: love, death, marriage, religious and other ceremonies and rituals, work and handicraft, nature, migration and nostalgia, imprisonment and soldier's life, legends and heroes, historical events, teasing and satire, and lullabies and children's songs (Başgöz 2008: 33; Büyükyıldız 2009: 151; Uğurlu 2009; Kaya n.d.a; n.d.b).

Case Study: The Music of Emirdağ

Emirdağ, the hometown of the majority of Belgian Turks, has a rich and flourishing music culture. The music of the town and its villages constitutes an important part of the Turkish folk music heard and performed in Ghent. At the same time, its documentation is scarce, and limited to a few endeavours in Turkish – except for a CD booklet. Publications from the past years include an article by Satı Kumartaşlıoğlu (2018), books reissued by Ömer Faruk Yaldızkaya (Yaldızkaya 2006, 2018), a CD booklet written by ethnomusicologist Melih Duygulu accompanying a double CD issued by Kalan (Duygulu 2012), and a master's thesis by Erdem Özdemir (2008).[12] Two other sources provide ethnographic descriptions of mystical rituals in the village of Karacalar (İstanbullu 2017; Kor 2018).

Although Emirdağ is administratively assigned to the Aegean region (as is the whole province of Afyonkarahisar), culturally and musically it is more closely related to the region of Central Anatolia. The town is situated 190km southwest of Ankara and 230km northwest of Konya – two important centres of Central Anatolian culture (see Figure 3.2). As of 2016, the population of Emirdağ is approximately 37,000, equally distributed between the town and the villages ("Emirdağ" 2018). Ethnic diversity is the main feature of its population, which consists largely of Turkmens. The area had been conquered in the twelfth century by the Seljuks from the Byzantines and was subsequently populated by Turkmens (Yaldızkaya 2006: 6).[13] The majority are Sunni but there is a substantial Alevi minority, which is chiefly concentrated in the village of Karacalar but also found in Emirdağ itself.[14] Emirdağ has been and still is mainly dependent on agriculture and animal husbandry. Due to its altitude (ca. 1000m) and harsh climate with its warm, dry summers and cold, snowy winters, the agricultural possibilities are rather limited. This economically unrewarding situation caused a massive emigration starting in the 1960s, first to urban centres in Turkey and later to Europe. As shown in Figure 3.3, another defining trait of the sociocultural configuration of Emirdağ is the large size of its territory and the quantity of its villages and municipalities (Duygulu 2012: 21–22; De Gendt 2014: 30–31).

Figure 3.2: Location of the province Afyonkarahisar (https://commons.wikimedia.org/wiki/File:BlankMapTurkeyProvinces.png)

Figure 3.3: Map of Emirdağ and its villages (www.afyonkarahisar.net.tr)

As elsewhere in Turkey, the *bağlama* has gained importance in Emirdağ during the past three or four decades (Duygulu 2012: 13). Today, it is the most commonly used instrument in wedding and circumcision parties (in its electric form) and other events requiring (semi-)professional music-making. Yet it has not penetrated the amateur level as thoroughly as in larger urban environments. The clarinet has also gained a central place in the Emirdağ style. It is played by the *abdals* and has replaced the *zurna* in the traditional combination with the *davul*. This combination is used in different kinds of celebrations with a ritual component. The "oriental" synthesizer is now used in many public or private musical events. *Kaşık* (wooden spoons) are commonly used in dance tunes. Instruments belonging to the realm of Turkish (light) classical music, such as violin, *ud*, *cümbüş* (hybrid between *ud* and banjo), and *darbuka*, have entered the musical practice of the *abdals*. Here, the boundary between classical and folk repertoires and styles is crossed. The absence of the *bağlama* in the traditional practice of the Emirdağ *abdals* renders a different and rather uncommon character to this group of professional musicians, compared to other *abdal* groups (most eminently the culturally important Kırşehir *abdals*). Amateur music-making usually does not involve any instruments or is limited to the use of some kind of percussive instrument. Women (except Alevi women) usually do not play musical instruments, although traditionally they sometimes accompany themselves on a metal dish or the lid of a pan called *def* or *tef* after the musical instrument (frame drum). The *kaval* or shepherd's flute has almost disappeared but is still played by a few people.

Three types of "traditional" performers of folk music in Emirdağ and its villages can be identified: "ordinary" people, *aşıks*, and *abdals*[15] (Duygulu 2012: 11). While the first and second category are also original "creators" (*üretici*, *yakıcı*) of folk songs, the importance of the *abdals* is their status as performers (*icracı*) of the existing traditions and their ability to play instruments (Özdemir 2008). While the three types still continue to exist – the *aşıks* nevertheless being limited to three or four persons and the *abdals* to a few families – a new type of performer should be added: people born in Emirdağ having studied in an urban centre and learned music autodidactically or through formal or informal music lessons. They typically perform a repertoire broader than the regional folk songs and dances, incorporating music from neighbouring regions or even the whole of Turkey in a performance style modelled on that of the conservatoires (the "academic" style), commercial artists (a popularized style), or the TRT (an official style incorporating academic as well as popularized stylistic elements). The *bağlama* plays an important part in this type of musician's musical performance and in *aşık* practices. Today, it is also played by *abdals*, notably in lengthy performances during weddings and other festive occasions, although it still remains entirely extraneous to the traditional musicking of common people.

Rhythmic and melodic similarities to the music of Kırşehir can be observed, and certain songs are close to the idiom of the typical *uzun hava* genre of Kırşehir, the *bozlak*. These commonalities appear in the music of the *abdals*, which can be interpreted as a possible sign of interaction or interrelation between the *abdal* families of both regions. Other observable influences are the resemblances to certain genres belonging to Southeast Anatolia (the region of Şanlıurfa) – a stop on the *abdal* route from Khorasan to Central Anatolia. The prevailing modal structures are *kürdi*, *hicaz*, and *hüseyni* (Aydemir, i/v, 14 and 15 June 2011) (see Figure 3.4).

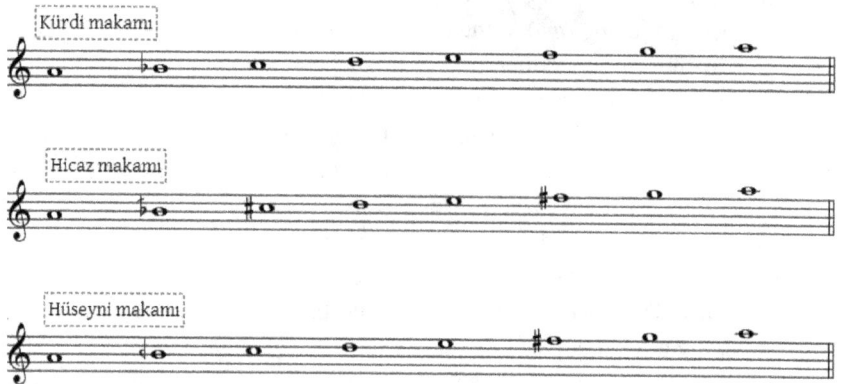

Figure 3.4: Frequently used modes in Emirdağ (Liselotte Sels)

Traditional occasions for which songs were created, and themes expressed in songs include: sowing (*ekin*), harvesting (*harman*) and time spent on the *yayla*, and the separation (*ayrılık*) sometimes accompanying these periods of the year; the rituals of henna night (*kına*) and wedding (*düğün*); love – often unrequited or complicated love – and separation from the beloved; social pressure and gossip (*dedikodu*); departure for military service (*askerlik*) and the separation it entails; migration and living abroad (inside or outside Turkey) (*gurbet*); and banditry (*eşkıyalık*) (Özdemir 2008). *Cems* and spiritual celebrations can be added to the list. One recurring theme is an imagined dialogue with birds, often a crane (*durna*), who are expected to bring (good) news about the distant beloved.

A persisting although gradually declining tradition is the singing of lamentations to express grief over a sad event. Those laments, called *ağıt* throughout the whole of Turkey, are almost without exception sung by women. Abdullah Özkürt from the village Suvermez is one exception, embodying the rare phenomenon of male *ağıt* singers in the region. Most typically, laments are created when a beloved person has died, often the partner, but also a sibling, child, or other relative. The death can have diverse causes: for example, illness, an accident, war. The *ağıt* improvises in free metre, narrating the qualities of the person who died or the circumstances of his/her death. If the deceased does not have a relative or friend who is able to lament him/her, this socially and morally mandatory task is fulfilled by specialized women (*ağıtçılar* or *ağıtçı kadınları*) who are respected for their lamenting abilities. While the majority of the *ağıts* are created for a close relative or friend, there is also a kind of *ağıt* which is made for the occasion of the death of an illustrious person, for example Atatürk. Another variant does not mourn about the death of a beloved person but is instead a personal plaint about an unfortunate situation. Examples of this kind in Emirdağ are provided by girls lamenting about their fate of being given to a boy they do not love.

Gaba hava is another non-metrical genre typical for the region of Emirdağ, corresponding to a local form of the generic type of the *uzun hava.* Another kind of improvisatory music-poetic creation in Emirdağ that has now disappeared is the singing of short quatrains or even distichs with brief verses of usually seven syllables (*maniler*). In the past, this type of song was improvised by girls or women during their collective work or sung in playful dialogue between boys and girls during wedding parties. In many cases, improvisation means creating variations on the lyrics of already existing songs. Common rhyme schemes are AAAB, AABA, and variants like AAABB. Musically, the most common metre is 2/4, but metres with five and nine beats also occur. Metrical changes within one song are not exceptional (Yaldızkaya 1990, 1995; Duygulu 2012; Özdemir 2008).

Some Remarks on the Theoretical Knowledge of Turkish Folk Musicians in Ghent[16]

Turkish folk musicians in Ghent possess theoretical and practical knowledge about the music they perform. Through a qualitative survey, I was able to learn more about the extent and modalities of their knowledge in the fields of music theory, performance practice, and context. Regarding music notation and reading skills, the majority of the interviewed musicians recognized their importance and mentioned greater musical insight and increased accessibility of the repertoire as their principal advantages. On the other hand, some musicians considered these skills superfluous, referring to their well-developed ear and memory. Most of the musicians were able to follow the contours of written music; some could write music as well. Many musicians admitted that their skills were becoming weaker due to a lack of practice.

The interviewed musicians' knowledge of music theory was generally implicit or practice-oriented, and was preferably illustrated on the *bağlama* or by singing, instead of through verbal explanation. The typical characteristics of the Turkish music system were usually articulated via a comparison with the "Western" system. *Horizontality* and *monophony* were often mentioned as characteristic features of Turkish music. The interviewed musicians were aware of the larger number of tonal subdivisions available in the Turkish tonal system compared to the Western system, although their exact position, distribution, and quantity were not always consciously known. For those smaller steps, they employed terms such as "commas", "microtones", and most frequently and inaccurately, "quarter-tones".[17] Some of the musicians mentioned the fact that microtones are not confined to Eastern music, but were also found in ancient Greek and Byzantine music. The tuning system was somewhat opaque for those interviewed: not everyone was aware of the difference between non-tempered tuning (with pure fifths/fourths) and the equal temperament of modern Western music. Some interviewed musicians asserted that folk music uses a smaller number of "microtones" than classical music, but also that this gamut can be extended according to the needs of the music or the performer. Other differences between the classical and folk music system remained unexplored. The *makam* system was relatively familiar to the Turkish musicians in Ghent. The classical musician defined it as "a system of rules for melody formation". Many musicians easily transplanted the *makam* system to the folk domain. The term *ayak* was known to some as the (academic) folk music equivalent of *makam*. The *makams* or *ayaks* of Turkish folk music were thought to differ in name and/or in number from the classical *makams*. Most of the musicians knew *makam* or *ayak* names and were able to recognize, play, or sing the most common modes.

Turkish musicians in Ghent often used the concept of "rhythm" in the sense of "metre", while the term "tempo" also caused some confusion. Rhythm and metre were recognized as important parameters, inherently connected to poetry and song texts, dance, and performance aspects such as plectrum strokes. The classical musician defined the Turkish metrical *usul* system as being cyclic in contrast with the rigid (divisive) Western system. Some musicians pointed out that all metres consist of combined units of two or three beats. The difference between symmetric and asymmetric metres was known, along with the possibility of different or alternating groupings under one "time signature". Almost all interviewees spontaneously named or illustrated typical kinds of metre belonging to certain regions or genres.

With rhythm being connected to the verses of song texts, the larger structures of poetry were thought to define the longer musical phrases and the general shape of Turkish folk songs. The interviewed musicians identified strophic forms (with repetitions) in addition to through-composed forms (without repetitions). Defining musical forms and genres proved to be an intricate task. From the musicians' explanations, it was not clear whether they associated specific genres with different regions, or if they identified more generic forms with different names across the different regions. Most musicians were aware of the existence of broad categories of Turkish folk music, such as *uzun hava* and *kırık hava*, or *türkü*. The characteristics of specific genres, however, proved difficult to describe. Genres were usually characterized either by extra- or meta-musical parameters such as region, instrument, and/or dance, or by musical parameters such as tempo and metre. The concept of "style" was mentioned by certain musicians, which in turn was defined by the parameters of rhythm, melody, and *tavır*. The concept of *tavır* was widely known and used to denote region-specific playing styles, involving plectrum techniques or (under the name of its vocal pendant *ağız*) singing styles.

Knowledge in the field of performance practice was easily illustrated on the instrument or by singing; verbalizing often unwittingly turned into too much abstraction. The interviewed musicians spontaneously mentioned a great number of concrete components of performance practice, such as (in order of importance): ornamentation and trills, dialect and pronunciation, singing techniques and *ağız*, plectrum techniques and *tavır*, tempo and phrasing.

On the conceptual level, different attitudes concerning performance practices of Turkish folk music emerged from the interviews. Attitudes situated on the "traditional" or "conservative" side included attempting to imitate the original performer, following the *tavır/ağız* of the region in question, relying on the scores published by the TRT, and using the appropriate regional instrumentation. Many musicians were aware of the impossibility of copying the specific *tavır* or *ağız* of another performer and of a region other than one's own region of origin. More "innovative" or "progressive" attitudes included transferring the music to alternative Turkish folk instruments, developing a personal style out of different examples, improvising based on existing repertoire, and adding Western techniques (amplification, electronic instruments or other Western instruments, harmonization, chordal accompaniment or polyphony, or other features of diverse Western music styles). The practice of musical variation was generally accepted, on the condition that it be restricted and idiomatic. Tolerated forms of variation were ornamentation, small additions or omissions, tempo fluctuations, and rhythmic variations. On the subject of improvisation, views differed more widely. The interviews did not make clear when improvisation opportunities occur, and there was no unanimity about the question of whether vocal or instrumental improvisation is more common. However, the introductory *uzun hava* form was acknowledged as the pre-eminent occasion for improvisation. Improvisation, like interpretation and performance practice in general, was considered to be based on the knowledge of existing models and repertoire.

When discussing the contextual domain relating to Turkish folk music, concrete knowledge was alternated with more general opinions. There was consensus about the impossibility of retrieving the exact context, occasion, and period of origin and the precise author of the largest part of Turkish folk music, apart from certain well-documented exceptions and the most recent repertoire. Information concerning the *kaynak kişi* ("source musician", in fact the transmitting musician) and the place and date of recording have only become known since the first half of the twentieth century, when Turkish state organizations began registering and notating Turkish folk music. Some musicians believed that traditional folk songs are still being collected today as they used to be earlier in the twentieth century, while others emphasized that nowadays only predictable, simple love songs are being added to the TRT repertoire (see the next chapter for more information about the TRT repertoire and its constitution).

The interviewed musicians perceived contemporary and historical meanings and functions of Turkish folk music as largely different. Certain musicians viewed present-day so-called folk songs as being composed in an artificial, non-functional way, for the sake of mere entertainment or even financial profit. Some complained about a loss of originality and quality. All the same, on another level, Turkish folk music was perceived as universal, still meeting present-day needs of listeners and musicians alike. (Unattainable) love, homesickness, war, farewell, and blood feud were mentioned as frequently occurring subjects. Regarding musical function, the musicians mentioned religious songs, lamentations, political or social songs, dance music (recreational or ritual), music within the marriage rituals, lullabies, children's songs, shepherd songs, market vendor songs, and walking songs. A recurring outlook on Turkish folk music was to view it as a way of life and as being closely related to all lifetime events and stages of life. The musical characteristics, lyrics, and dances of Turkish folk music were considered closely interwoven with cultural traditions and living conditions, such as the way of life, the environment, the economic situation, and the needs and cultural characteristics of the people concerned. *Aşık* duels and Alevi *cem* ceremonies were known as ancient traditions that continue to endure to the present day.

Song texts were considered vital in Turkish folk music, even if their interpretation can be challenging due to their connectedness with often distant or bygone specific traditions or contexts. Many musicians in Ghent experience difficulties with metaphoric or literary language used in song texts. A Belgian musician specializing in Turkish music mentioned the sometimes nonsensical or superficial nature of Turkish folk music lyrics.

Concluding Thoughts: Turkish Folk Music in Theory and Practice

It is a complex endeavour to construct a general picture of what Turkish folk music today entails and encompasses, taking into account its enormous stylistic, formal, and thematic diversity, the Atatürkian reforms and societal changes it underwent, its appropriation by the Turkish state and later (attempts at) reappropriation by various groups, and the scarcity of historical, scholarly, and European-language sources.

The music and musical life of Emirdağ, the town of origin of a majority of the Turks in Ghent, is seriously underdocumented and requires further focused, in-depth study. The starting point I have provided is based on limited fieldwork and few written sources. Limited availability of sources and resources also affects the theoretical knowledge of the Turkish folk musicians in Ghent. The knowledge of performers in the diaspora is often – although not always – implicit and practice-based and -oriented. A major resource in the diaspora as well as in Turkey is constituted by the musical scores and recordings made and distributed by Turkish Radio and Television, to be discussed and critically evaluated in the next chapter.

Chapter 4

Turkish Folk Music Notation and the TRT Archive

In cities and towns in Ghent and Turkey, Turkish folk musicians often use or mention an official folk music collection, commonly referred to as "*TRT repertuvarı*" ("the TRT repertoire"). The extensive Turkish Radio and Television archive consists of recordings and scores from the folk and art music domains. Its importance and influence can hardly be overestimated. The collection of the folk music archive has been a determining factor in defining what is considered the folk music of Turkey: the repertoire has become a kind of canon upon which most folk music practice and discourse are based in urban Turkey and the diaspora.

Turning an essentially oral, highly diversified, living, changing tradition into musical notation has far-reaching and potentially problematic consequences. The modernist and nationalistic aspirations of the young Turkish Republic led to systematic processing and remodelling of the rich musical heritage of the non-classical (non-Ottoman) domain. The regional and other specific styles and repertoires (including those belonging to ethnic or religious minorities) were systematized and subjected to both "Turkifying" and Westernizing modifications. My remarks on regional *tavır* and *ağız* (in the previous chapter) are to be embedded here in a larger discussion and evaluation of the Turkish state's archival endeavours and more specifically the TRT folk music archive.

History of the Folk Music Archive

The TRT folk music repertoire (*TRT halk müziği repertuvarı*) builds on the numerous collecting expeditions undertaken since the first years of the Turkish Republic, and it is still undergoing further expansion. A first collection trip was organized by the Ministry of Education in 1925, but since no recording device was available during that expedition, the transcriptions were erroneous. After a phonograph and other devices had been imported from Paris and Germany, several trips were made by the Istanbul Municipal Conservatory (formerly named Darülelhan) in the late 1920s and early 1930s, resulting in a collection of more than a thousand songs. In 1930, a national archive was established in Ankara, which would become the Ankara State Conservatory in 1935 with the assistance of Paul Hindemith, who was invited by the Turkish government. This institution would carry out nearly 20 fieldwork trips between 1935 and 1952, with the collection growing to 9000 folk songs as a result. In the 1930s, folk song collection was coordinated by the *Halkevleri* (People's Houses), urban institutions with a cultural and educational function.[1] In 1936, Béla Bartók was invited by the Ankara Halkevi to conduct a fieldtrip. Bartók's methodological and systematic approach resulted in 90 carefully notated songs and functioned as a model for subsequent work. While the focus of the Turkish endeavours had been on quantity rather than quality, Bartók's exemplary work involved careful selection of representative material, notation from the wax cylinder, and a notation technique displaying as much detail as possible in order to achieve greater objectivity. Since the 1960s, the TRT and the newly founded Milli Folklor Araştırma Dairesi ("Department of National Folklore Research") of the Ministry of Culture have been the primary collector of Turkish folk music (Stokes 1992a; Karahasanoğlu Ata 2002; Balkılıç 2005; Okan n.d.).

Composition of the Folk Music Archive

The TRT folk music repertoire in its current form consists of three subcollections: *kırık havalar* (metrical songs), *uzun havalar* (non-metrical songs), and *sözsüz oyun havaları* (dance songs without text). At present, more than 6500 pieces and songs are transcribed, but a large and ever-increasing number of recordings is still waiting to be notated. The repertoire includes not only pieces from throughout the Turkish Republic, but also music from now foreign regions, formerly belonging to the Ottoman Empire. A considerable part of the TRT archive consists of music collected in the Balkans (e.g., Skopje, Thessaloniki), Iraq (e.g., Kerkuk), Azerbaijan, and Cyprus. In addition to music collected in rural villages, urban folk music has been included as well. This urban repertoire is often closely related to (light) classical idioms, especially in Thrace, the Aegean region, and the southeast; in the case of music from Istanbul or the Balkans, the urban repertoire even displays (implicit) influences of the European tonal-harmonic system in its melodic conception.[2]

When I visited the Ankara TRT Radyo Evi (Radio House) in July 2012, I was shown the then-ultimate entry in the *kırık hava* section, bearing the number 4884: the song '*Akan dereleri gibi*' ("Like running streams"), collected in 1980 and examined in 2010 (see Figure 4.1). The number of archived classical works was said to be 21,637 at that moment. The DVD which was given to me at the same occasion contained 4,694 *kırık havalar*, 600 *oyun havaları* and 1,047 *uzun havalar*, but it was already outdated. The online repository "Repertükül" (*Repertuar Türküleri Külliyatı*) today contains 5,210 *kırık havalar*, 695 *oyun havaları*, and 1,076 *uzun havalar* (Akbıyık 2016).

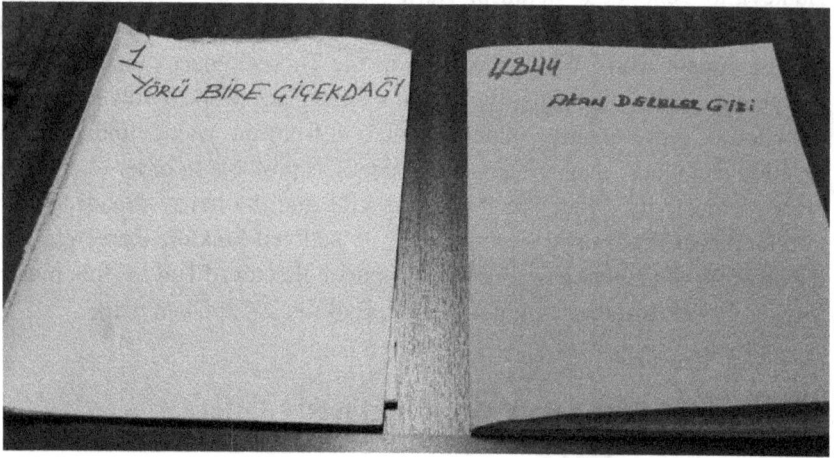

Figure 4.1: The first and last entry of the TRT archive in 2012, as kept in the Ankara Radyo House (photo by the author)

The same archive is kept in Istanbul, Ankara, Izmir, and Erzurum, where the four large Turkish radio houses with folk music choirs are located.[3] Newly collected tunes are numbered chronologically and distributed to the different radio stations. All scores contain the following information (see Figure 4.2 and Table 4.1):

T R T MÜZİK DAİRESİ YAYINLARI
T H M REPERTUAR No : 1
İNCELEME TARİHİ : 7. 6. 1970
2. İNCELEME TARİHİ : 1990
YÖRE
SİVAS / Şarkışla
KAYNAK KİŞİ
Âşık ALİ İZZET ÖZKAN
SÜRE : ♪ = 116

YÖRÜ BİRE ÇİÇEK DAĞI

DERLEYEN
NİDA TÜFEKÇİ

DERLEME TARİHİ
1967

NOTALAYAN
NİDA TÜFEKÇİ

(SAZ– –

Figure 4.2: Sample score of the TRT repertoire (www.repertukul.com/YORU-BIRE-CICEKDAGI-1, reproduced with permission)

Table 4.1: Information on TRT scores

TRT Müzik Dairesi Yayınları – THM repertuar No	TRT Music Department Publications – Turkish Folk Music Repertoire Number
İnceleme tarihi	Date of examination
(2. inceleme tarihi)	(Date of second examination)
Yöre	CITY/district or village
Kaynak kişi/Kimden alındığı	Source person: the person performing the piece while recorded
Derleyen	Collector: the person collecting/recording the piece
Derleme tarihi	Date of collection/recording
Notalayan/Notaya alan	Transcriber of the piece

The Turkish Folk Music Repertoire Committee (*Türk Halk Müziği Repertuar Kurulu*), consisting of seven to eight experts, decides which proposed pieces are to be included in the repertoire. The decisions are made on the basis of explicit evaluation criteria (*değerlendirme kriterleri*):

THE CONDITIONS REQUIRED BEFORE A WORK CAN BE EVALUATED

1. It should be accompanied by a recorded interview/report.
2. The recording should be clear and understandable.
3. It should be anonymous. Non-anonymous tunes (tunes belonging to a particular individual) cannot be included in the folk music archive, but can possibly be considered for inclusion in the art music archive.
4. The source person should be indicated and adequate/qualified.
5. The transcription should be correct and follow the recording.

MATTERS TO BE TAKEN INTO ACCOUNT IN THE EVALUATION

A. REGARDING THE TEXT

1. Should be in accordance with the Constitution, Turkish Radio and Television laws, other laws, general and specific principles of the Turkish Radio and Television, relevant regulations, circular letters and directives.

2. Should be in accordance with the structural features of Turkish folk poetry.

3. The specific and local expressions should be explained.

B. REGARDING THE MUSIC

1. Should carry the features of the region to which it belongs (*seyir*,[4] *uslüp*,[5] *tavır*,[6] and *ağız*[7]).

2. Should not be previously accepted in the repertoire.

3. Should not be similar to other pieces in the repertoire (except in the case of variants).

REMARKS

1. Pieces from audio, video or printed sources can be taken into consideration.

2. The realizations in the field of Turkish folk music, the accumulation of knowledge and the experience of the applicant will be assessed, and it is possible that an evaluation will be made only on the basis of the score.

3. Pieces performed in the Turkish radio of which recordings exist in the archives can be taken into consideration if approved by the relevant committees.

4. Pieces existent in the TRT Turkish Art Music Repertoire of which the composer is unknown and which are recognized as folk music, can be taken into consideration …

5. Pieces generated by *Halk Aşıkları*[8] can be taken into consideration, if they satisfy the conditions displayed above. (Türk Halk Müziği Repertuar Kurulu n.d.)

During my visits in July 2012 to the Ankara TRT Radio House and the TRT General Management in Ankara (see Figures 4.3 and 4.4), several informants provided valuable insight into the principles and procedures governing the composition of the TRT archive. New songs from throughout Turkey are still being added to the repertoire, and it is believed that there is still a vast resource to be discovered. An example of remaining rich sources of new folk songs are henna ceremonies. When people come to the TRT to propose a tune for inclusion in the repertoire, an interview is conducted, and an information file is set up. Questions are asked about who the source person is, whether the tune is anonymous, whether people dance to the tune, whether a recording has been made of the tune, and so on. The persons responsible for the admittance of new songs are said to virtually know the whole TRT repertoire, thus being able to judge whether a tune is really "new" ([TRT employee], i/v, 25 July 2012). New songs can be added to the repertoire through different channels: via experienced individuals diffused throughout Turkey (e.g., professional musicians or individuals attached to cultural associations), via musicians employed by the TRT who collect music from their own region of origin, or via old recordings or old musical scores (Dökmetaş, i/v, 25 July 2012).

In particular cases, an exception can be made to the prerequisite of anonymity. As Kubilay Dökmetaş[9] and the late Altan Demirel[10] explained, songs of *aşıks* can be included in the repertoire, on the condition that the melody and the lyrics carry the characteristics of the region to which the song belongs.[11] If a song is "too far removed from being authentic or traditional" (*otantik veya geleneksel olmaktan uzak*), it will be rejected. Judging this is indeed an intricate task requiring a lot of experience and thus can only be accomplished by "folk music experts" (*halk müziği uzmanları*) (Demirel, i/v, 25 July 2012; Dökmetaş, i/v, 25 July 2012).

Regarding the different versions of a particular folk piece, it was asserted that the first version reaching the TRT is regarded as the official version. In case different versions reach the TRT at the same time, a combination is constructed resulting in a single version. When a new transcription is finished, it is inspected by the Repertoire Committee (Sabuncu, i/v, 24 July 2012; Demirel, i/v, 25 July 2012). The process of transcription was described by Altan Demirel and Sabri Sabuncu.[12] If possible, transcriptions at the TRT are made by playing the recording at normal speed in order to keep the general impression. Great importance is attached to small details in the performance such as inflections in the voice and trills. It was claimed that knowing the *tavır* and *ağız* belonging to the region is a prerequisite to be able to make a proper transcription. The fast rhythms of the Black Sea music are considered difficult to recognize for non-experts (e.g., a 7/16 metre could be perceived as 2/4). The "microtonal" pitches are identified by ear, also in accordance with regional practices. The "instrumental parts" (to be played on the *bağlama*), which punctuate the vocal parts, are constructed after completion of the vocal parts. Mistakes or missing parts in the recordings are corrected or added in the scores. These decisions are motivated by considerations related to practices and principles applied in the discipline of art restoration: not more than

10 to 15 per cent of the artwork should be restored (Sabuncu, i/v, 24 July 2012; Demirel, i/v, 25 July 2012).

Figure 4.3: The Ankara TRT Radio House, downtown Ankara (photo by the author)

Figure 4.4: The Ankara TRT General Management, uphill Ankara (photo by the author)

Turkish Music Notation

In Ottoman history, different kinds of music notation systems existed, mainly in the classical music domain, but sporadically involving the notation of folk melodies as well. The earliest notation systems utilized numerological notation (with letters standing for figures, indicating pitches) and were used in theoretical works. Around 1700, new systems were introduced by Europeans at the Ottoman court. The Moldavian Wojciech Bobowski also known as Ali Ufki (1610–75) introduced European staff notation (from right to left according to the Ottoman writing) and made an extensive anthology containing religious and secular, instrumental and vocal, and classical and folk music. The Polish Dimitrie Cantemir also known as Dimitri Kantemiroğlu (1673–1727) used letters to indicate pitches in combination with figures to indicate duration. He applied this system to the composition of 40 pieces and to the notation of 350 instrumental pieces from the religious, secular, and military domain. The Armenian Hamparsum Limoncuyan also known as Baba Hamparsum (1768–1839) developed an ingenious notation system involving symbols to indicate pitches, durations, rests etc., for the first time written from left to right, and also compiled a state-of-the-art musical anthology. Giuseppe Donizetti also known as Donizetti Paşa (1788–1856) left a strong mark on Ottoman musical life, introducing European music in the Ottoman army and palace, organizing European-style concerts, and teaching European notation, composition, and instruments. His endeavours formed the basis for modern Turkish music notation (Emnalar 1998: 12–14; Karakaya 2012).

Anatolian folk music has been notated and published since the nineteenth century by Armenians, Greeks, and Hungarians, and subsequently by Turkish researchers (Greve 2017: 129). Since the establishment of the Turkish Republic, modern methods of notation of classical music and folk music have developed separately in certain respects. Both are derived from the modern, standard European system with extra accidentals added. In the classical domain, important contributions have been made by Rauf Yekta[13] (1871–1935), Suphi Ezgi[14] (1869–1962), and Hüseyin Sadettin Arel[15] (1880–1955), among others. The Ezgi-Arel system is a further development of Yekta's system. The difference between both systems is that they are based on different reference scales/*makams*, which results in a different conceptualization of natural and inflected tones, and subsequently a different use of accidentals. In the Ezgi-Arel system, a scale without accidentals exclusively involves intervals of a whole tone and four commas (Signell 1977: 39–40).

The notation system for Turkish folk music was developed by Kemal İlerici[16] (1910–86) and Muzaffer Sarısözen (1899–1963).[17]

Figure 4.5 shows the system of accidentals used in modern Turkish music notation.

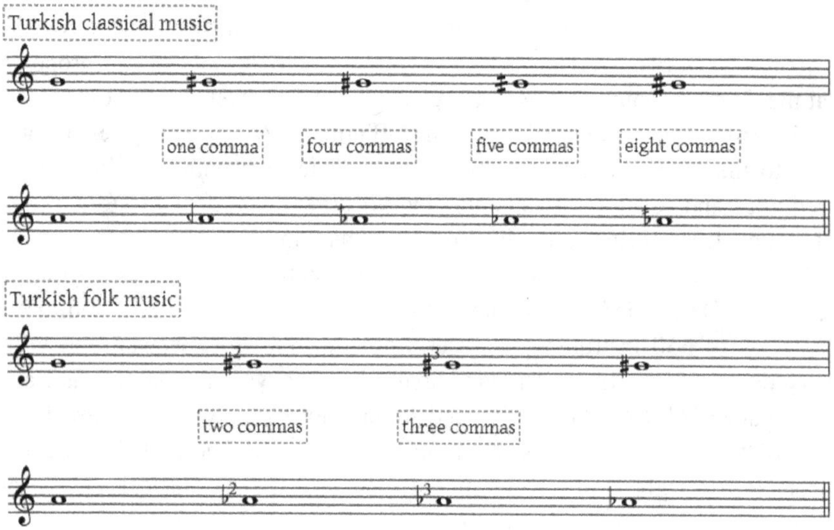

Figure 4.5: Accidentals used in the notation of Turkish classical and folk music (Liselotte Sels)

Folk music notation by official Turkish institutions (notably the TRT and universities) can differ greatly with respect to the amount of detail reproduced. The difference can be so great that some scores can be considered "descriptive" (e.g., the score in Figure 4.6), while others can be regarded as "prescriptive" (e.g., the score in Figure 4.7).[18] Nevertheless, a tendency towards complexity can typically be discerned, which in some cases hinders readability. These kinds of scores, which are in fact ossifications of a possibly accidental, probably one-off version of a certain piece or song at a specific moment in a particular context, are nevertheless considered by some folk music experts as standard or canonical representations of the music, which should be followed as closely as possible.

Figure 4.6: Sample of descriptive notation from the TRT repertoire (www.repertukul. com/SEKER-DAGI-NIN-HIC-EKSILMEZ-GICISI-353, reproduced with permission)

Figure 4.7: Sample of prescriptive notation from the TRT repertoire (www.repertukul. com/IZMIR-IN-KAVAKLARI-337, reproduced with permission)

Critical Evaluation of the TRT Repertoire

A critical examination of the practices and principles governing the selection and transcription of the TRT folk music repertoire, reveals multiple unsolved questions and contradictions:

- The criterion of anonymity leaves the door open to discussion and is not watertight as a determining factor for incorporation. Anonymity is an arbitrary criterion and an outdated concept in the scholarly study of folk music. It is generally accepted that folk tunes have an author, and the fact that the author is forgotten (or maybe concealed) does not render the tune anonymous. Anonymity as a feature of a tune is not inherent to the tune but is rather attributed by a deliberate decision. As a consequence, the exceptions ingrained in the evaluation system are just as arbitrarily decided based on unstable, adaptable criteria.

- In some cases, the first version is considered the official version, while in other cases, variants are also included in the repertoire; still in other cases, a combination of variants is constructed.
- While some transcriptions in the TRT repertoire are very detailed and specific (descriptive transcriptions), others are rather rough and general (prescriptive transcriptions). While the former may be based on one specific version of a piece, the latter may be the result of the combination of different versions.
- Mistakes in the recordings are corrected in the score, and missing parts are added. The result is that it is not clear to what extent the score reflects the reality of the concrete musical performances of the source persons. Can the resulting score still be considered as "belonging to the people" or "belonging to our country" (*yurdumuza ait*)?
- The instrumental parts, absent in the original recordings, are fully invented and constructed, in order to make the collected songs fit into the historically developed aesthetics of the Turkish Republic folk song collection.
- The pitches of the microtones are determined by ear and considered as flexible or approximate. This relaxed attitude is in contradiction to the often-heated debates about the exact pitches and intervals of the Turkish tone system in Turkish academic discourse.

Critical analyses of the TRT repertoire policy can be found in the literature as well. Seyit Yöre claims that "[t]here are many songs classified as anonymous of which the owner is known and still alive" (Yöre 2012: 566).[19] Based on an analysis of the types of folk tunes incorporated in the TRT repertoire, according to criteria of musical creation and stylistic features, he discerns three categories: "anonymous-authentic folk music, individual-authentic folk music, and populist-individual folk music" (ibid.).[20]

Zeki Büyükyıldız makes a similar analysis, discerning four categories of Turkish folk music: (1) anonymous folk music (separate from *aşık* music); (2) anonymous *aşık* music; (3) folk music created by traditional folk artists; (4) *aşık* music with a known author. Motivating the inclusion of *aşık* music – of which the author is usually known – is its embeddedness in a historical tradition involving a distinct, regionally defined melodic and literary style. The same principle is applied with regard to non-*aşık* music with a known author: if the musical style and lyrics are close enough to the regional idiom (which is considered to be authorless), the piece can be considered "close enough to anonymity". *Abdal* Neşet Ertaş from Kırşehir is the most obvious example[21] (Büyükyıldız 2009: 139–43).

Atınç Emnalar points to the ambiguity of the concept of the "source person" (*kaynak kişi*) and asserts that in many cases the person indicated as "source" (in the meaning of the person who transfers the – anonymous – piece) is in fact the creator of the piece. Mentioned examples are Aşık Veysel, Muharrem and Neşet Ertaş, and others. According to Emnalar, the TRT's criteria for deciding on the acceptance of a piece with a known author are arbitrary and unsatisfactory:

> According to some experts ..., the creators [*yakanlar*][22] of *türküler* should be uneducated and illiterate, and they should perform *ozanlık* in the cafés and on the village wedding parties. People who have studied or have not, villagers or city dwellers, have the same blood and origins and experience the same emotions. Why shouldn't they create *türküler*? (1998: 596)

Martin Stokes dwells at length on the topics of "individuality and invention" and "notation" in the context of the official TRT repertoire. In 1992, he also observed a field of tension between the official policy of incorporating only anonymous and *aşık* music, and "the great pressure on young musicians … at the TRT to get their [invented] pieces accepted, since their names are included in the repertoire [as source persons] and are often announced when they are performed on radio or television" (1992a: 55–56). The problems related to TRT music notation are identified by Stokes as manifesting on different levels and domains. As a consequence of the omnipresence and centrality of the *bağlama* in Turkish folk music since the establishment of the Republic, all collected music has been transformed into music that can be played on this instrument: "Notation is bound by that which can be played upon the *bağlama*, and the *bağlama* is bound by that which can be represented in notation" (Stokes 1992a: 58). This results in a monophonic, simplified notation that ignores the often rich and complex textures of authentic folk music (e.g., the polyphonic Black Sea *kemençe*[23] music). On the rhythmic-metrical level, drastic simplification sometimes takes place. Again, Black Sea music is used as an example. This extremely dynamic and flexible music often involves two or more unequal beats and many and quick changes in metre; yet it is notated as if it were, for example, a stable 5/8 metre consisting of two units of three and two sub-beats. A third level is the modification of the lyrics, which can also influence rhythmic and melodic development (Stokes 1992a: sec. 3.3). Stokes gives a clear impression of the possible impact of such aesthetic choices:

The Black Sea *kayde* is essentially improvised dialogue over a fixed, but open-ended melodic ostinato. The *türkü* required by the TRT is a formally closed, repetitive, and monologic verse-chorus structure. In the process of transformation from one to the other, what is officially deemed to be the same song has radically changed its nature. It is no longer an improvised demonstration of social wit and verbal skill, but an anonymous product of "the folk". (Stokes 1992a: 69)

Özlem Doğuş Varlı and Mahmut Cemal Sari provide other examples of how dance tunes and folk songs, traditionally played on *kaval*, *davul* and *zurna*, or *ud*, are adapted to fit into *bağlama* idioms. While the new *bağlama* versions apply certain techniques to evoke or imitate some of the idiosyncrasies of the "original" performances, they unavoidably alter the whole musical text and the perception thereof (Varlı and Sari 2017: 307–11).

The incompatibility of the often-extreme versatility of musical metre in Turkish folk music, and the regularity of the TRT notational system, is also demonstrated in Figures 4.8 and 4.9, juxtaposing the TRT score and my own (basic) transcription of the same song.

To summarize, the TRT repertoire which is so central to urban and small-town folk music performance (in Turkey as well as in the diaspora) presents itself – after close and critical examination – as an important, fascinating, hybrid, and problematic musical archive. Although notation of indigenous music (including some folk music) already existed in the Ottoman Empire, the new, systematic approach applied by the Turkish Republic, based on Western concepts and practices, was a game changer. Nationalistic and modernizing motives led to the constitution of a vast folk music archive, presented and, if needed, refashioned as essentially "Turkish" (despite the inclusion of minority, foreign, and urban musics).

Although the TRT employs highly skilled and knowledgeable musicologists and musicians, the constitution and notation of this archive remain inherently challenging and troublesome tasks. Changes and standardization procedures are often applied with regards to metre, instrumentation (voice and *bağlama*), microtones, form, and *tavır* and *ağız*. Arbitrariness exists in the choice of versions, the application of corrections, and the issue of prescriptive versus descriptive notation. The criterion of anonymity, with its exceptions, is also problematic.

Figure 4.8: Official TRT transcription of the song 'Uzun ince bir yoldayım' by Aşık Veysel, with a regular 4/4 metre (www.repertukul.com/UZUN-INCE-BIR-YOLDAYIM-2973, reproduced with permission)

Figure 4.9: Alternative transcription of the song 'Uzun ince bir yoldayım' by Aşık Veysel, showing the greatly versatile metre (Liselotte Sels)

The information and insights offered in this and the previous chapters, about the specific diaspora context of Ghent and its Turkish folk music network, the ways in which Turkish folk music manifests itself today in theory, performance, and notation, and the ways in which it has – in some respects thoroughly – changed during the past century, provide contexts and vantage points to understanding the ethnographic descriptions and analysis offered in the next chapters, which zoom in on musical events in Ghent and Turkey featuring the studied repertoire.

Chapter 5

Turkish Folk Music Events in Turkey and Ghent

This chapter, as well as the three ensuing chapters, take a closer look at a series of musical events I attended in 2011 and 2012 in Turkey and Belgium.[1] The events are analysed from different angles to gain more insight into how Turkish folk music functions and manifests itself in the early twenty-first century in a world characterized by the dynamics of migration, diaspora, and cosmopolitanism. Although the diasporic events are by default urban (happening in or around the city of Ghent), the fieldwork in Turkey purposefully extends to small-town and rural contexts to complement the urban focus.

Many kinds of Turkish folk music events in Turkey have a counterpart in Belgium. Life-cycle events such as weddings and circumcisions maintain their role and significance in the diaspora as much as in the motherland, and folk music is as much an integral part of these events in Ghent as it is in Turkey. The same applies to the *cem* ceremonies performed by the religious-cultural minority of the Alevis. Rural and urban festivals involving various kinds of folk music are transferred to the diaspora in a similar way, as are Turkish folk music concerts and café concerts, such as *türkü* nights (sometimes indicated as "Turkish evenings", thereby meeting the frame of reference of the autochthonous population).[2] Other events are specific to either the motherland or the diaspora context. For example, one might observe a folk dance lesson with live musical accompaniment and the training of *aşıklık* skills in Turkey, and a benefit evening for a Turkish village and a celebration of 50 years of Turkish migration in Ghent.[3]

Before going into the ethnographic details of the above-mentioned "common" and "specific" events selected in view of meaningful comparison and analysis, an overview of social occasions typically linked with folk music performance is offered. These occasions, mostly grounded in ritual, include nursing, circumcision, leaving for military service, marriage, decease, fasting, and certain types of spiritual or social gatherings. The connection between folk music and these occasions is rooted in history but is still current, and although strongest in the motherland, it manifests in the diaspora as well.

Traditional Occasions for Folk Music Performance

Nursing

Lullabies or cradle songs (called *ninni* or *nenni*) are sung by mothers after birth when alone with their babies. Given the limited possibilities for Turkish women in traditional society to express their feelings, these moments of privacy are a rare opportunity for a mother to "voice her desires, dreams and problems" (Duygulu 2006a: 46). Singing lullabies functions as "a time of thinking aloud, a concentration of emotions. [The mother] puts what comes to her mind, an extension of what she has experienced" (2006a: 47). By singing, the mother forms an emotional bond with her child and establishes a relationship with the Turkish language (2006a: 47).[4] Amil Çelebioğlu has categorized the diverse subjects which can be expressed through the lyrics of ninniler as follows: "(1) Religious, sacred or intellectual subjects; (2) Legends and laments; (3) Wishes or desires; (4) Love and related subjects; (5) Praise and satire; (6) Complaints and sorrow; (7) Separation, exile; (8) Promises, pledges; (9) Threats and frightening" (Çelebioğlu 1982: 20, as cited in Duygulu 2006a: 49). Existing lullabies can be passed down through generations, new ones can be created by improvisation, or combinations of existing and new elements can be made.

Circumcision

Circumcision is an important rite of passage in Turkish society. Although boys today are often circumcised as infants, traditionally, this ritual took place during the period of primary education,[5] or, in any case, before puberty. The organization of a large celebration ceremony (*sünnet düğünü*[6]) is considered a societal duty of the parents, through which they gain social respectability. Most often, modern celebrations are held on Saturdays or Sundays. Typical is the special outfit worn by the boy, consisting of a white cloak, napkin, and headgear, all embroidered with gold. A few days before the ceremony or on the day of the ceremony, the boy and his friends are paraded around the village or neighbourhood on a horse (or nowadays a car), upon which he receives gifts. Traditionally, the operation of circumcision was performed by a *sünnetçi*, a specialist who often belonged to the social group of the *abdals*, but today it is done by a doctor in the hospital. While in the past, the actual operation was integrated into the celebratory ceremony, today the party is usually organized a considerable time (sometimes even several years) after the operation (Turkish Cultural Foundation 2014a).

Military Service

For Turkish young men, fulfilling military service is considered an important societal duty and a rite of passage. A man who has not joined the army is considered immature and has not gained a proper position in society. Leaving for military service is celebrated ceremonially in an *asker uğurlama* or *asker düğünü*, depending on the region. Various farewell rituals are performed. First, the young man receives visits and presents. A few days before leaving, a banquet with his relatives and friends is organized, accompanied by dance music performed by *davul* and *zurna*. Sometimes the young man is paraded around the village or neighbourhood, during which he can receive gifts and "good luck money" can be put in his pockets (Turkish Cultural Foundation 2014d; "Asker Uğurlama" n.d.).

Marriage

Marriage is considered the cornerstone of society. In the past, wedding celebrations (*düğün*) were "almost the only opportunity for organized merry-making" in traditional communities, and the societal significance of this event was illustrated by its high costs, which could equal an annual income. Variations in how wedding celebrations unfold depend on factors such as "social standing, ... social distance between the parties, and ... area" (Stirling 1994). Many changes have occurred in the wedding traditions of Turkey, and many old forms of marriage (including polygamy) have disappeared. The custom of paying a dowry (*başlık*) is almost extinct, and the age deemed appropriate to marry has risen significantly. At present, young people usually marry just before or after military service, or after graduation from higher education. Although Stirling (1994) reports that the (early or late) winter used to be the appropriate season for wedding parties, today the vast majority are held during the summer months. Traditional wedding ceremonies consist of different stages, which begin a long time before actual marriage. The website of the Turkish Cultural Foundation (USA) identifies the following stages:

A) Before the wedding: Matchmaking and asking for the hand of a daughter; Verbal agreement to betrothal; Sherbet; Engagement; Quran-accompanied wedding gift announcement; Sending and exhibiting the trousseau; Bridal bath.

B) Wedding: Henna night (bride henna–groom henna); Receiving the bride; Marriage; Bridal Chamber; After the Bridal Chamber.

C) Practices after the wedding. (Turkish Cultural Foundation 2014c)

In the past, women from the family of the young man who was ready to marry paid visits to the family(s) of the prospective bride(s), and in the case of a positive evaluation, the prospective father- and mother-in-law would formally ask for the girl's hand in marriage. This custom is called *görücülük* or *dünürlük*. If the family of the bride agreed with the proposal, the betrothal was sealed with a verbal agreement (*söz kesme* or *söz kesimi*) and a small ceremony.

The official engagement ceremony traditionally takes place in the bride's home, although the costs can be paid by the groom or the bride's family. Male and female guests used to celebrate separately. The ceremony included music and dance, a lunch, the handing out of jewellery (*takı*) and other gifts, and the engagement rings. The bride wore a special engagement dress. The modern engagement party has maintained many of these elements, but the context is different: a wedding hall is often rented, men and women celebrate together, and sometimes the engagement party is even integrated into the wedding party itself.

The actual wedding celebration traditionally takes place from Tuesday to Thursday (according to the Islamic calendar), or from Friday to Sunday (which is the modern standard) and lasts three or even four days. Today, especially in urban contexts, wedding celebrations are often shortened to two days or even condensed into one day or evening. The expenses of the wedding party are met by the family of the groom. Between the engagement and the wedding, a period of one week to several years may pass. A few days before the marriage, a wedding flag is planted in front of the groom's house to announce the forthcoming marriage. During the first days of the wedding celebration, separate smaller or larger parties are held by the families of the groom and the bride.

The last night before the actual marriage, the henna night (*kına gecesi*) is held at the bride's home in exclusively female company, consisting of the female relatives of the bride and groom, and friends of the bride. In some cases, a similar ceremony is held in the groom's house by the groom and his friends and male relatives. The henna night is sometimes a sad occasion punctuated with lamentations by the relatives of the bride, but there is also room for joyful songs and dances. It is believed that crying by the bride brings good fortune. In the past, the henna night was a framework for the formal meeting of the bride and her mother-in-law. The bride wears a sumptuous dress and a special ornamented, red veil. The henna is brought on a silver tray with candles by female family members of the groom. Songs and hymns about henna and its symbolic value are sung while the hands (and sometimes feet) of the bride are adorned with henna by a woman with a happy marriage, but not before the mother-in-law has placed a gold coin in her hands to evoke prosperity and the responsibility of the groom's family. Henna is also put on the hands of the bride's friends, to effectuate timely marriage. Many of these elements and procedures persist today.

The day after the henna night involves the bride's farewell from her family and fetching her from her home to the groom's house (*gelin alma*: "taking the bride"). Sometimes the bride is paraded around the village on a horse (in the past) or a car (today), accompanied by traditional *davul* and *zurna* performances. Upon arrival at the groom's house, many ritual actions are performed to provide happiness, such as tying a red ribbon around the bride's waist (the "maidenhood belt" or "belt of perseverance"), holding up a mirror behind the bride as a symbol of a bright life, tossing coins or sweets as a wish for abundance, and spreading honey or butter on the threshold of the house to evoke sweet harmony. Subsequently, the bride enters the house. The same day, the groom goes to the mosque for the evening prayer, during which a *hoca* performs a religious ceremony in the house, and the fathers of the bride and groom seal the marriage in the presence of an *imam*, a ritual called *nikah* (Stirling 1994). Then, the newly married couple proceeds to the nuptial chamber. In some cases, the day after the marriage (bridal veil day) involves a small celebration by the women of the new house of the bride (Stirling 1994; Ustuner, Ger, and Holt 2000; Turkish Cultural Foundation 2014b; 2014c; 2014e).

Decease

When a person dies, the partner, relatives, and friends of the deceased come together for condolences, after or sometimes before the funeral. On this occasion, the sadness intensifies, and everyone is expected to participate in the ritual of mourning. Some people sing or speak an improvised lamentation (*ağıt*), which is a highly emotional act. This is traditionally done by women. In case no close family or friends of the deceased are able to create such a lamentation, "professional" *ağıtçılar* are engaged. These women, with the necessary experience and skills in textual and melodic improvisation, are generally not paid for their duties. The *ağıts* can also be created in dialogue between the *ağıtçılar* and the mourning person(s). The singing of *ağıts* is a ritual with important societal value, "socializ[ing] the family crisis" (Yaldızkaya 1990; Başgöz 2008).

Ramadan

During Ramadan, *davul* players in some places fulfil the duty of circulating through the streets to wake up the people just before dawn (*seher*) by playing loudly on their drum. While in some places this task is carried out by *abdals* or Roma, in other places poor amateur musicians take the initiative.[7] A communal ritual meal (*sahari* or *sahur*) is then consumed before all food and drinks are to be renounced during the day. After sunset, a second communal ritual meal (*iftar*) is eaten to break the fast. The *davul* players are traditionally paid a small amount of money by the people of the neighbourhood; today, this is sometimes done by the municipality ("Emirdağ Da Bu Ramazan Davul Yok" n.d.).

Alevi Rituals

In traditional society, Alevi *cem* ceremonies took place secretly in private places or lodges, to avoid confrontations with the dominant Sunni majority, which looked down upon the Alevis and did not consider them to be "proper" Muslims.[8] Today, cities and villages with an Alevi population sometimes have specially built *cem* houses (*cemevi*). Men and women are considered equal and participate in *cem* ceremonies together. Music belongs to the very heart of Alevi religious worship, and the *bağlama* performs a symbolic function.

Social Gatherings

Typical occasions for musical performance throughout Anatolia are social gatherings, often held in the evening or at night in private houses or properties. The winter is the preferred season. Different names are used to indicate these musical occasions, such as *oturak* ("sitting") in Konya, *yarenler meclisi* ("friends' gathering") in Çankırı, *cümbüş* ("merrymaking") in

Ankara, *muhabbet* ("affection") in Kırşehir, *sıra gecesi* ("turn night") in Urfa, *barana* in Balıkesir, *sohbet* ("conversation") and *keyif* ("pleasure") in Antalya and Isparta. Traditional *sohbet* meetings have been inscribed on the UNESCO List of Intangible Cultural Heritage of Humanity (Ataman 2009; "Nomination File No. 00385" 2010).

Traditionally, and even today, only men come together in this kind of gathering. Conversation, collective and individual singing, poetry reading, storytelling, and dancing belong to the performed activities. Usually, a meal and drinks are consumed, and in some cases also alcohol. Exceptionally, female dancers are involved. In addition to their divertive function, these gatherings fulfil important social and cultural functions. Denise Gill recognizes that such gatherings contribute to the development of moral and aesthetic aspects of "true manliness": "learning to become a man" (Gill 2018: 182, 198).

Other Occasions

This overview of traditional occasions involving folk music performance in Turkish society is not exhaustive. Other traditional occasions include the changing of seasons (specifically, the beginning of spring or summer), labour (e.g., sowing or harvesting, shepherding, doing handicraft, peddling), welcoming an important visitor (*karşılama*), and *aşık* activities (e.g., in *aşık* cafés or private homes).

A Comparison of Events in Turkey and Ghent

Two Wedding Parties

Boztepe and Mucur. It is Friday afternoon, the ideal time to start off a three-day wedding party. The places to be are alternately Boztepe and Mucur, both semi-rural districts of the Central Anatolian city of Kırşehir. At both locations, everything is prepared and ready. Both at the bride's (*gelin*) and the groom's (*damat*) places, large tents with tables and chairs are set up in front of the house, while in the yard, a PA system is provided, and plastic chairs are scattered around. During the three days of celebrations, there will be a lot of driving back and forth by the families, who are invited at particular moments by the family-in-law, while the rest of the time is spent with their own relatives. Both families have three musicians at their disposal: a traditional *davul–zurna* duo performing at important stages and welcoming newly arriving guests, and an indefatigable all-around musician entertaining all attendees for three days with regional dance music performed on strongly amplified *bağlama* combined with synthesizer and vocals. The *davul* and *zurna* players belong to the social group of the *abdals* and are in fact "seasonal workers" who move from South to Central Anatolia each summer to perform music during the countless wedding parties. They obtain their income largely from the tips of the guests, whom they accompany only as long as required to make them bring out their purses. The other musicians ("one-man ensembles") are well paid for their work but work long days without a moment of rest.

On Friday, the two families initially celebrate separately. There is a lot of dancing, chatting, eating (at any time of the day or night, arriving guests always receive a meal), and (alcohol-free) drinking. In the evening, the bride's family is invited by the family of the groom for the traditional *çiğ köfte* (a dish of spiced raw minced meat). The preparation of the *çiğ köfte* involves the singing of *maniler*, simple traditional songs, by the women.

Saturday is an important day; in the afternoon, the "engagement ceremony" (*nişan töreni*) is held, and in the evening, the "henna night" (*kına gecesi*) takes place. During the engagement ceremony, the groom's family visits their family-in-law to hand over their wedding gifts in the presence of the district mayor and accompanied by the obligatory gunshots. After this ceremony, both families move to the site of the groom, and in the evening, they once again travel in convoy to the bride's home for the famous henna night. This is an intimate moment when the amplified music ceases and gives way to the singing of the girls who bring the henna and apply it on the hands of the wedding couple in the dim light of many candles (and the flashes of the cameras nervously trying to capture everything). The bride wears a red veil, and the groom a green cloth. After this relatively intimate moment, the party goes on as before until everything comes to an end at the stroke of midnight.

That is to say, for most of the attendees. For the closest friends of the bride's father, the best is yet to come; they are invited for an "after party" in the form of a *rakı* night with mezze. The table and chairs are ready in the garden, and the mezze are quickly provided by the women of the family, who do not join the men's circle but keep their own private party in the kitchen of the house. The musicians on duty join in and play much more sensitively now than in the busyness of the previous days. The emotions often run high, also under the influence of alcohol. Many a man lets his tears flow freely, not least the father who will have to say goodbye to his daughter the next day. However, there is room for fun and joy as well, which is reflected in the cheerful dances, the many jokes that are swapped, and the funny, creative ways of asking for and giving *bahşiş* (tips).

The next and final day, Sunday, is more serious. In the morning, the family-in-law calls at the bride's place with only one goal: to fetch the bride to her new home. The red veil will be replaced by a white one today. A whole series of rituals is performed, such as holding a mirror and crying before the bride gets carried away by the family-in-law's loudly honking convoy of cars. Upon arriving at her new home, a vase is smashed on the ground, petals are tossed, hands of the family's elderly are kissed, a chicken is decapitated, and its blood is applied to the forehead of the bride, which she undergoes filled with horror. The "belt of maidenhood" is tied around her waist. After a short dance, accompanied by the completely exhausted musician in duty, the newly married couple enters the house, thus marking the end of the long wedding ceremony.

Nazareth. A second wedding celebration takes places on Easter Sunday at 6 pm; the party is about to start in the large party hall with the Turkish name "Ömeroğlu Düğün Salonu" (Ömeroğlu Wedding Hall), situated in Nazareth on an expressway connecting Ghent and Oudenaarde in the province of East-Flanders. The party hall consists of different sections and is highly decorated. The chairs are festively covered, and the tables are set and display mezze and fruit. The guest list includes family, friends, and some colleagues of the married couple, more than 300 people in total. Male and female guests are equally proportioned, and all kinds of people are present, from little children to elderly people, from girls wearing glittery or loud dresses to girls with long skirts and headscarves. The non-Turkish guests are given a place at specific tables with bottles of wine. Notable is the presence of a group of young fans of the musicians, not having any relationship with the married couple.

Similar to the wedding in Turkey, two bands are present: the traditional *davul–zurna* duo (in this case, a father and his young teenage son who have come along from the eastern part of Flanders) and a local band consisting of four young men (two keyboard players, a singer accompanying himself on the *bağlama*, and a soundman). The sound is electronic, and the keyboards are used to evoke *zurna*, clarinet, *darbuka*, and other "Turkish" or "Eastern" sounds. This wedding party is one of the band's first commissions, and the musicians are determined to establish their reputation, with unremitting energy and goodwill. The singer-*bağlama* player acts as a "master of ceremonies", creating a good atmosphere, smiling and talking to the attendees, asking for applause, and taking only a few minutes' rest from time to time. The people in the party hall are having a good time, eating, drinking, dancing, and chatting.

After a while, the married couple make their entry between two rows of girls holding a "dome" of flower garlands, accompanied by the traditional *davul–zurna* duo and the enthusiastic encouragements of the attendees. Fireworks are lit, and petals are tossed up. The bride and the groom perform the opening dance, and soon the other guests follow – at this stage, no live music is involved. The band then takes over again, and people dance enthusiastically to uptempo dance music from Ankara (where the bride has her roots) and Emirdağ (where the groom originates from) and to *halaylar* (quick line dances) from Eastern Anatolia. Men and women dance together, but at certain moments, one of the groups steals the scene with special male or female dances. Short, slower songs are inserted, to catch a breath for a moment.

The next stage in the celebration is the "henna ceremony" (*kına gecesi*) (see Figure 5.1). The family members and female friends of the bride wear red shawls and kerchiefs, carry candles, and form a long procession, circling the married couple sitting on two chairs in the middle of the hall. The bride wears a red scarf, and the groom a green cloth, just like in Turkey. The henna is put on the palms of both their hands as well as those of some of the couple's close relatives.

After the henna ceremony, the counterpart to the Turkish "engagement ceremony" (*nişan töreni*) is performed. This means publicly handing out the gifts with the assistance of an ad hoc masters of ceremonies, who announces the gifts and those who bestowed them.

At certain times, a DJ takes over the role of the live band, playing mainly Turkish, but also some Arab and American pop music. Nevertheless, it is clear that the live performance of popularized Turkish folk music is favoured by the attendees. Around midnight, the festivities wrap up with some slow dances to pre-recorded Turkish songs, followed by a live performance of uptempo folk music from Ankara to end in style.

If both wedding celebrations are compared, it becomes clear that some of the differences are inherent to the contrasting settings (motherland versus diaspora, semi-rural versus urban, outdoors versus indoors), while many other social and cultural factors also play a part.

Figure 5.1: Henna ceremony during wedding party in Nazareth (photo by the author)

In Turkey, wedding parties are typically organized in the summer and celebrated in the open air. The location can be private property (yards, gardens, fields), sometimes complemented by public space (streets or fields adjacent to the house), or specific places in the village, town, or city intended for events and celebrations. Private party rooms or halls for indoor celebrations are found in both Turkey and the diaspora. Traditional weddings are celebrated in multiple locations: the place where the bride comes from and the place where the groom lives. A large part of the celebration is performed separately by the two families, who only come together at well-defined, fixed moments in the ceremony.

Typically, a wedding celebration in Turkey lasts several days. The more traditionally it is conceived, the longer it takes. Three days is still a normal duration in many parts of Turkey. Another possibility is to organize a two-day party. In large Turkish cities, as well as in the diaspora, the duration is usually reduced to one day or one evening. The *nişan töreni* ("engagement ceremony") is sometimes incorporated into the actual wedding party (as was the case in the Boztepe-Mucur wedding); in other cases, it is celebrated separately some time in advance. The wedding ceremony in Boztepe-Mucur displayed several clearly distinguishable stages of the traditional ritual: the first day with mutual family visits, the second day with the *nişan töreni*, mutual visits, the *kına gecesi*, and the *rakı* night, and the third day with the *gelin alma* (which involved many rituals, including the tossing of petals). Many of these stages were also performed in Nazareth but sometimes in a different order and in brief, "miniature", and indoor versions. The diasporic one-evening sequence included the entrance of the couple (involving the tossing of petals, among other acts), the *kına gecesi*, the *nişan töreni*, and the cutting and distributing of the giant wedding cake. The celebrations at both settings thus result in the completion of a formalized series of rituals – albeit different in conception. In the described celebration in Turkey, the symbolic rituals are more prominently present, and the long-drawn-out event is closer to its dramatic original. Traditional Turkish wedding ceremonies have in fact much in common with theatrical plays. In this respect, other interconnected dimensions appear to be absent from the diasporic celebration, such as the interplay between the private and the public, and the explicit anchoring of the rituals in public social life. In Turkey, the development of the wedding ceremony was distributed between public (streets within towns, roads between towns) and private places (houses, yards, gardens). The convoy was a very explicit act of communication about the wedding to the social environment. The official component of that environment was represented by the district mayor who directly participated in the *nişan töreni*. Further, the gun shots during that ceremony, and maybe even the loud *davul* and *zurna* playing during the *rakı* night (which caused a police intervention!), can be considered as "public announcements" of the wedding.

Throughout the plethora of possible manifestations, meanings, and functions, certain constants can be identified. Whichever form a Turkish wedding may adopt, and whether a traditional or a modern conceptualization lies behind it, there is a clear tendency towards large-scale and extensive celebrations with many guests. The famous hospitality of the Turks is maintained in the diaspora, and a wedding party is an excellent showcase for it. Certain roles among the guests are equally maintained regardless of the wedding setting, such as the female *yenge* ("sister-in-law") who dresses in red and male *sağdıç* ("groomsman") who wears green; today, these roles are usually taken by the bride and the groom's best friends, who accompany and assist the couple throughout the ceremony (Ustuner, Ger, and Holt 2000; Aydemir 2013: 631–33). The "belt of maidenhood", which represents the shift from dependency on the father to dependency on the husband, is maintained as an important symbol, referring to virginity and also perseverance (Tuna 2006).

Corresponding to Islamic regulations and especially Sunni ethics, the consumption of alcoholic drinks is still considered unfavourable and is avoided in many weddings, even in the diaspora. Possible exceptions are the musicians and non-Muslim guests. Another constant is the position and role of the music and the musicians. Music at wedding parties has both a ritual and an entertainment function, and dancing is one of the main activities performed during any type of Turkish wedding. Musicians usually fulfil an active role as a kind of "master of ceremonies", guiding and animating the whole celebration. The types of music ensembles and the assignment of their tasks is also relatively constant: an average wedding party engages a traditional *davul–zurna* duo and a modern band featuring at least a *bağlama*, keyboard, and voice. The only difference is that while in Turkey the (readily available) *davul* and *zurna* are indispensable and omnipresent, their presence in the diaspora is considered non-essential and depends on availability. If no live performing duo is available, it is easily replaced by its electronic equivalent on the synthesizer.

Two Circumcision Parties

Milas. In a small street in a central neighbourhood of Milas, a town in the province of Muğla in the southwest Aegean Sea region, a circumcision party has just started (see Figure 5.2). The choice of the particular date, a Friday in June, has been motivated by several considerations. The actual operation took place one year ago when the boy was eight years old. Although *sünnet düğünleri* are usually organized on a Saturday or Sunday, it was decided to bring this specific party forward to Friday because of the general elections taking place on Sunday that week. The guests are relatives of the boy, most of whom live in Milas, while some of them have come from Izmir. The group is relatively small, consisting of approximately 20 persons with an equal gender division. Most attendees are clothed in a rather sober way; only some of them are dressed up. According to tradition, the boy is clothed in the characteristic white-and-gold furry costume and hat, especially bought or hired for the occasion.

The party proceeds in four distinct stages. The first takes place in the street of the celebrating family, a small alley that has been covered with a large canvas for the occasion. On both sides, a row of plastic chairs is placed. The music is provided by three professional Roma musicians from the region. To be specific, they come from Dibekdere, a Romani village just outside the city, where every male (from early childhood on) plays *davul* and/or *zurna*.

All families of the Milas region rely on musicians from that special village for their traditional celebrations. During circumcision parties and other ritual celebrations like wedding parties in this region, the standard ensemble formation involves two *zurnas* and one *davul*. Typical for the Aegean region are the large *zurnas*, called *kaba zurna*, which sound relatively low. While one *zurna* provides the fundamental tone, the drone (*dem*), the other one plays the melody. The musicians are very experienced and play beautifully and perfectly together. Many attendees are dancing to the regional *zeybek* dances; others are chatting or observing.

During the second stage of the festivities, the celebrated boy is driven around in a car in order to be seen by the whole neighbourhood. The car carrying the boy is followed by that of the musicians, who continue their performance of *zeybek* music through the open windows. Some of the guests also join this small convoy.

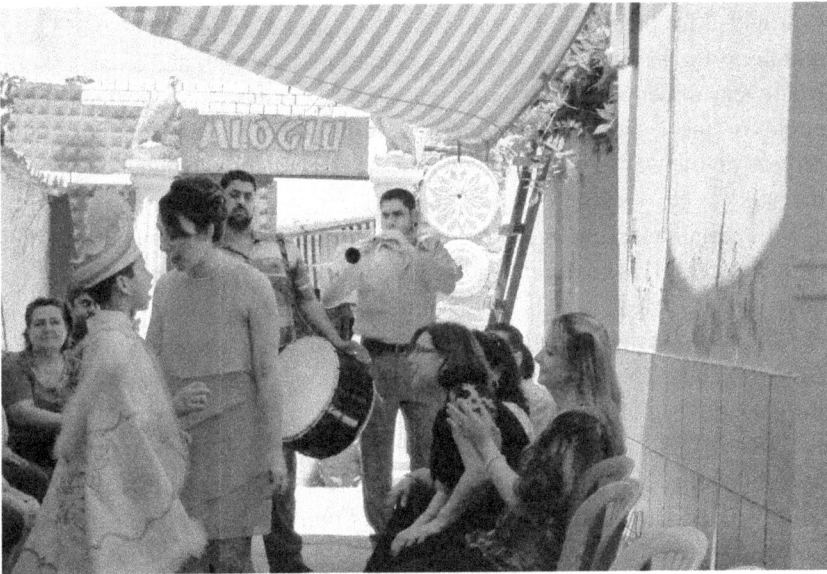

Figure 5.2: Circumcision party in Milas (photo by the author)

The third stage of the ceremony involves a *hoca* (an imam or other religious functionary) reciting Quran verses and other suitable prayers. This is a more serious part of the ceremony compared to the two previous phases, which were very cheerful. For the first time, there is a certain degree of separation between the men and the women. While the men sit close to the *hoca* in the covered alley, the women listen to the recitations from the adjacent garden of the house. They now wear headscarves when they can be seen by the men's group, unlike in the previous phases, where none of the women had their heads covered.

The fourth stage, concluding the ceremony, consists of a simple meal in which the musicians and the *hoca* take part as well.

Rupelmonde. A second circumcision party is organized by a family from Ghent in a party hall in the town of Rupelmonde, approximately 45km from Ghent. It takes place two years after the actual operation on the two celebrated boys. Although the name of the venue is "Salons De Schepper", it is now run by Turks and oriented towards a Turkish public (see Figure 5.3). The large family – a few hundred guests from diverse Belgian and even Dutch cities – is gathered on a Saturday evening in the large hall filled with ornamented chairs and tables on which drinks and fruit are displayed. A kind of throne is provided for the two boys, who wear their special *sünnet* costumes. In the middle of the hall, there is a stage occupied by the band, and a dance floor, where tens of people are performing a *halay* (a fast dance performed in large circles or lines). The dance is filmed and projected in real time onto two large screens on the wall. The celebrated boys are elated and run and dance across the hall.

At a certain moment, the two boys are carried around on a palanquin decorated in red. This represents an indoor, small-scale variant of driving the boys around by car, which is still done quite often in Turkey but rarely in the diaspora. At the same time, red ribbons are tied to the arms of the boys' closest friends. The red colour, the colour of blood, is an important symbol in the performance of life-cycle rituals.

Turkish folk music from diverse regions is performed all night long by two alternating bands, one invited from the Netherlands and one all the way from Turkey. The first band, a trio, employs two synthesizers and an electric guitar that imitates the sound of an *elektrosaz*; the second band, a quartet, consists of two synthesizers, a *bağlama*, and a singer. The Turkish band is more experienced and acts more professionally, at the same time displaying a greater hierarchy between the band members. The singer is a master of creating atmosphere, and when he leaves the stage to dance along with the attendees, he manages all the action from the middle of the circle, setting the pace, accelerating and slowing down the dancing group and the band. The sound is heavily influenced by a pop idiom with loud bass and a stereotypical style. At certain points, the synthesizers evoke the traditionally required *davul–zurna* duo.

In more than one respect, the whole setting resembles an urban indoor wedding party: the location, decoration, and clothing are similar, the music is of the same kind, and the course of events, involving dancing, eating and drinking, and traditional ritual procedures, is comparable. Such indoor wedding and circumcision celebrations thus represent a contemporary, urban way of dealing with and interpreting Turkish tradition.

Figure 5.3: Circumcision party in Rupelmonde (photo by the author)

Elements common to the two attended (and probably to most) contemporary manifestations of this kind of event were the traditional costume and objects, the offering of food to the guests, the importance of folk music, the ritual act of carrying the celebrated boy around, the practice of holding the celebration long after the actual operation, and the option to organize the party with two or more families together. The fact that the party in Turkey was performed outdoors and the diasporic party indoors was one but certainly not the only factor determining the different ways in which the same kind of event manifested itself.

The events I attended exemplify two different conceptions of the phenomenon of circumcision parties. While the event in Turkey was characterized overall by sobriety and modesty, a clearly structured succession of ritual stages, adherence to tradition, and integration into the larger social environment, the diasporic event displayed abundance, a loosely defined ritual development, departure from tradition, and relative disconnectedness from the larger social environment. The party in Milas only attracted around 20 family members, while in Rupelmonde hundreds of guests were present; still, the food provided was simpler in Turkey than in the diaspora. While the event in Turkey consisted of four clearly distinct stages (dancing, the convoy, the *hoca*, and the meal), there was no clear successive development in Rupelmonde; the food was not served at a particular moment, and there was no religious intervention. The only ritual actions performed were the carrying of the boys around the hall and the tying of the red ribbons to the arms of their best friends. In Turkey, adherence to tradition was realized through a combination of factors: the exclusive engagement of local *davul* and *zurna* players performing exclusively Aegean regional music to which exclusively regional *zeybek* figures were danced, and the actual driving around of the boy across the neighbourhood with loud musical accompaniment. In Rupelmonde, the music was provided by two bands invited from abroad, who performed highly popularized versions of folk music from diverse regions of Turkey. Another important difference, identified in the analysis of the two wedding parties, is the divergent use of public and private space in the development of the ritual celebrations. While the event in Turkey established explicit communication with and positioning towards the social environment by means of the loud convoy and the overall use of public terrain, the whole celebration in the diaspora proceeded in the remotely situated party hall.[9]

Two cem *Ceremonies*

Beypınar. On Sunday, 3 July 2011, a celebration is held for the opening of a new *cemevi* in Beypınar, a remote village 60km from the small town of Zara in the province of Sivas. The date of the celebration is not arbitrary but related to the anniversary of the "Sivas massacre" or "Madımak massacre" (*Sivas katliamı* or *Madımak katliamı*), which happened on 2 July 1993. During that event, 35 people were killed by an arson attack on the Madımak hotel in Sivas. The target group of the Islamist fundamentalist attack was the Alevi intellectuals and artists who had gathered to attend the Pir Sultan Abdal Festival.[10]

The newly built, two-storey venue is situated in an open field and has several rooms: a dining room, a kitchen, toilets, and an abattoir on the ground floor, and the actual *cem* room on the first floor. The Karabel Cemevi is dependent on the main *cemevi* of Sivas, and the event has been organized cooperatively. There is even a connection to the Alevi institutions of Istanbul, as the *dede* (literally "grandfather"), the spiritual guide and leader of the *cem*, has been delegated from Istanbul. The *zakir*,[11] the musician accompanying the ceremony on the *bağlama*, is the regular *zakir* of the Sivas *cemevi*. More than 50 Alevis from Sivas, Zara, and even Istanbul have come to attend the first *cem* in the new *cem* house. The attendees have a heterogeneous ethnic background and include Kurds and Zazas.[12] In addition to these "intrinsic" attendees, there is a presence of dignitaries, press, and even the military for this occasion. Prior to the actual start of the *cem* ceremony, an official pro-gramme has been carried out since noon, involving a tour of the building, inauguration speeches, the consumption of a communal meal, and a rehearsal for the *cem* by the group of young people who are to perform the ritual dance (*semah*).

The actual *cem* takes place in the late afternoon and lasts two hours (see Figure 5.4). Most (though not all) women put on a headscarf when the cer-emony starts. There is no strict gender separation, although there clearly is a concentration of men on one side of the room and women on the other. Large pictures hang on the wall, depicting Pir Sultan Abdal, Ali (cousin and son-in-law of the prophet Mohammad, considered by the Alevis as his rightful successor), and Haji Bektash Veli (thirteenth-century Persian mystic, founder of the most important form of Alevism in Turkey). The *cem* cere-mony involves the development of a fixed, elaborated "liturgy", nevertheless providing room for specific, topical, occasion-related sections. Spoken and sung prayers – all in Turkish – are sometimes performed by the *dede* and the *zakir* alone, but in most instances, the worshippers participate partly or entirely. Because of the size of the community, it is practically impossible to give every attendee the opportunity to perform the *semah* and other ritual acts. A group of young members of an Alevi association has been assigned a leading role in performing the rituals of the ceremony. One boy adopts the role of *bekçi* ("guard, guardian"), whose task it is to assist the *dede* by ensuring that everything proceeds smoothly and correctly. One girl functions as the *süpürgeci* ("sweeper"), the person symbolically keeping the *cemevi* clean.[13] The *semah* is performed by a group of girls and their male leader. The dance gradually develops, beginning with small and modest movements to slow music and building towards greater and more active moments to fast music. The music, which is at the same time complex and transparent, inti-mate and emotional, is beautifully played and sung by the *zakir*, who knows his job very well. The repertoire belongs to a standard corpus of "liturgical" pieces, of which the performance style is fixed. These features justify the view of Alevi ritual music as being largely "pre-composed". While throughout the whole ceremony the worshippers have displayed great engagement and participation involving active response to the music – exteriorized by moving and singing along – the most intense interaction occurs during the *mersiye* (religious lamentation) in remembrance of Alevi martyr Hussein, the son of Ali. Standing in a large circle holding hands, many members of the community let their tears flow freely during the account of the battle in Karbala, in which Hussein was killed. Without doubt, the remembrance of this tragedy suffered by the Shiite community evokes feelings of sadness and anger related to the difficulties lived by the Shiites in present-day Turkey and particularly to the dramatic event of 1993.

Figure 5.4: *Cem* in the newly opened Karabel *cemevi* in Beypınar (photo by the author)

Ghent. In Ghent, on a Friday evening, a *cem* ceremony is held in a ballroom of Intercultural Centre De Centrale. The room is decorated for the occasion with a portrait of Atatürk next to pictures of Ali and Hussein, and carpets are placed on the floor. The rather small space is becoming crowded with more than 50 men, women, and children, all Alevi, and all with roots in the wider Emirdağ region. Everyone has brought some food or drinks to consume at the end of the session. Although there is no strict gender separation, most of the men are seated on one side of the room, and most of the women on the other. Only very few women wear headscarves.

The service is led by the *dede*, who recites most of the prayers. On his side sits a befriended musician of the *abdal* family of Emirdağ, who carries the title of *zakir* for the occasion. He plays the *bağlama* during the sung prayers of the ceremony, in which everyone takes part. Besides the *dede* and the *zakir*, another man fulfils the role of *bekçi* and carries a stick and wears a cap, in that way evoking tradition. The traditionalism is also represented by the clothes worn during the "official" parts of the ceremony: the ritual *semah* dances. The women put on headscarves and loose wide trousers; the men caps and waistcloths. First, three couples perform ("turn") the *semah*, which consists of two parts: a slow part involving stamping with the feet and upward movements of the arms, and a faster part in which the man and woman whirl around each other. During a short break, drinks and snacks are passed around. Then, two couples again perform the dance, among whom the *zakir* who is temporarily substituted by a family member. Subsequently, a variant of the *semah* is performed by groups of four people. In particular, the quick part differs from the duo variant: three people dance around a fourth person who stands in the middle with his hands folded above his head, and they clap their hands to each other's hands. After two hours, there is a break of ten minutes, giving the opportunity to smoke a cigarette or use the bathroom. After the break, it is the turn of the children and young people to perform or learn to perform the *semah*. The ceremony finishes with a lamentation (*mersiye*) remembering Hussein, sung in a circle with everyone holding hands. At the end, there is a communal meal, after which the room is cleaned up swiftly and the whole group leaves the building in an orderly fashion.

Many parallels or constants can be discerned in the two attended *cem* ceremonies. The overall structure and underlying principles are the same. The minimum requirements for a contemporary *cem* to be performed are a closed space where the participants can feel safe and comfortable, with carpets to sit on, and pictures of Alevi saints on the wall. Since Alevis are less orthodox than Sunnites, headscarves are worn less often, even during religious service, but still most women will put on a scarf during the *cem*. There is also a much less strict gender separation than during Sunni services in mosques, although a rough separation of men and women is maintained during the *cem*. Every *cem* is conceived of as a social gathering as well, and the consumption of a communal meal (of whichever kind) is one of its essential features. The liturgy of different *cems* is also highly compatible, although certain variations may occur due to regionally defined differences, differences related to the branch of Alevism, or in connection with current events or topicalities. The liturgy consists of a succession of sung and spoken prayers, a ritual dance (*semah*), and a closing lament for Hussein. The music is highly standardized to the extent that it can be considered "pre-composed", though it is not always written down (except the poems). Every *cem* involves the fulfilment of (some of) the 12 roles, of which the roles of *dede, zakir*, and *bekçi* are generally most prominent and active. Differences between the two manifestations of a *cem* ceremony concern the type of public (heterogeneous in Beypınar; homogeneous in Ghent) and the distribution of the roles within the public (only a small, preselected group actively performs most of the rituals in Beypınar; everyone actively participates in the liturgy in Ghent).

Although the similarities regarding the course, structure, and philosophical-spiritual background of both *cems* are strikingly significant, an important difference between the manifestation in Turkey and that in the diaspora relates to the larger sociopolitical environment in which they are embedded. In Turkey – particularly since the disaster of 1993 – Alevis have begun to seek political, social, cultural, and religious emancipation. The proliferation of recently built *cemevis* in urban and rural environments is a clear sign of that ongoing emancipation. Although people used to be reluctant to claim their Alevi identity and practised their religious activities in secret, nowadays a tendency towards openness and assurance can be discerned. Although this tendency can be observed mainly in larger cities on the one hand, and in villages, towns, or cities with a substantial Alevi population on the other hand, it can be expected to gain strength and expand towards other sociopolitical environments. In present-day Turkey, being Alevi – and especially openly being Alevi – is a political statement. The left wing in Turkey's political system is largely occupied by Alevis. The described *cem* inaugurating the new *cemevi* in Beypınar, protected by the military and patronized by the authorities, should be understood as an act of emancipation and assurance in a quickly developing sociopolitical context.[14]

The *cem* ceremony held in De Centrale in Ghent is to be situated in a totally different sociopolitical context. Although the traditional dividing lines of Turkish society (Alevi/Sunni, Kurdish/Turkish, Kemalist/Islamist, etc.) are transferred to the diaspora context, the distinctions are less pronounced as a consequence of the changed relationship with the surrounding political, social, and cultural environment. Being (openly) Alevi in the Turkish dias-pora is much more a sociocultural and religious statement than a political one. The sociocultural and religious emancipation of the diasporic Alevis proceeds very slowly, not receiving much support from either non-Alevi Turks and Turkish associations or non-Turks and non-Turkish associations and authorities. A special venue destined for the performance of *cems* is still a distant dream for the Alevis in Ghent. While continuing their quest for a convenient and free place, they currently perform their *cems* in private homes again, like it was/is done in Turkey before emancipation took/takes place.

Two Rural Festivals

Ocaklı. The Ocaklı Köyü Lişer Yaylası Soğuksu Şenlikleri (Cold Water Festival of the Lişer *yayla* of the village of Ocaklı) is an annual event organized on 7 July by the village of Ocaklı. This village is attached to the town of Maçka in the province of Trabzon in the eastern Black Sea region. The *yayla* (summer pasture) where the festival takes place is situated on a plateau with an altitude of almost 2,000 metres. A few brick and wooden structures are provided as basic facilities for its users. During the festival, the whole terrain is dotted with stalls and stands, forming a huge market. A small, covered stage has been set up, and a small, covered seating area for the obligatory dignitaries has been provided. Hundreds of people, displaying a great diversity, have gathered for the festival. Many of them, particularly the elderly, are wearing traditional Black Sea clothes.

The programme proceeds from noon to evening. Before the official part starts, people visit the extended market, and the enthusiastic sounds of the *davul* and *zurna* liven up the atmosphere. The official part consists of speeches by dignitaries and organizers; as a guest and researcher from Belgium, I am also invited to say a word. The musical programme opens with a *davul–zurna* duo accompanying a girls' folk dance team dancing the *horon*. The musicians on duty are experienced elderly men from the area who are regularly invited to play at cultural events and parties. The Black Sea *zurna* is much smaller and higher in pitch than the large *zurna* played in, for example, the Aegean Sea region. The *davul* is constructed with membranes of animal skin, and sounds rather muffled compared to the more transparent sound which nowadays has become the standard. Both musicians play the exceptionally vivid music of the region in a virtuoso way.

The next performance is of a completely different nature. A singer who is closely involved in the organization of the event sings his own songs, accompanied by recorded music, in a highly popularized style that bears only a slight resemblance to the traditional regional music. The popular style is perpetuated in the next performance by a female singer accompanied by two musicians playing synthesizer and *kemençe*. The blond singer, announced as the Madonna of the Black Sea, wears black and white clothes with accessories belonging to the traditional costumes. She sings popularized versions of well-known regional folk songs, during which many people dance the *horon* in lines or circles. Next is a short solo performance of the *kemençe* player who sings at the same time; a performance closer to traditional idioms. The last part of the programme consists of *horon* music played by the same musicians (*kemençe* and synthesizer) and another singer. Again, the lively *horon* is tirelessly danced in the blistering sun (see Figure 5.5).

While the musical programme on the stage continues, *davul* and *zurna* are played elsewhere on the terrain, to which even more people are dancing in sometimes huge circles consisting of hundreds of people of different ages and genders. At certain times, smaller circles of dancers are formed in the middle of the large circle; at other times, the large circle falls apart into different – for example, gender-defined – groups. People unable to participate in the dancing, or needing a rest, sit on the ground in the middle of the circle. The appetite for dancing and the dynamism of the people of this part of Turkey are striking. The feeling of solidarity and oneness, evoked by hundreds of people dancing together and holding hands, is remarkable.

Figure 5.5: Collective *horon* dancing during the Lişer Yaylası Soğuksu Şenlikleri (photo by the author)

Wachtebeke. The diaspora version of the rural festival is exemplified by the annual *seyran* organized by the non-profit organization Posküder (Posof Cultural Association). On a Sunday afternoon in May, this "folkloric event" or "intercultural folk festival" takes place on a large field in the Puyenbroeck provincial domain in Wachtebeke, approximately 20km from Ghent. Puyenbroeck is a large recreation park, parts of which can be rented to organize events. The rent, which is quite high, necessitates sufficient income from sponsors (mostly Turkish but also Belgian companies) and subsidies. Admission to the festival is free; those who want to sit on a chair or at a table can hire one for a small fee. On one side of the field, a large tent is installed, while on the other side, a bounce house has been set up for the many children present. Small stalls and tents are scattered on the terrain, selling snacks, food, drinks, and other products. Every year, the diaspora from Posof, a small town at the border with Georgia, gathers at this event, with some coming from the Netherlands and Germany. However, people originating from other regions of Turkey also attend the festival. The public is diverse, as are the clothing styles – displaying Islamic clothing as well as short dresses and skirts. The *seyran* appears to be a family event par excellence. Children are having a great time, playing football or cycling across the field.

As is customary, the actual programme begins with some speeches, in which the sponsors are also thanked. When the Istiklal Marşı ("Independence March", the Turkish national anthem) resounds, everyone stands up. Next, the live music programme starts with a performance of a band from the city of Antwerp that specializes in wedding parties. Their set-up consists of a *bağlama* player-singer, a keyboard, and a guitar. The repertoire is varied, alternating between music from different regions, such as East Turkey and the Black Sea region (the larger area in which Posof is situated), but also Central Anatolian Kırşehir (from which the music is universally popular in Turkey and the Turkish diaspora alike). The band performs the folk songs in a highly popularized, rather monotonous style. The audience dances when favourite songs are performed. From time to time, the programme is interrupted for a tombola and other announcements. Later in the afternoon, the loud, amplified pop sound alternates with the acoustic sound of a traditional *davul* and *zurna* duo, which has also come from Antwerp. Their *halaylar* are much appreciated, particularly by the young generations, who try to perform the row dance in an enthusiastic but inexperienced way. It is clear that the cultural heritage of regional folk dances has been partly forgotten by the youth of the Posof diaspora. But a few men of age beautifully show how the dances should be danced, thus teaching the "third generation" post-migrants a cultural lesson (see Figure 5.6).

Figure 5.6: *Halay* dancing during the *seyran* in Wachtebeke (photo by the author)

Rural festivals such as the *yayla* festival in the Black Sea region and the imitation of a Posof *seyran* in the provincial domain near Ghent are rooted in ancient rituals celebrating the seasonal change and its influence on social, cultural, and economic aspects of the lives of the people. Moving to the high summer pastures (*yayla*) was an annually recurring activity marked by a large celebration.

These kinds of celebrations, whether occurring in Turkey or in the diaspora, involve long, lively programmes taking a whole day or several days. The entrance is usually free, but an economic aspect is present as well in the form of a market or stalls selling food or other products. To lend an official character to the event, speeches by dignitaries, or at least the organizers, are delivered. Traditional music of the region is indispensable – in its purest form performed by the traditional festive outdoor musical ensemble of the *davul* and *zurna*. Nowadays, this traditional performance is complemented by popularized interpretations of the regional repertoire or even of a pan-Turkish repertoire by modern bands. As in many other musical events, the activity of social dancing is an important part of the celebration.

Although the settings of the rural festivals in Turkey and their diasporic counterparts differ greatly, and the diasporic event can be seen as a more limited imitation of the "original" (regarding functionality and natural beauty of the environment, scale and duration, and musical quality), many essential features are also maintained. Although the ritual aspect may have become weaker in the diaspora than in Turkey, and weaker in contemporary modernized Turkey than in former agrarian or nomadic communities, the festivals celebrating spring or summer can still be considered as markers of the natural undulations of human life on an individual as well as on a social level.[15]

Two Urban Festivals

Kaman. On a Wednesday afternoon in June 2011, the annual Abdallar Şöleni (*Abdal* Feast) is held for the second time in Kaman, a town in the province of Kırşehir in Central Anatolia, approximately 50km from the province capital. This year, the festivities have a dual motive: celebrating the beginning of the summer (which could be an implicit as well as an explicit motive) and inaugurating a new cultural association. The association, called "Kaman Abdalları – Eğitim, kültür, sanat, araştırma ve dayanışma derneği" (Kaman *Abdals* – Education, culture, art, research, and solidarity association), was established the previous year. Although no official figures or estimates are known, observation of *abdal*-oriented events such as this festival suggests that the *abdals* represent a substantial part of the general population of the town. Of the hundreds of people present for the event, the majority could be associated with either the *abdal* or the Romani people. They are dark-complexioned, often with light green or blue eyes. Some of them could be taken for Indian people or meet the "Gypsy" stereotype. Most women do not wear a headscarf, which indicates an undogmatic approach to Islam and, in this case, probably means that they are Alevi (the religious identity of the *abdals* in Turkey). The fact that a special *abdal* festival is organized by the municipality and that the *abdals* are supported in having their own association and meeting-place is rather exceptional in Turkey, where this section of the population is sometimes still regarded as second-class citizens. Here, it is a direct result of their culturally and numerically significant presence in this region.

The festivities start at the Kaman petrol station, where a large group of *abdal* musicians have gathered in front of their new venue. Some of them wear the costumes of a historical Ottoman military band; others wear elegant clothes appropriate for the performance they will give a bit later. The Ottoman military band, called *mehterhane* ("house of *mehters*"), *mehteran* ("*mehters*"), or *mehter takımı* ("*mehter* band"), consisted of elite (*mehter*) musicians-servicemen and was an important imperial institution. It was mobilized to add lustre to routine as well as special activities of the sultan and his court, and to deter the enemy and motivate the Ottoman troops during battles. The most common instruments included *zurna*, *davul*, *boru* (trumpet), *zil* (cymbals), *kös* (large double kettledrum), and *nakkare* (smaller double kettledrum). The *mehterhane* was suspended during the period of reforms of the 1820s and experienced a revival in the second half of the twentieth century (Klebe 2008: 65–66; Reinhard 2002). Nowadays it has regained importance as a nationalist symbol of the illustrious Turkish history. In contemporary Turkey, the *mehterhane* is regularly deployed to add lustre or an official aura to different kinds of events, as is the case in Kaman.

After a few short speeches by important figures of the *abdal* association, the march proceeds through the streets of Kaman and ends on the square in front of the town hall, where a large stage has been set up. As always, a special place for the dignitaries is provided, in this case a covered tribune with adorned chairs. A fence is placed to keep the common audience (everyone except the dignitaries and the press) at a distance from the stage. The first part of the programme is a continuation of the military show on the stage, which is in fact rather unusual. One of the obligatory marches is the Independence March (the national anthem). The programme proceeds with an exceptionally long-drawn-out series of speeches and lectures delivered by dignitaries and a few scholars on the subject of *abdal* culture, and in relation to the present event. It is remarkable how patiently the audience waits for the actual *abdal* musical programme to start. The first real *abdal* performance involves a combination of very young *davul* players and adult *zurna* players. The Kırşehir *zurna* is a large size, like the Aegean Sea *zurna* but unlike the Black Sea instrument. One of the children performs a *davul* dance, one of the specific dance forms typical of this region. After the children's performance, a *halay* is danced by a group of young men, accompanied by an experienced *davul–zurna* duo. The next group is a trio consisting of a violin, *darbuka*, and *bağlama*, a typical formation in the folk music of the Kırşehir region. After a while, four senior *abdals* join in and beautifully perform a regional folk dance to lively and energetic dance tunes. This act is followed by a large ensemble of eight *davuls* and eight *zurnas*, on which again *halays* and *davul* dances are performed (see Figure 5.7). True to the tradition, the dancers are symbolically rewarded with bank notes (in this case, old dollars) attached to their clothes. The concluding act and "grand finale" of the event is a performance by *bağlama* player and singer Tufan Altaş, born in Kaman and one of the popular representatives of the Kırşehir *abdal* music at present. He is accompanied by three musicians playing *darbuka, kaşık, def*, and *bendir.* The rhythm section joins in when the non-metrical, melancholic *bozlaks* give way to uptempo, energetic dance tunes. Notwithstanding the relative distortion of the highly amplified *bağlama*, a traditional sound is maintained due to the rest of the set-up, avoiding, for example, the otherwise omnipresent keyboard.

Figure 5.7: *Davul* dance accompanied by *davul* and *zurna* during the Kaman *abdal* festival (photo by the author)

Ghent. On a Sunday afternoon in Ghent in October 2011, a one-day "Cultural Festival" (*Kültür Şöleni*), organized by the city in cooperation with the Turkish Union of Belgium and sponsored by Turkish firms, is taking place on a public square in the city centre. A similar concept – a showcase of the cultural activities of the member organizations of the Turkish Union and of the Belgian-Turkish diaspora in general – has been performed in other cities before. In Ghent, it is the first time that a Turkish event of this scale has been organized in the heart of the city. It attracts a substantial though not overwhelming audience of a diverse nature, consisting of Turkish and non-Turkish inhabitants of Ghent complemented by some tourists. A large stage, many food and drinks stalls, and a bounce house occupy the square.

Around two in the afternoon, a *mehterhane* from Rotterdam tumultuously launches the event (see Figure 5.8). The similarities with the Ottoman military band in Turkey are striking. True to the Turkish tradition, the actual programme on stage begins with speeches by the organizers of the event and by dignitaries, including the mayor of Ghent. Subsequently, a long series of diverse cultural showcases passes in review. A first musical performance is given by singer Melike Tarhan, accompanied by a Flemish guitarist and saxophonist. They give a jazzy interpretation of traditional folk songs. Next, a group from Rotterdam enters the stage and surprises the public by evoking the mystical ritual dance of the Mevlevi whirling dervishes in a fast, popularized version of the original calm, classical music. The loud beats and synthesizer sounds, close to the *arabesk* idiom, form an unusual combination with the *ney* (the reed flute originally used in this kind of music) and the transverse flute (a contemporary interpretation of the *ney*). Another unusual addition is the folk *bağlama*. Subsequent performances include a Balkan band and a street dance group (both non-Turkish) and a short Turkish-language stage play. The final two concerts involve the performance of popularized folk music. While the first ensemble, featuring singer Bülent Gök accompanied by *bağlama*, drums, and synthesizer, displays a rather modestly popularized style, the last ensemble, consisting of singer-guitarist Kürşat Zengin accompanied by keyboard, *bağlama*, drums, and bass guitar, shows heavy influence from pop music. While the first ensemble limits its repertoire to traditional Turkish folk songs, the second ensemble includes *özgün müzik* and Dutch- and Turkish-language pop songs. Only when guest singer Fakı Edeer, distinguished expert on the folk music of Emirdağ, enters the stage, is a shift again made towards the folk repertoire.

Turkish organizations and media closely follow the event, and a lot of filming and interviewing is going on. The whole event has great significance for the performers on stage and for the Turkish population in Ghent. An occasion like this, presenting the Turkish cultural heritage and contemporary developments to a broad, general audience and initiating interaction with this audience, is rare. The musicians, who are well known and already popular within the Turkish part of the audience, seize the opportunity to act as representatives of the Turkish diaspora towards the Belgian majority.

The two described urban festivals differ from each other in several respects. While the event in Kaman was highly specific, focusing on the *abdals* and their music, the cultural festival in Ghent had a broad, general orientation towards diverse musical genres and other art forms. While the performance style in Turkey can be conceived of as more or less "traditional",

the different groups in Ghent (except the *mehterhane*) presented contemporary and hybrid-popularized interpretations. This different conception can be
partly explained by the festivals' embeddedness in the context of the motherland versus the diasporic. In the diaspora, it is less likely that an event will be
organized that shines the spotlight on a particular subsection (e.g., a cultural,
religious, linguistic, or ethnic minority) of the Turkish population. Turkish
cultural organizations in the diaspora are often either unspecific in their orientation or they are oriented towards the (cultural, religious, linguistic, or
ethnic) majority. As seen in the case of the Alevis in Ghent, minorities are not
always well represented in the sociocultural city fabric, and they experience
difficulties in manifesting and emancipating themselves. The cultural festival
in Ghent, being supported by the city government, was possibly consciously
conceived to have an unspecific, general orientation. The fact that this festival was organized in cooperation with the city government was an exceptional situation for Ghent (and more generally the diaspora). The festival in
Kaman was also organized by the local authorities, which in itself would be a
completely normal situation, were it not that *abdals* in general have difficulties manifesting and emancipating themselves in the sociocultural landscape
of Turkey. The organization of a specific *abdal* festival by Turkish authorities
can thus be considered an explicit recognition of their cultural (and conse-
quently also social) significance.

Figure 5.8: *Mehterhane* during the cultural festival in Ghent (photo by the author)

Other similarities and dissimilarities between the two described urban festivals can be discerned. Both events involved a long programme starting with a *mehterhane* procession followed by initial speeches by dignitaries, and a further development consisting of a whole series of featured performance groups. The *mehterhane* procession, adding lustre to the events, displayed many similarities in both contexts. However, the identity of the band members diverged significantly: the *mehterhane* in Kaman was an ad hoc constellation of local *abdals*, while the *mehterhane* performing in Ghent was an existing band from Rotterdam, the Netherlands. Both events were regarded as highly important, especially by the minority groups who were given the chance to manifest themselves in ideal circumstances: with moral and material support by the authorities. Both the *abdals* in Kaman, belonging to a minority group in dominantly Sunni Turkey, and the Turks in Ghent, belonging to a post-migrant minority group, received (at least temporary) official recognition through these events. The official nature was explicitly represented in both events by the dignitaries involved, but in contrast to Ghent, where the mayor mingled with the audience, the greater hierarchy governing in Turkey was explicitly reflected in Kaman in the form of the separate grandstand for the VIPs.

Two türkü *Nights*

Izmir. On a Monday evening around 9 pm, a *türkü* night starts in Şafak Türküsü – Türkü ve Şiir Evi ("Daybreak Song – *Türkü* and Poetry House"), a *türkü* bar in Bornova, the student district of the metropolis of Izmir (see Figure 5.9). The café, established on the ground floor of an apartment building, offers live music every evening. It has a partly covered terrace and is situated in the liveliest part of the district, being surrounded by many other cafés, restaurants, shops, and so on. The interior of the café is decorated with posters displaying poems written by the owner of the venue, pictures, candles, and *nazar boncukları* (typical Turkish amulets against the "evil eye"). The chairs are benches covered with traditional kilims.

The musician on duty, a singer accompanying himself on the *bağlama*, is a Turkish music student at Ege University in Izmir. He performs in this venue twice a week. Playing in cafés like this gives him the opportunity to practise his acquired knowledge of the Turkish folk music repertoire. His playing and singing are beautiful, clean, and clear in a slightly pop-influenced style, from time to time involving chords or flamenco-like elements. The clientele of this evening, fluctuating between 10 and 20 people, mainly consists of students, complemented by a few people of more advanced age. Intense interaction between the performer, the owner of the café, and the audience is maintained. The audience also participates in the musical action by singing along or by making requests for specific songs. Alevi music constitutes the principal part of the performed repertoire and is the preferred repertoire by the musician – being Alevi himself – and the public. It is complemented by a few songs from the Aegean Sea region and Eastern Anatolia, but the second important part of the programme is constituted by *özgün müzik*, also associated with leftist political orientations. The owner of the venue is an atheist with a progressive, leftist political persuasion, which causes the venue to attract a clientele of similar opinions.

Figure 5.9: *Türkü* night in Türkü ve Şiir Evi Şafak Türküsü (Bornova-Izmir) (photo by the author)

Ghent. In December on a Friday evening in Ghent, like every Friday evening, the small stage of the Muzikantenhuis music café is occupied by Turkish folk musicians: two *bağlama* players who also sing (one of them is the owner of the café), and a percussionist playing *darbuka* and *bendir* (see Figure 5.10). The venue is situated in the centre of Ghent at the edge of one of the Turkish neighbourhoods and is surrounded by Turkish and African shops, services, and cafés. The interior is abundantly decorated to create an explicitly Turkish atmosphere. The furniture is rustic, and the walls and ceiling are completely covered with rural Anatolian utensils, kilims, bookshelves, and wall paintings of Turkish poets and musicians. The wall behind the musicians on stage is decorated with a painting of Aşık Veysel, the most popular Turkish *aşık* of the twentieth century. The musical programming of the café is diverse and broad, but Turkish folk music is a fixed and important part of it, generally performed on Friday night but also on other evenings at the close of other performances. The café's clientele is as diverse as its programming – Turks being a fixed and important part of it as well.

This evening, the number of attendees varies between 12 and 20 people, almost exclusively of Turkish origin; one man is of Kurdish origin. Only one woman is wearing a headscarf. A fellow musician (a regular customer of the café and friend of the musicians on duty, who also performs in the same venue) is also present and listens attentively. From time to time, he participates in the musical action by singing along in a loud voice or by drumming on the table. There is plenty of interaction between the musicians and the audience, and between the musicians themselves. The setting is very informal, and the artistic quality of the performance seems to be of relatively little importance. Even while performing, the musicians chat with the attendees and with each other, laugh at funny situations, and drink tea. Various musical mistakes are made, such as forgetting lyrics, starting in the wrong tempo, singing out of tune or off beat, or starting to sing too late, but no one from the public worries about it and the musicians laugh at it. It is clearly a part of the setting; the musicians are not expected to have reached a high level of musical perfection. The sociocultural aspect prevails over the artistic.

The performance style can be called traditional though somewhat pop-influenced. The repertoire consists of folk music from different regions of Turkey – the music of Emirdağ occupying a prominent position – complemented by *özgün müzik*. Although the non-Turkish customers are a very small minority, the song 'Uzun ince bir yoldayım' (a highly popular song of Aşık Veysel) is rendered in a bilingual version, its lyrics being partly translated into Dutch.

Comparing *türkü* bars and *türkü* evenings in the motherland and the diaspora points to similar differences in political connotations as exhibited by the *cem* houses and performances. The majority of *türkü* bars in Turkish cities have an Alevi background and thus leftist orientation (Erol 2009: 174). This is also possibly the case in the diaspora, where the concept of the *türkü* bar is imitated, but the small number and great diversity of the diasporic Turkish music cafés make it difficult to pin them down to one political or ideological orientation. It is perhaps not unlikely for a *türkü* bar or Turkish music café in the diaspora to have a nationalist (and thus conservative, right-wing) background.

Figure 5.10: Turkish evening in Muzikantenhuis (Ghent) (photo by the author)

Whichever may be the underlying political-ideological preferences of the owner, clientele, and/or musicians of the *türkü* bars, the concrete manifestations display a great similitude with respect to both form and content. A *türkü* bar or Turkish music café can be accommodated in a variety of buildings or venues, but the interior design and decoration always bear resemblances. Every *türkü* bar, being a café, serves drinks, including alcohol, and in many cases also some meals or snacks. The ambiance is intimate, stimulating social interaction among the listeners, and between the listeners and the performers. Musical participation by the listeners, expressed by singing or dancing, is encouraged. The repertoire consists of Turkish folk music (including Alevi music) and the related genre of *özgün müzik*; the performance style usually stays relatively close to tradition but also display influences from popular music or "world music" (e.g., flamenco).

The embeddedness of the *türkü* bars in the respective sociocultural contexts of the motherland and the diaspora, and the concomitant difference in frames of reference, result in certain different accents. An example is the fact that some *türkü* bars in Turkey (like the bar in the student quarter of Izmir) programme live performances every day of the week, while their equivalents in the diaspora concentrate their activities on the weekend. A more signifi-cant difference is the level of musical artistry and professionalism. In Turkey, young professionals or music students of the Turkish music conservatoires often perform in *türkü* bars with the intention of acquiring necessary stage experience. Their (semi-)professional attitude matches the expectations of the audience, which consists of people with a special preference for and knowl-edge of the performed repertoire. In Belgium, no professional education in Turkish folk music exists, and many performers are even self-educated. The musical level, not being able to match the standard in Turkey, still suffices for the clientele of the music cafés, consisting of a general public, unspecialized music lovers, and possibly fellow musicians or teachers.

Events Bound to the Motherland Context

A Folk Dance Lesson in Kırşehir

During the summer holidays, folk dance lessons for children are organized every Tuesday and Wednesday afternoon in the venue of Hoy-Dek–Halk Oyunları Derneği (Hoy-Dek–Folk Dance Association), which is situated on the second floor of a building in the city centre of Kırşehir. The teachers and musical accompanists serve as volunteers. The atmosphere is open and wel-coming; fellow teachers, friends, and new pupils walk to and fro. Traditional clothes belonging to the region are displayed, and the room is abundantly decorated with traditionally designed furniture, flags and banners, pictures, press cuttings, and all kinds of certificates and distinctions. This is clearly an active and ambitious association, regularly participating in the folk dance competitions which are so important in Turkey.

The musicians are friends of the teachers, and young local residents seizing every opportunity to develop their musical skills and to present themselves to a possible market. The two youngsters flexibly pass their instruments, an *uzun sap* (long-necked) *bağlama* typical for the region and a *darbuka*, onto each other. While doing their best to play as beautifully and in time as pos-sible – with a stable tempo and clear rhythm – they clearly enjoy themselves and have a lively interaction with each other and the teachers. Everything proceeds in a very informal way, for a large part excluding the children, who are nevertheless given sufficient attention. The four pupils, one boy and three girls, play at different levels, but all make progress thanks to the diversifying approach of the teachers. The main teacher is professionally involved in music, working part-time in a music shop and part-time as a folk dance teacher.

The music performed is exclusively Kırşehir music, which is extremely rich and exceptionally passionate. Logically, the performed repertoire mainly involves dance music in the characteristic quick 2/4 metre. But the dance tunes do not stand alone; they are always preceded by a *bozlak*. Muharrem and certainly his son Neşet Ertaş (see Chapter 3) are clearly an inspiring example for everyone involved in these folk dance lessons. The transmission of the music, poetry, and dance patrimony of Kırşehir is assured, thanks to the great enthusiasm of the numerous music lovers and specialists in this extraordinarily music-minded city.

Training of aşıklık Skills in Sivas

We are on the first floor of a building in the busy city centre of eastern Central Anatolian Sivas in a nicely decorated room with a wooden floor, seats covered with traditional pillows, tables with traditional tablecloths, and an enormous number of pictures and posters on the wall (see Figure 5.11). The plate above the door says "Sifahod–Sivas Fasıl Heyeti Aşıklar ve Halk Oyunları Derneği" (Sifahod–*Fasıl* ensemble, *Aşık*, and folk dance society). The association is thus active in different fields of Turkish popular and high culture: Turkish classical music, folk and classical poetry, the tradition of *aşıklık*, and folk dance. Three men are ready, with their *bağlamas* at hand, to perform certain subdisciplines of the *aşık* and *ozan* traditions. Tea is provided for the whole (exclusively male) company of *aşıklar*, *ozanlar*, poets (*şairler*), teachers, and the president of the society.

The improvised programme starts with the performance of some self-written (pre-composed) folk songs of the *türkü* type. The three musicians take turns and support each other by softly singing along. The attendees listen attentively and occasionally express their approval by singing along or applauding. After the *türküler*, the *taşlama* (satire, literally "stoning") or *atışma* ("quarrel, battle of words") phase begins. This subdiscipline involves trying to defeat one's opponent poetically and musically in a humorous way. This is done through instantaneous improvisation and as such is reserved for the persons carrying the title of *aşık*. Often an impetus is given by someone from the audience by presenting a particular verse as a starting point, or by suggesting a certain thematic thread. The *aşıks* give the best of themselves and sing and play in their own personal style, which is also recognized and appreciated by the audience. The man self-identifying as *ozan*, who is not supposed to improvise and thus refrains from participating in this exciting artistic game, calmly performs a self-written *türkü* by way of variation. The last subdiscipline is *leb değmez* or *dudak değmez* ("lips should not touch"), which involves a blunt needle inserted between the lips and the gums, preventing the use of certain consonants, namely b, f, p, m, and v. Again, the attendees are allowed to participate by giving the musicians a challenging task.

By practising and perfecting these and more subdisciplines of the *aşık*-art in the closed setting of the association, the artists in question get ready to present themselves on the stages of formally organized *aşık* festivals in which colleagues from all over Turkey and sometimes even from neighbouring countries take part. In this way, an important part of Turkish (and broader Turkic) music culture is conserved for the present and future generations.

Figure 5.11: *Aşıks* in their association in Sivas (photo by Sohrab Jabbari)

Bound to the context of the motherland, both described events can be understood as fitting into a general predisposition for the conservation and transmission of Turkish cultural traditions, and the concomitant professionalization of their current and future practitioners. This predisposition, a result of sustained nationalistic endeavours (initiated by Atatürk almost a century ago), is nowadays maintained and realized by, on the one hand, all levels of the Turkish state system and the institutions related to it, and, on the other hand, individuals and institutions belonging to civil society. This collective (sense of) responsibility and mission regarding cultural heritage penetrates all levels of society, and educational and (socio-)cultural institutions in particular are always prepared and equipped to make their contribution to this cause. The folk dance lesson in Kırşehir is an example of (extra-official) education with a cultural and social component. The artistic training of the *aşıks* in Sivas is an example of cultural conservation, transmission, and further development within an (extra-official) cultural association. The degree of penetration of the ideals of traditionalism and cultural nationalism is illustrated by the interior design and decoration of both the Hoy-Dek and the Sifahod rooms.

Events Bound to the Diaspora Context

Suvermez Night in Temse

On a Saturday evening in May 2012, one or two months before the annual exodus of a part of the Turkish diaspora to spend the summer in their place of origin, Emirdağ, a special event aimed at this target group is organized. The Central Anatolian town of Emirdağ, including its surrounding villages, has been suffering from massive migration to Europe. The money spent by *Emirdağlılar* from Europe every summer represents a substantial part of the town's economy. In order to raise more funds for the village of Suvermez, a benefit evening is organized by its *muhtar* (elected head), assisted by a few friends living in the diaspora. The event takes place in a party hall run by Turks in Temse, a town 45km from Ghent (see Figure 5.12). Since it is a benefit evening, there is an entrance fee (20 euros), and the food and drinks are to be paid as well. In addition to the financial motive, this event has a social and cultural goal: bringing together the dispersed Suvermez community and keeping the cultural traditions alive. Gathered on this day are approximately 400 *Suvermezliler*, mostly families, from different places in Belgium (mostly Ghent and Brussels) and neighbouring countries such as the Netherlands and France. Apart from the *muhtar*, there is a small delegation from Turkey. The audience consists of a mix of different ages and types; clothing styles are partly modest-Islamic, partly posh-Western, but always dressed up.

The organizers have set up an extended, entertaining programme with plenty of variation. Most of the guests arrive between 6 and 7 pm; at 7 pm, the actual programme starts with a welcoming speech by the *muhtar* of Suvermez and the screening of a short video about the village. More speeches follow by the *muhtar* and other respected *Suvermezliler.* Around 7.45 pm, the first musical performance takes place. Fakı Edeer (see Chapter 2), a poet-musician and respected former inhabitant of Emirdağ, recites and sings self-written poems as an ode to his hometown, before switching to the Emirdağ and Suvermez "classics" – the established repertoire of the region. He is accompanied by two members of the "Ibıdık" family of *abdals* (see Chapter 1) on *bağlama* and clarinet, and a keyboardist providing a harmonic and rhythmic substructure. Subsequently, the *bağlama* player takes the microphone and continues the performance of folk songs of the region. Like Fakı Edeer, he walks around the hall in the middle of the people while singing. The next performance involves a set-up with synthesizer, *davul* (played by the versatile *abdal* musician), and clarinet (the other *abdal* musician); the Macedonian singer is the first non-Emirdağ musician of the evening. His interpretation is heavily pop-influenced and ignores the regional stylistic characteristics (*tavır*), which makes the music (mostly from Emirdağ and Kırşehir) sound atypical. The audience does not mind and dances enthusiastically. One hour later, the roles change again, and the singer becomes an accompanist on the *bağlama* for the next singer, a young woman from Brussels, while the other accompanists continue their duty. The repertoire is broad and includes music from various regions of Turkey. This is also the case during the performance of the next female singer, the first guest from Turkey. Nuray Hafiftaş (deceased in 2018) is an established name in the Turkish folk scene and acts like a star. She reprimands her accompanists when they accidentally slip up their parts or react somewhat slowly to her impulses. Although the public disapproves of her behaviour, she nevertheless receives a gift from the organizer and is invited to sing at the next Suvermez festival.

At 11.15 pm, an intermezzo is inserted into the programme, consisting of a small show of traditional clothes of the region and another informative speech. Emirdağ expert Fakı Edeer appears on the stage for a second time, again reciting and singing traditional folk poems, but also initiating a particular song called 'Düz Oyun' ("plain dance"), a female dance reminiscent of *semah*. Subsequently, plane tickets for a Turkish Airlines flight to Eskişehir, the closest airport to Emirdağ, are handed over to the winner of the organized tombola. At midnight, the final performance begins, featuring a second guest from Turkey, Ankaralı Coşkun, who sings and plays the *bağlama*. He has problems with his voice, for which he apologizes several times. The extreme loudness of the music does not make the situation easier. The risk of ear damage and hearing loss during events like this is real. Many people start to leave around 1 am, but a select company of deeply involved people keeps on celebrating until the early hours.

Figure 5.12: Suvermez night in Temse (photo by the author)

Celebration in Ghent of 50 Years of Turkish Migration

On a Sunday evening in October 2013, a concert programme celebrating 50 years of Turkish migration to Belgium takes place in Intercultural Centre De Centrale. The concert evening is part of a larger event starting in the afternoon and involving a reception and an exhibition of traditional kilims from the region of Emirdağ and artworks by post-migrant Turks in Flanders. The whole event, organized by Türk Ocağı Gent ("Turkish Hearth") and ATEP (Avrupa Türkiye Emirdağ Platformu – "Europe-Turkey Emirdağ Platform"), does not belong to the official programming of the intercultural centre, nor to the series of official migration festivities scheduled for 2014. The involved organizations clearly want to be the first ones to put the anniversary – and themselves – in the spotlight. The event is sponsored by the umbrella organization FZO-VL (see Chapter 2) and the entrance is free. A large audience of approximately 350 people has come out exceptionally early and fills the concert hall half an hour before the actual starting time. The setting is rather chaotic, with adults and children respectively walking and running to and fro, and the organizers are noticeably nervous.

Five minutes before the scheduled starting time, the "Ibıdık" family starts performing a repertoire of light classical songs on *darbuka* and *davul*, clarinet, *ud*, violin, and *cümbüş* (see Figure 5.13). At 7.15 pm, when the official programme starts, it becomes clear that the performance by the *abdals* from Emirdağ was just a kind of warm-up. True to the Turkish tradition, a long series of speeches proceeds, delivered by the presidents of the three organizing bodies and a few honoured guests, including Flemish and Turkish politicians. A plaque of honour is presented to Belgian and Turkish people of importance for or within the Turkish diaspora in Ghent. Next on the programme are speeches by Maurice Maréchal of the integration services of Ghent, who has assisted probably thousands of newcomers in multiple situations, and by Johan Vandewalle, a linguist teaching the Turkish language at Ghent University. The speeches take turns with other interventions, such as a recitation of humorous-sarcastic poems or an academically inspired, polemical lecture on migration. The talks are too long, and the audience is losing its patience.

Figure 5.13: Performance of the Ibıdıklar during the celebration of 50 years of Turkish migration to Belgium (photo by the author)

The musical part starts around 9.30 pm. Different groups and artists appear in revue with short performances in which folk music forms the principal part. The first group features singer Bülent Gök, who has developed into an experienced entertainer. With his band consisting of *bağlama*, synthesizer, and electronic drums, he brings popularized folk music with jazz influences. Next, Hilde De Clercq, the only non-Turkish musician on the programme, sings a few Turkish folk songs while accompanying herself on the *darbuka*. Both try to establish interaction with the almost-dozing-off audience and encourage them to sing along. The programme continues with a reappearance of the Ibıdıks, this time performing folk music from Emirdağ. A young female singer and an old name – the ubiquitous Fakı Edeer – conclude the long Sunday evening.

Both events bound to the diaspora context combine social and cultural endeavours and involve an (almost) exclusively Turkish target audience. The celebration of 50 years of migration creates a partial rapprochement with the non-Turkish public, in the form of select invited individuals who have proven their merits in enhancing mutual understanding between the Turkish minority and Belgian majority populations. Publicity for both events is made almost exclusively in Turkish. This approach is not exceptional; many events organized by Turks in Ghent are oriented towards their own population in form as well as in content, which can be regarded as an illustration of a subsisting sociocultural field of tension (an "ethnic boundary") between the Turkish and Belgian populations.[16] Both activities are organized by Turkish individuals and associations in the diaspora in cooperation with individuals and associations from Turkey, which illustrates the strong transnationalist tendencies of the Turkish diaspora. In the case of the celebration of 50 years of migration, one of the aims of the organizing Turkish individuals and associations in Belgium, in addition to a nationalistically motivated sociocultural agenda, appears to be the reinforcement of their bonds with their backing or target public.

Features typical of events in Turkey maintained in the diaspora context include the importance of speeches by dignitaries lending an official aura to the event, and the length of the drawn-out programmes. The strict hierarchy prevailing in Turkey is often reflected in a milder form in Belgium. Typical for events organized in a diaspora context is the limited availability of professional or at least semi-professional musicians able to perform the duty. As a consequence, certain familiar and reliable musicians are ubiquitous in different kinds of events, in different time and space settings, and for different occasions; examples are the Ibıdık *abdal* family, but also singers such as Bülent Gök or Fakı Edeer. A last observation concerns the fact that many events organized by Turks in Ghent adopt similar forms with many features and procedures common to contemporary urban Turkish wedding parties; the benefit evening for Suvermez was a clear example of this case.

General Observations on Turkish Folk Music Events in Turkey and Ghent

Besides context- and setting-related differences characterizing events in Turkey and their counterparts in Belgium – motherland/diaspora, rural/ urban, outdoors/indoors, more/fewer resources, and so on – many social, cultural, and political factors are at play. The strong association of certain types of events or settings with ethnic, cultural, or religious minorities in Turkey often dissolves in the diaspora, where the Turkish presence in its entirety can be (and de facto is) considered as a minority. Correspondingly, political connotations also disappear or change. In Turkey, ritual components often prevail more strongly and are often more tightly socially integrated than in the diaspora. A diasporic tendency towards convergence exists in the design and style of events, often adopting features common to wedding celebrations. Hierarchic relations are often less strongly observed or displayed in the diaspora.

However, many constants can be observed: general conceptions and designs are mostly and purposely retained, while the concrete details of the way in which the events unfold can show similarities or be adapted to the context. The position and role of the music and musicians are comparable, considering that qualitative and quantitative factors can show considerable variation.

Events tied to the homeland context typically bear witness to the widespread commitment to the Turkish cultural traditions and the project of their preservation and transmission, grounded in Atatürk's nationalistic state design. Events typical for the diaspora possess the potential to depart from this embeddedness in the Turkish culture, but in the observed reality, in many cases they maintain an intra-Turkish (often transnationalist) orientation.

Following the above ethnographic description and in-depth discussion and analysis of selected examples of musical events from my fieldwork in Turkey and Ghent, the scope is to be widened again. A more systematic, comparative analysis will review a range of contextual and musical aspects of the 46 attended musical events in Chapters 6 and 7, to be further framed by a consideration of their musical functions in Chapter 8.

Chapter 6

Contextual and Musical Aspects of Performances in Turkey and Ghent

The most systematic part of my research concerned the participant observation of a broad range of 46 musical events qualifying as non-educational social events with live performance of Turkish folk music. They took place in 2011 and 2012 in Ghent and its close surroundings, and in different rural, small-town, and urban places of the Aegean Sea region, Central Anatolia (Emirdağ and Kırşehir), the Black Sea region, and eastern Central and Eastern Anatolia. An ethnographic working method based on structured notes, documentation, and interviews was able to provide some insights in the general and specific properties of performances of Turkish folk music in the motherland and the diaspora context of Ghent, and their commonalities and differences. These insights are presented below, in a mosaic of contextual and musical aspects, regarding the kind of event (or use of the performance), occasion, set-up, financing, time and place, commissioners, listeners, and performers, performed music, performed Turkish folk music, used instruments, way of creation, performance quality, and performance style.

Kinds of Events (Uses of Performances)

Alan Merriam argues that a clear distinction should be made between the concepts of "use" and "function" of musical performances, but he also stresses their complementarity. He defines the use of music as "the situation in which music is employed in human action" while "'function' concerns the reasons for its employment and particularly the broader purpose which it serves" (1964: 210). Bruno Nettl adds two proposals to the discussion. The first analytical model is the "pyramid model", which consists of "a base, a tip, and something in between, moving gradually from uses to functions".[1] Uses and functions of music are represented as two ends of a continuum ranging from the concrete-specific to the abstract-general (2005: 251–54). His second contribution is the "coin model", involving an analytical distinction between "the culture's and the analyst's statements" of uses and functions of music (2005: 249–51).[2]

Table 6.1 groups the 46 events I attended in 2011 and 2012 into generic categories. In this way, the variety of events in which Turkish folk music is used comes to the fore.

Table 6.1: Categorization by kind of event (use)

Kind of event/use	Turkey	Ghent
Artistic training	Training of *aşıklık* skills with peers	[Not observed[3]]
Dance education	Folk dance lesson	[Not observed]
Concert[4]	[Not observed[5]]	*Türkü* night
Café concert	*Türkü* night	Turkish evening; *türkü* night; café concert
Festival[6]	Summer festival	Cultural festival; open day of intercultural centre; student festival of world music school; open-air festival (*seyran*)
Celebration of life-cycle event	Wedding party; circumcision party[7]	
Celebration of specific event	Celebration of end of school year	Celebration of 50 years of Turkish migration to Belgium
Official opening	Official opening of cultural association; official opening of *cemevi*	Official opening of music café
Religious ceremony	*Cem*[8]	
Formal social gathering	Musical evening of soccer supporters club	Suvermez night (benefit evening); karaoke evening of student club
Informal social gathering	Spending time with friends, colleagues, family or acquaintances; visiting old friends	Jam session

Occasions for Performance

My field research in Turkey revealed a broad range of occasions calling for folk music performances. The rituals of marriage and circumcision belong to the core of Turkish society and are important forums for the performance of

Turkish folk music. Folk music performances also elicited other occasions with a ritual component, such as graduation or the end of the school year, the official opening of a new sociocultural organization, or celebrations accompanying the changing of seasons (in this case the start of summer). Another specific occasion in some cases involving spontaneous performance of folk music is a reunion with old friends after a long period. Apart from this range of more or less specific occasions involving folk music, many performances happen outside of special occasions, such as regular cultural activities organized by cultural organizations, or informal social gatherings accompanied by music.

The parallel research in Ghent yielded similar results. I encountered the same specific occasions, namely marriage, circumcision, and the opening of a new organization. An occasion typically occurring in the diaspora is the celebration or commemoration of migration. The changing of seasons functions as an occasion in a similar way to Turkey. The same kinds of events occur without specific occasion: regular cultural activities organized by cultural organizations, and informal social gatherings.

Set-up of Performances

In Turkey as well as in Ghent, most events were planned in advance. In Ghent, only one event could be considered as spontaneously initiated: the jam session in a music café, involving a small group of friends and acquaintances of whom some played a musical instrument or were able to sing. All other folk music performances were not only planned in advance, but also commissioned. In some cases, however, musical performance was partly self-initiated, involving spontaneous musical participation by the attending people. Among these are Turkish evenings or *türkü* nights in music cafés. A specific case is the Alevi *cem* ceremony, during which the attendees regularly participate in the ceremony by collective singing, which proceeds in a similar way in Ghent and in Turkey.

Spontaneously self-initiated performances in Turkey were informal social gatherings (spending time with friends, colleagues, family, or acquaintances) on the one hand, and the artistic training session performed by a small group of *aşıks* in the venue of their association in the presence of some acquaintances, on the other hand. All other attended events were planned in advance and commissioned by a third party. In some cases, the external assignment was combined with an internal stimulus to participate in the performance: besides the *cem* mentioned above, this was the case in parties celebrating a specific event, and in a formal social gathering of soccer supporters in their clubhouse – all settings characterized by a safe and positive atmosphere.

Financial Aspects[9]

Various financing channels sustain or facilitate the performance of Turkish folk music: support by governmental authorities (municipal, provincial, regional, or state authorities[10]), sponsoring by private companies, investment by the organizing body, private financing, and recuperation via the audience (ticket sales and/or consumables). The majority of the attended events were supported by an authority, almost always complemented by other financing channels. The events without authority support were the wedding and circumcision parties, the karaoke evening of the student club, the *seyran*, the official opening of the new music café, and the celebration of 50 years of Turkish migration to Belgium, the latter being an "unofficial" early celebration organized by Turkish non-profit organizations in Ghent. The wedding and circumcision parties were financed by private means; every Turkish family invests in these celebrations of important life events (rites of passage) of their young family members. The events without support from the authorities were financed by the organizing body. In some cases, additional funding was provided by sponsoring from private companies (in the case of the *seyran*) or recuperation via consumables (in the case of the karaoke evening). The events supported by the authorities were usually co-financed by the organizing body's fund as well as a recuperation of the costs via the audience. Events sponsored by private companies in addition to support from the authorities and recuperation via the audience or investment by the organizing body were the cultural festival and the Suvermez night (benefit evening).

Time-related Aspects

A particular event's timing can be accidental (unintentional) or non-accidental (intentional). Regarding the events observed in Turkey, it became clear that occurrences in the spring or summer months were non-accidental in many cases. In Ghent, however, the outcome was different, which is in part due to the specific kinds of events which were observed. In Turkey as well as in Ghent, the choice for a weekend day was in most cases intentional. While in Turkey, the attended events were equally divided between the week and the weekend, in Ghent fewer events took place during the week. This difference possibly reflects an actual concentration of performances of Turkish folk music during the weekend in the diaspora, but may also be related to the fact that a large part of the systematic research in Turkey was conducted during the summer holidays.

The part of the day during which the events take place, as well as the duration of the events, varies substantially, both in Turkey and in Ghent. In both contexts, most settings are situated in the evening (in some cases already starting in the afternoon). Many events in Turkey were short or very short, while others lasted more than four hours or even longer than eight hours. In Ghent, most events lasted between two and eight hours, the remainder lasting less than two hours or more than eight hours.

A time-related factor present in Turkey but not in the diaspora is the call to prayer (*ezan*) five times a day, during which all music should temporarily cease.

Table 6.2 shows the time-related aspects of the observed events. The settings with the longest duration were the wedding parties (Turkey), certain festivals (Turkey, Ghent), and the benefit evening (Ghent).

Table 6.2: Time-related aspects of the musical events

Parameter		Turkey	Ghent
Season	Spring	9	10
	Summer	17	0
	Fall	[not observed]	4
	Winter		6
Day of the week	During the week	13	2
	During the weekend[11]	13	18
Time of day	Whole day	1	0
	Morning[12]	1	0
	Afternoon	6	2
	Afternoon + evening	6	3
	Afternoon + evening + night	0	1
	Evening	10	10
	Evening + night	1	4
	Night	1	0
Duration[13]	Less than 2 hours	7	3
	2–3 hours	11	6
	4–7 hours	3	8
	More than 8 hours	5	3

The last time-related aspect concerns whether a certain event is single (once-only) or recurring, a parameter largely dependent on the kind of event and the occasion. In Turkey as well as in Ghent, most of the attended events were recurring, either in a defined way (with the timing of the next occurrence already known) or in an undefined way (with the timing of the next occurrence not yet known). Most recurring events with defined timing were regular cultural activities organized by cultural organizations, including festivals and religious ceremonies. Typical single events were private family celebrations (wedding and circumcision parties) and official openings both in Turkey and in Ghent, as well as particular kinds of cultural activities organized only once in Ghent, such as a cultural festival or a celebration of 50 years of migration.

Aspects of Place

One of the most significant aspects of defining the setting is the distinction between an urban and a rural context. The intention of the research conducted in Turkey was to take into consideration the widest possible range of contexts. I attended 11 urban settings, three small-town settings, and nine rural settings. Particular kinds of events (weddings and festivals) were studied in both urban and rural contexts, which offered an opportunity to obtain a more complete view regarding many context-related aspects. Most of the observed events could equally well appear in urban as in rural contexts, while a few events were typically urban, such as *türkü* nights in music cafés, and folk dance lessons in folk dance associations. Almost all events researched in the diaspora took place in the city of Ghent itself, thus in an urban context. A few observed events occurred in non-urban contexts: the wedding party and the circumcision party were organized in party halls in smaller towns respectively 40km and 15km from Ghent, and the *seyran* took place on a large field in a rural environment 20km from Ghent. The choice to hold these events outside of the city was motivated by the specific requirements of the events.

A second distinguishing parameter is outdoors (open air) versus indoors (closed space). In Turkey, wedding and circumcision parties are typically organized in spring or summer, preferably in the open air, as are many other festivities for special occasions and large-scale annual festivals. Moreover, during a large part of the year in Turkey, social life almost completely takes place in the open air, and as a consequence, almost all social happenings involving the performance of Turkish folk music are transplanted from the interior to the exterior. In contrast to the events observed in Turkey, most events in the diaspora happened indoors, except for festivals. This difference could be explained by the fact that the research in Turkey was conducted in June and July, while the research in Ghent was conducted throughout the year, but it could also be due to the different weather and climatic conditions in Belgium and Turkey.

A final distinction is the one between private and public places. A public place can be defined as a place where anyone is allowed to come, without invitation or without asking for permission. A private place is a place belonging to a certain person or group of persons, which should not be entered without an appropriate reason, an invitation, or permission by the owners or their representatives ("Public Space" 2014). In Turkey, courtyards, gardens, or rooms belonging to houses or hotels and club houses, or rooms belonging to associations are examples of settings belonging to the private sphere. Public locations include different kinds of cafés and restaurants, streets, squares, and fields. Venues for religious service such as a *cemevi* are situated on the edge of the public and the private spheres. Many of the public and private locations in Ghent were similar to those in Turkey. Private locations typical for the diaspora are the large halls that are hired for wedding or circumcision parties (reluctantly organized indoors, instead of outside), and a room in an intercultural centre functioning as a replacement for an appropriate venue for religious service. Concert halls are an example of public locations where the performance of Turkish folk music was regularly observed in the diaspora.

Commissioners

Some events in Turkey were initiated by the musicians themselves and did not involve any form of commission or employment. However, the events in Ghent all involved a commissioner, except the jam session. This difference certainly does not imply the non-existence of self-initiated musical events in the diaspora, but nevertheless provides an indication of the omnipresence and more spontaneous use of Turkish folk music in its motherland.

Commissioners can be private persons, organizations, or authorities (see Chapter 2). In Ghent, most commissioners were (related to) organizations. Private commissioners in the diaspora as well as in Turkey typically occur in private celebrations such as wedding and circumcision parties. In Ghent, a tendency could be discerned involving one person within an organization deciding semi-independently about the "employment" (formal or informal, paid or not) of musicians. Typical examples of such persons within organizations are owner-managers of music cafés structured as non-profit organizations, and concert organizers operating in larger concert halls. The overwhelming majority of commissioners was male and Turkish, in the diaspora as well as in Turkey.

Typically, in Turkey as well as in Ghent, commissioners conduct an active role in leading the events as a kind of "master of ceremonies", welcoming the attendees, looking after the well-being of attendees and musicians, and connecting people with each other. Usually, commissioners also participate in the general action of the event, for example by performing religious rituals (*cem*), dancing, eating and drinking, or talking. In some cases, the role of commissioner (temporarily) coincides with the role of performer, as in the case of musician-owners of the music cafés, or in the case of commissioners being the teachers of the pupils participating in the event.

Listeners

Formal or informal audiences (see Chapter 2) appear in various forms involving substantial differences regarding gender, size, and age. Nevertheless, the majority of the observed events in Turkey as well as in Ghent displayed an equal distribution of male and female listeners. The size of audiences ranged from very small (one or a few individuals) to very large (several hundred people). In Turkey, exclusively male audiences were common, while in Ghent only mixed-gender audiences were encountered. Regarding age, in Turkey as well as in Ghent, many events involved audiences of a wide age range. Other events (mainly) involved middle-aged listeners or young people, or different combinations of age groups. In Ghent, audiences involving substantial numbers of elderly people were encountered less often than in Turkey.

Events in Ghent involving a clearly mixed audience of Turkish and non-Turkish people were the cultural festival in the city centre, and particular activities in the intercultural centre. In most other cases, the audience was predominantly or exclusively Turkish.

General audiences (see Chapter 2) were notably identified during the open-air festivals in Ghent and Turkey. Specific audiences encountered in Turkey and in Ghent involved acquaintances, family, friends, students, or colleagues of the commissioner(s) or performer(s), regular guests of the venue where the performance took place, or members of a club (e.g., the soccer supporters club in Turkey and the student club in Ghent) or a community (e.g., Alevi communities in Turkey and Ghent and people from Suvermez in Ghent).

Regarding the listeners' place of residence, in both research contexts, the majority of cases involved only listeners from the region, city, or village in which the event took place. In some examples, this local audience was supplemented by listeners from other places in the same country. In exceptional cases, people from other countries also attended the event. This situation was observed during the summer festival in the city centre of Sivas (where some tourists attended the activities), during the circumcision party in Rupelmonde (where family members from the Netherlands joined the party), and during the benefit evening (which was attended by *Suvermezliler* from the Netherlands and France).

In general, both in Turkey and in Ghent, listeners are actively involved in the event and the setting. Only formal concerts display a more silent and "passive" audience. In other kinds of events, listeners often join in by singing, clapping hands, clicking fingers, moving in response to the musical meter and rhythm, dancing, responding verbally to the musicians, or applauding. In some cases, they have a drink or something to eat, or chat during the performance. In certain events, the audience actively influences the musical performance by making requests for particular pieces or for a certain style or genre. Dancing occurred in many kinds of events in Turkey and in Ghent, such as parties and celebrations, festivals, formal and informal social gatherings, and concerts (including café concerts). Singing along was observed during informal social gatherings, the artistic training of the *aşıks*, many concerts and café concerts, the circumcision party, and evidently the karaoke evening in Ghent. A particular case was constituted by the *cem* ceremonies, in which active participation of the community members by singing prayers and performing the *semah* is part of the religious ritual.

Performers

Some events in the diaspora – all taking place in the aptly named intercultural centre – displayed a collaboration between Turkish and non-Turkish performers: the open house, the student festival, café concerts, and the celebration of 50 years of Turkish migration. These activities not only involved a mixed set-up, but often a mixed audience as well. Regarding gender, female participation turned out to be much higher in Ghent than in Turkey, where most events involved exclusively male performers. This difference could possibly be related to the fact that public musical performance by women was not easily accepted in traditional Turkish society, except in exclusively female company or in particular communities such as Alevis or Roma. This restriction can still be observed in rural and conservative communities, although the situation is gradually changing, and in large cities, it is completely normal for a female amateur or professional musician to play an instrument. A typical example of "institutionalized" female music-making is the henna night, during which female family members and friends of the bride sing songs circling around the bride and groom before applying the henna.

The number of performers ranges from a single performer to almost 50 people. In Turkey, events involving only one performer were regularly encountered, in contrast to Ghent. In Ghent as well as in Turkey, several events displayed small ensembles of two to five performers. Events featuring more than five performers are rarer and, in most cases, concern festivals. The official opening of a cultural association in Kaman as a part of a summer festival featured the largest number of performers (almost 50). In Ghent, two festivals and a *türkü* night involving a performance by the pupils of the world music school, featured 20 or more performers.

The performers of most of the events in Turkey were (mainly) middle-aged; the other events involved (mainly) young performers, (mainly) elderly performers, a combination of middle-aged and elderly people, or a mixture of all age categories. In Ghent, many events displayed young performers or a combination of young and middle-aged people; the remainder involved either (mainly) middle-aged performers or children, sometimes in combination with young and middle-aged people.[14]

Regarding their place of residence, the vast majority of the events in Turkey exclusively involved performers from the region, city, or village where the event took place. In a few cases, musicians from the same province were combined with performers from another province, for example during the wedding party in Kırşehir, where "seasonal" musicians from Adana were employed along with a local musician, and during certain large festivals, where musicians from Istanbul were engaged. Performers from abroad were not encountered, except in the case of a musician living abroad who had returned to his town of origin for his summer holidays. In Ghent, the same parameter showed a broader range: musicians from the region or city were regularly combined with musicians from other cities in Belgium, or even from other countries (the Netherlands and Turkey), while the circumcision party and certain *türkü* nights or Turkish evenings exclusively featured musicians from other cities and countries (the Netherlands, Germany, and Turkey).

Regarding professionalism (see Chapter 2 for a discussion of the concept), the categorization of the musicians as amateur, semi-professional, or professional was based on a combination of my personal judgements based on musical criteria, and information gathered through interviewing the musicians (self-perception and descriptions of their professional situation). In Turkey, many events involved exclusively professional or semi-professional musicians. This was less often the case in Ghent, where the degree of professionalism among musicians varied considerably. These differences reflect a larger percentage of professional musicians in Turkey, compared to the Turkish communities in Ghent.

Professional musicians in Turkey often belong to one of the categories of traditional specialists, namely *aşıks*, *abdals*, or Roma (see Chapter 3). This is usually the case during tradition-oriented events such as wedding and circumcision parties, and other ritual celebrations, but sometimes also during café concerts, or informal or formal social gatherings. Although the number of these categories of musicians is smaller in the diaspora, they are usually very active as performers. In Ghent, *abdal* musicians participated during the Suvermez night, the *cem*, and the celebration of 50 years of Turkish migration.

In general, both in Turkey and in Ghent, the performers behave in an informal way, directed towards creating a relaxed atmosphere. Generally, the interaction with the attendees proceeds in a convivial and engaging manner, without strict separation between performers and listeners. In the case of amateur or occasional performers, no formal musician-role is undertaken; on the contrary, they adopt an unpretentious attitude. Most events involve a musical programme punctuated by breaks, during which the performers participate in the social action of the attendees. As the musical programme is usually structured in a loose and improvisatory way, mutual communication between the musicians during the performance commonly occurs. It is also common for performers to be open to requests from the public, even in more formalized concerts with more distance between the audience and the performers.

The Music Performed

Many of the attended events were not purely confined to the performance of Turkish folk music. The combination of Turkish folk music with other musical genres or other art forms seems to occur more often in Ghent than in

Turkey: in Ghent, two-thirds of the observed programmes were mixed, while in Turkey two-thirds of the events were confined to Turkish folk music.

In Turkey, Turkish folk music was combined with popular music (wedding party in Milas, celebration of the end of the school year/graduation in Emirdağ, *türkü* night in Kırşehir), with *özgün müzik* (*türkü* night in Izmir, celebration of the end of the school year in Emirdağ), with Islamic prayers (circumcision party, *cem* ceremony), with military music (inauguration of the Kaman *Abdal* association), and with Turkish classical music (informal social gathering in Milas). Typical events exclusively displaying Turkish folk music are wedding parties, cultural activities such as folk dance lessons or training of *aşıklık* skills, certain kinds of festivals, and formal and informal social gatherings.

In Ghent, events exclusively involving Turkish folk music were the circumcision and wedding parties, the Suvermez night, the *seyran*, a Turkish evening in Muzikantenhuis, and the *cem*. The most common combination is an alternation of Turkish folk music and *özgün müzik*. Almost all Turkish evenings or *türkü* nights displayed this pattern. Turkish folk music was also combined with popular music (karaoke evening), with several other genres (café concert and student festival in De Centrale), with other art forms (open house at De Centrale and cultural festival), and with pieces from the Turkish classical repertoire (concert by Erkan Oğur and Derya Türkan[15]).

The Performed Turkish Folk Music Repertoire[16]

A closer look at the Turkish folk repertoire performed during the events attended in Turkey clearly points to the locally anchored importance of regional music. Every attended event involved repertoire belonging to the region in which the event took place, in many cases even exclusively. This was the case in all events taking place in the Central Anatolian province of Kırşehir, which gives an indication of the large popularity of the music of that region. The fact that this popularity reaches beyond its own region was evidenced by the appearance of music from Kırşehir and Ankara[17] in several events in other provinces. The ubiquity of this music is possibly due to the popularity of *abdal* folk singers such as Neşet Ertaş and the expressive quality of the folk music of the region. The remaining musical events featured a mix of music from the region where the event took place with music from other regions, be it music from neighbouring regions, music from more distant Turkish regions, or even from beyond the borders of the Turkish

Republic (Azerbaijan or the Balkans[18]). A typical example of the appearance of a wide range of regions within one event was the cultural festival in Sivas, which involved a display of the folk dances from the diverse regions of Turkey. The range of regions featured during a wedding party in Milas (Aegean Sea region) illustrates the degree of cross-region penetration and intermingling sometimes occurring in Turkey: besides *zeybek* music from the Aegean Sea region, dance music from Central Anatolia, Eastern Anatolia, and the Mediterranean Sea region was performed.

In Ghent, the combination of folk music from many different regions of Turkey within a single event is standard. The only homogeneous event was the *cem*, logically confined to liturgical Alevi music as used in the region of Emirdağ. Figures 6.1 and 6.2 show the (approximate) occurrence of regional and transregional musical styles across the whole range of attended events in Ghent.

The prevalence of the music from Central Anatolia is clear, mainly involving music from the central provinces of Ankara and Kırşehir (from which the music is popular not only throughout Turkey but also in the diaspora), and from the town of Emirdağ (where the majority of the Turkish population in Ghent has its roots). The relative importance of the music from the province of Sivas is largely due to the popularity of the music of iconic *aşık* Veysel Şatıroğlu (1894–1973) (see Chapter 3). Other dominant regions are Eastern Anatolia and to a lesser extent Southeast Anatolia and the Black Sea region. (Transregional) Alevi music is popular as well.

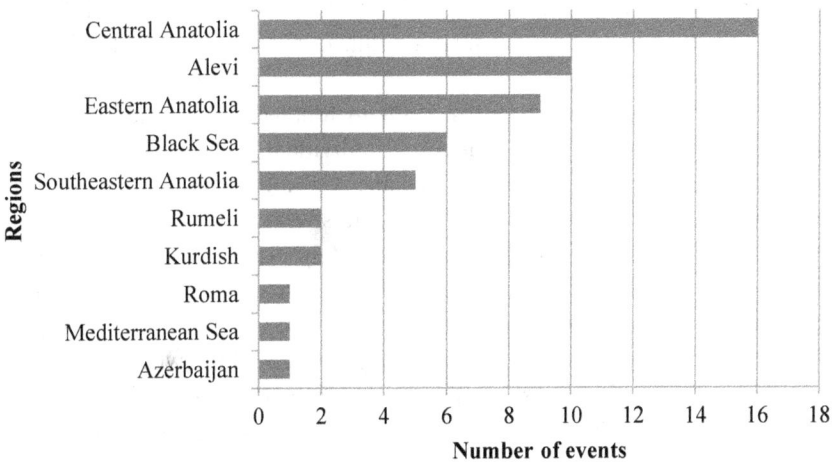

Figure 6.1: Occurrence of the regional and transregional styles in the attended events in Ghent (Liselotte Sels)

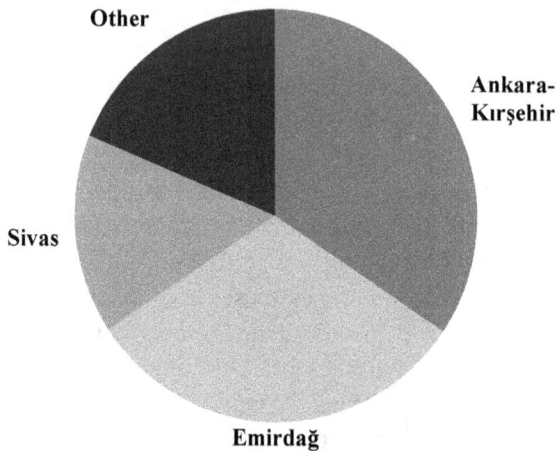

Figure 6.2: Occurrence of the Central Anatolian sub-styles in the attended events in Ghent (Liselotte Sels)

Instruments Used

The line-up (instrumentation) throughout the event can be either variable or fixed. The majority of observed line-ups was variable, in Turkey (almost all) as well as in Ghent (all). In Turkey, a fixed line-up was observed in a *türkü* night in Izmir (a single singer-*bağlama* player), a wedding party (a fixed band) and a circumcision party (a *davul–zurna* trio) in Milas, and an informal social gathering involving one man singing in the company of family and acquaintances.

A variable line-up can manifest itself in four ways: variation of instruments played by one person; variation of individual performers; variation of instruments within one group of musicians; variation of ensembles. Typical examples of variation of individual performers were an informal social gathering in which some of the attendees alternately played or sang folk songs, and the training of the *aşık*s in their association. A specific case of variation occurred in the *cem* ceremonies in Turkey and in Ghent, where the recognized musician (the *zakir*) played and sang throughout the whole ceremony, except for the small time-span wherein he himself performed the *semah*. Variation of ensembles and variation of line-ups within one ensemble occur very often, both in Ghent and in Turkey. These variations belong to standard procedures during many kinds of celebrations, including wedding and circumcision parties, and typically during festivals.

The most commonly used instrument in Turkey is the *saz* or *bağlama*, often used to accompany oneself while singing, followed by the standard combination of *davul* and *zurna*. "Oriental" types of synthesizers (keyboards), featuring "microtonal" scales and specific instrumental timbres, are the third most important instrument, typically appearing in wedding parties and other kinds of parties and celebrations.[19] Wedding parties in the province of Kırşehir engaged one-man-orchestras involving singers accompanying themselves on synthesizer and *bağlama* simultaneously. The *darbuka* was used several times in Kırşehir. Instruments such as the *kemençe* (Black Sea region), the violin (Central Anatolia), the clarinet (Emirdağ), and the *kaşık* (Central Anatolia) are used in specific regions; the guitar is sometimes used to add a specific timbre or flavour to the music.

In Ghent, like in Turkey, the *bağlama* was clearly the most prevalent instrument (most commonly combined with singing). The *bağlama* was followed in importance by the synthesizer (keyboard). The guitar, clarinet, *davul*, *bendir*, *def*, and *darbuka* appeared regularly as well, but the combination of *davul* and *zurna*, highly common in Turkey, was observed in only two events in Ghent: a wedding party and the *seyran*. The explanation for this striking difference is twofold: on the one hand, *davul* and *zurna* are open-air instruments that produce very loud sounds, inappropriate for indoor use, while on the other hand, there is a lack of good *zurna* players in Ghent. Many other instruments are sporadically used: Turkish instruments such as the *kemençe*, *kaval*, *mey*, *kaşık*, *cura* (small *saz*), *bendir*, as well as non-Turkish instruments such as the bass guitar, electric guitar, electric piano, cajon, and so on (see Figure 6.3 for an account of the occurrences).

In many cases, the acoustic *bağlama* is replaced by a semi-electric or electric instrument. The semi-electric or "Fishman"[20] *bağlama* is an acoustic instrument provided with a pickup in order to amplify it. The *elektrosaz* was designed in the late 1960s by rock musician Erkin Koray and *arabesk* musician Orhan Gencebay and modelled on the electric guitar. This dependence on the guitar model and the use of magnetic elements originally developed for the guitar point to the weakness of the *elektrosaz*, which is considered as having not yet obtained its optimal construction and sound. The different forms of the *elektrosaz* all serve their own ends: semi-electric instruments replace the acoustic ones in more intimate settings than settings preferring the electric instrument. While a higher velocity and volume can be obtained on the *elektrosaz* than on the acoustic instrument, and the sound can be sustained, it also has an important disadvantage: the regional *tavırs* cannot be rendered in an appropriate way (Murer, email to author, 24 July 2014; Volkan 2011; Toprak 2012). I did not encounter the real *elektrosaz* (an electric instrument without sound box) very often during the fieldwork. It is only used in some festive contexts such as large family celebrations.

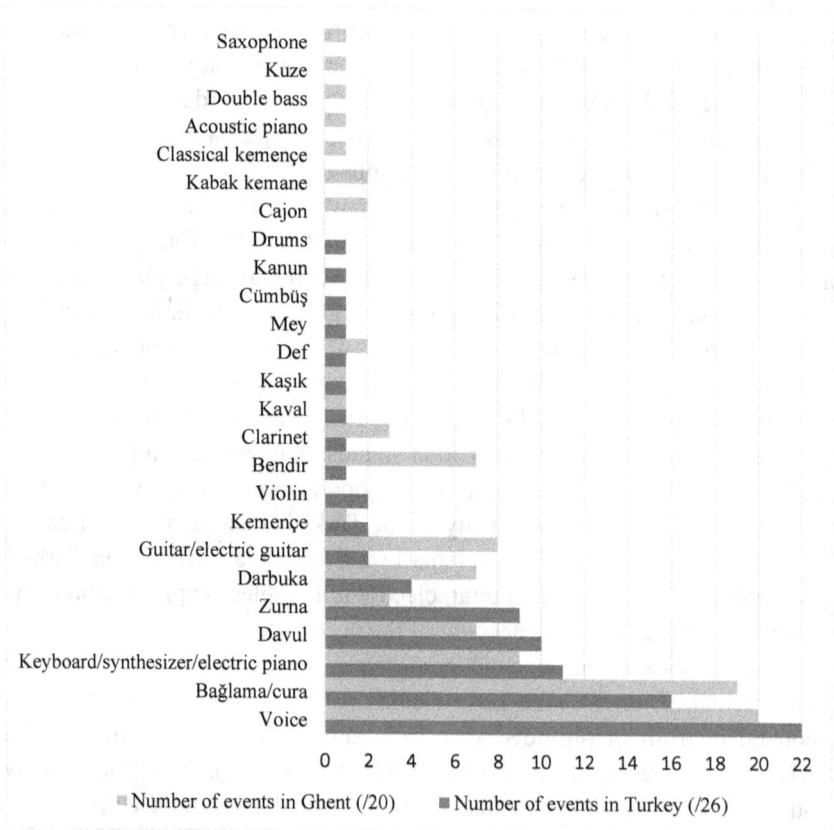

Figure 6.3: Occurrence of instruments in Turkey and in Ghent (Liselotte Sels)

Way of Creation

By "way of creation", I mean the extent to which the performance is improvised versus composed in advance. The vast majority of the performances in Turkey were semi-improvised, which means that the performance is based on known songs or pieces that are interpreted in a free way, according to the stylistic-ornamental and formal (structure-related) preferences of the performer. Certain events in Turkey involved compositional aspects, namely the performance by the *aşıks* of particular pre-composed songs (which alternated with improvisations of other songs) and the *cem* ceremony, which included fixed liturgical prayers and musical interventions. Besides the *cem* ceremony, compositional aspects only manifested themselves in Ghent in the student festival and open house of Intercultural Centre De Centrale – two events at which students (mostly children) performed a thoroughly rehearsed repertoire – and in certain café concerts involving extensive preparation and rehearsals.

Performance Quality

The quality of musical performance involves technical as well as expressive aspects. Measuring performance quality is highly subjective. A technically qualitative rendering of a piece meets the ideals regarding stylistic idiom, clarity, sound characteristics, pronunciation of the text, rhythmic stability, and so on, and depends on the aesthetics particular to the sociocultural context, such as the setting, the taste of the performer, the regional style, and the genre specificities. Professional pop-style renderings, for example, will maintain "ideals" completely different from regionally grounded, traditional amateur renderings. In many cases, both qualitative aspects are mutually unrelated: a technically deficient rendering of a piece can bear great expressive qualities, and a technically perfect performance can lack any emotion or expression.

An example of an emotionally expressive (though technically imperfect) performance was at an informal social gathering in a private home in the village of Kırşehir, involving an intimate setting in which an 80-year-old man performed the song of his life in the company of his wife and two acquaintances. Although his voice trembled and some notes were a bit out of tune, much of this was because of the great emotion he expressed in this heartfelt, nearly 30-minute song. A technically good but emotionally poor performance was encountered during the *seyran* in the Ghent area, with a band playing the repertoire smoothly and professionally, but without much expression and in a rather monotonous way. Examples of technically and expressively less-convincing performances were a jam session held in the music café Muzikantenhuis and the contribution of a musician during a karaoke evening of a student club, both in Ghent. Both examples involved aspiring musicians with an insufficient mastery of the repertoire and singing/playing techniques. An exceptional, technically and emotionally high-level performance was at an informal gathering with friends in a mountain town in the Black Sea region, in which Ziya Aytekin, a professional musician living in Sweden and having returned to his hometown for the holidays, played music from all regions of Turkey on diverse wind instruments all night long.

Performance Style

A single Turkish folk song or dance tune can be performed in manifold ways. A possible way of classifying the diverse performance styles is by defining them according to the absence or presence of elements extraneous to the Turkish music tradition. Performance styles avoiding influences from extraneous styles involve locally grounded "traditional" styles on the one hand and academic traditionalist approaches derived from them on the other hand. The second category, an agglomerate of diverse kinds of hybrid performance styles, involves the incorporation of elements from various kinds of Western or non-Western, popular, folk, or classical styles. The first category could be labelled as (supposedly) "mono-cultural"; the second category could be conceived of as "poly-cultural" (see below). The two categories are not mutually exclusive: in some cases, overly mono-cultural performances can be temporally interspersed with flashes of styles belonging to the second category. The reverse, although less likely, is also possible.

Existing Conceptualizations

Dorit Klebe has made a related conceptualization, distinguishing a category of "traditional or pseudo-traditional music performances and/or reconstructions" from a category of "multipart arrangements as well as fusion styles related to predominantly heterophonic traditional Turkish music by adding 'western' elements" (2008: 69).[21]

The inter-combination of elements derived from extraneous styles can be conceived of as occurring in different layers, as has been showed by Karahasanoğlu and Skoog who distinguish a "superstructure" (consisting of main melody, mode, and text) from a "substructure" (consisting of instrumentation, texture, form, and rhythmic configurations) (2009: 63). Although the use of the designations "superstructure" and "substructure" could be contested, the proposed grouping of musical elements into an essential (content-related or content-defining) and a decorative (style-related or style-defining) category is an adequate and useful tool for musical style analysis. While the superstructure (as conceived of by Karahasanoğlu and Skoog) is mostly maintained throughout the different performance styles, the substructural elements differ for each performance style. If the tone system is affected as well, the superstructure of the piece is changed.

With reference to folk music performance around 1990 in urban Turkey, Martin Stokes has identified three performance styles, which I here link to the previous conceptualization: (1) an academic-regional performance style involving a central role of *tavır* [= substructural element: texture and rhythm], (2) an *elektrosaz* [= substructural element: instrumentation] style that is a simplification of the first style without *tavır* [= substructural element: texture and rhythm], and (3) a recording studio style involving large ensembles [= substructural element: instrumentation], antiphony [= substructural element: instrumentation and texture], and simple harmonizations and counterpoint [= substructural element: texture + superstructural element: mode] (Stokes 1992a: 83–98; 1992b: 97–99).

Martin Greve, in his account of the twenty-first-century Turkish musical landscape (centring on Istanbul), distinguishes two approaches, which also often interact. The first involves performance with superficial changes such as new instruments or instrument configurations, new playing techniques, Western tunings, and the integration of Western elements such as "differentiated articulation, glissando, vibrato, trills, tremolos, harmonics and chords" (2017: 170). The second approach involves more drastic changes such as harmonization and synthesis of Turkish and non-Turkish traditions (either Western or non-Western) (2017: 171–72).

Mono-cultural Performances

The category of "mono-cultural performance styles" (or indigenous Turkish styles) is an amalgam of diverse conceptions and practices regarding Turkish folk music. A first stylistic sub-group involves so-called "traditional" performances by amateur or professional performers, usually embedded in a rural context or with a background of recent rural-urban migration. This style has undergone relatively little influence from urban conceptions and practices. The second sub-group exactly concerns these urban conceptions and practices, involving a "secondary" interpretation of the tradition that is a direct or indirect product of the Turkish Republic's official approach regarding Turkish folk music. In particular, the large-scale academization of folk music, involving scholarly research and higher education, has resulted in the formation of a standardized *bağlama*-oriented performance style extracted from the traditional regional (and transregional) performance styles of Turkey. This style often adopts aspects of art music performance, not only on the level of aesthetics and technique (cleanness, clarity, virtuosity, reproducibility), but also on the level of social use and presentation (performance by "artists" in formal listening contexts). The distinction between these two types of mono-cultural performance styles is by no means absolute; it seems to be more adequate to consider them as a continuum of indigenous styles, displaying fewer or greater influences from official, academic conceptualizations and practices.

Mono-cultural traditional or tradition-derived performance styles are monophonic in essence, incorporating idiomatic kinds of polyphony: the use of drones (either a single tone or a dyad) or (structural or ephemeral) diaphony in parallel fourths. These styles develop within the flexible and rich pitch and metrical systems of Turkish folk music. Region- or style-defined melodic or rhythmic elements, ornamentations, instrumental or vocal timbres, dialects, and playing techniques are an essential characteristic.

In Turkey, more than half of the attended events displayed a rural or urban traditional or tradition-derived performance style, in some cases combined or alternated with other performance styles. I observed rural styles (relatively) uninfluenced by urban conceptions and practices during various informal social gatherings and in *davul* and *zurna* performances during circumcision and wedding parties and festivals. Standardized urban, tradition-derived performance styles were encountered during the *cem* and the *aşıklık* training in the province of Sivas, the *türkü* night in Izmir, various informal social gatherings, the folk dance lesson in Kırşehir, and festivals. The *bağlama* performance and singing during the *rakı* night of the wedding party in Kırşehir (the celebration of the father of the bride with his male friends and relatives) occupied an intermediate position between a rural and urban performance style.

In Ghent, I observed a standardized urban tradition-based performance style during the open house and the student festival at De Centrale, involving the rehearsed performance of folk pieces by pupils of the world music school, and during certain Turkish evenings in music cafés. Instances of performances closer to rural idioms (performances relatively less influenced by urban conceptions and practices) are the *cem* ceremony, and the *davul* and *zurna* performances during the wedding party and the *seyran.*

Poly-cultural Performances

This category involves influences from diverse musical styles, such as Western or non-Western classical music, jazz, pop, or folk. The use of these elements can possess a permanent (structural) or temporary (ephemeral) quality throughout the duration of the piece or the programme.

The adoption of elements from Western classical music, often in a performance in twelve-tone equal temperament, can involve tonal harmonizations, the addition of second voices in simple counterpoint, or parallel thirds or sixths. Typical procedures are the insertion of virtuoso phrases, scales or arpeggios, classically flavoured ornamentation, and chromatic passages. Possible elements defining this style are listed in Table 6.3.

Table 6.3: Elements defining a performance style influenced by Western classical music[22]

Twelve-tone equal temperament	Superstructural element: mode
Tonal harmonizations, second voices in simple counterpoint or parallel thirds or sixths	Superstructural element: mode + Substructural element: texture
Virtuoso passages, scales or arpeggios, classical ornamentations, chromatic passages	Substructural element[23]

In Turkey, this performance style occurred in the form of brief flashes during longer performances, for example during the wedding party in Kırşehir. In Ghent, I observed certain traits of it in performances of guest musicians from Turkey, such as Erkan Oğur. An example of a brief episode of influence from Western classical music is provided in Figure 6.4, representing a fragment of a song performed during the *rakı* night of the wedding party in Kırşehir. It concerns the insertion of a tonal chord [= superstructural element: mode + substructural element: texture], which does not fit in the modal context, by way of punctual accompaniment of a cadenza-like melody.

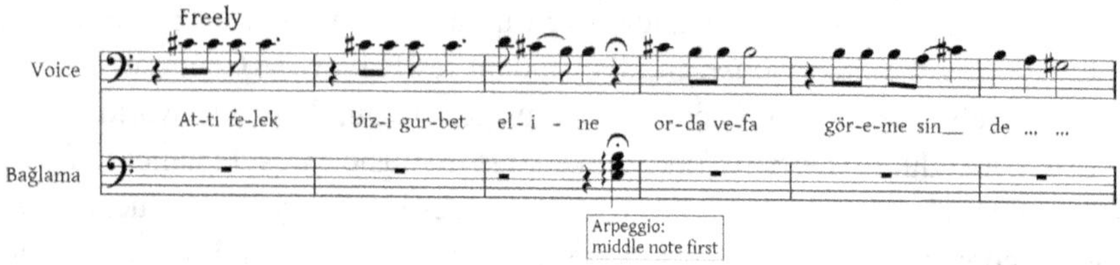

Figure 6.4: Example of ephemeral influence from Western classical music (fragment) (transcription by the author)

Influence from the jazz idiom can manifest itself through the use of jazz scales, chords and harmonies, jazz metres and rhythms (e.g., swing), formal structures belonging to the jazz genre (exposition of the theme – improvisatory development – recapitulation of the theme), and so on. In most cases, these elements will occur in a tonal context based on Western tuning (equal temperament), in some cases involving a line-up and playing/singing techniques explicitly associated with jazz music (e.g., involving jazz guitar or saxophone, or pizzicato playing on double bass). Possible elements defining this style are listed in Table 6.4.

Table 6.4: Elements defining a performance style influenced by jazz music

Twelve-tone equal temperament	Superstructural element: mode
Jazz scales, chords and harmonies	Superstructural element: mode + Substructural element: texture
Jazz metres and rhythms	Substructural element: rhythm
Jazz forms	Substructural element: form
Jazz line-up and playing techniques	Substructural element: instrumentation

In Ghent, this performance style occurred during the cultural festival in the city centre, during a concert and café concert in De Centrale, and during the celebration of 50 years of Turkish migration, also in De Centrale. An example of a jazz-influenced idiom is provided in Figure 6.5, which represents a fragment of a performance during a café concert in De Centrale, involving a Belgian female singer-*darbuka* player and a Turkish double-bass player [= substructural element: instrumentation] interpreting a Turkish folk song using playing techniques [= substructural element: instrumentation] and harmonizations [= substructural element: mode + superstructural element: texture] belonging to a jazz idiom.

Figure 6.5: Example of a jazzy interpretation of Turkish folk music (fragment)[24]
(transcription by the author)

A lightly popularized style displays vocal and instrumental timbres belonging to an Eastern or Western pop or rock idiom, and a general sound based on increased amplification. Generally, acoustic and indigenous instruments are retained, but complemented by electr(on)ic and/or Western instruments. Pop or rock harmonizations occur, and if *bağlama* playing is involved, typically chords and configurations originating from a guitar idiom are used. "Microtonal" intervals are standardized or disappear in favour of equal temperament, rhythms are simplified, the metre is usually regular, repetitions are common, and riffs are used. Simplification is also manifest in the abandonment of regional characteristics and idiomatic ornamentation (*tavır*). An overview of possible elements defining this style is provided in Table 6.5.

Table 6.5: Elements defining a lightly popularized performance style

Standardization or elimination of "microtonal" intervals	Superstructural element: mode
Pop or rock timbres, amplification, mixed acoustic-electr(on)ic Turkish-Western line-up	Substructural element: instrumentation
Pop or rock harmonizations	Superstructural element: mode + Substructural element: texture
Guitar configurations on *bağlama*	Substructural elements: texture and rhythm
Simple, regular rhythmic-metrical structure	Substructural element: rhythm
Repetitions, riffs	Superstructural element: melody + Substructural elements: form and rhythm
Abandonment of *tavır*	Substructural elements: texture and rhythm

In Turkey, I encountered this performance style at *türkü* nights, at various kinds of parties and celebrations, and in festivals. In Ghent, it occurred during Turkish/*türkü* evenings and during the karaoke evening. Figure 6.6 provides a brief example of a manifestation of this style during the performance of Grup Tını during a *türkü* night in De Centrale. While the *bağlama* in some places retains its traditional rhythmic configurations in dialogue with the voice, in other places it joins the harmonic function [= superstructural element: mode + substructural element: texture] of the synthesizer [= substructural element: instrumentation] and the guitar [= substructural element: instrumentation].

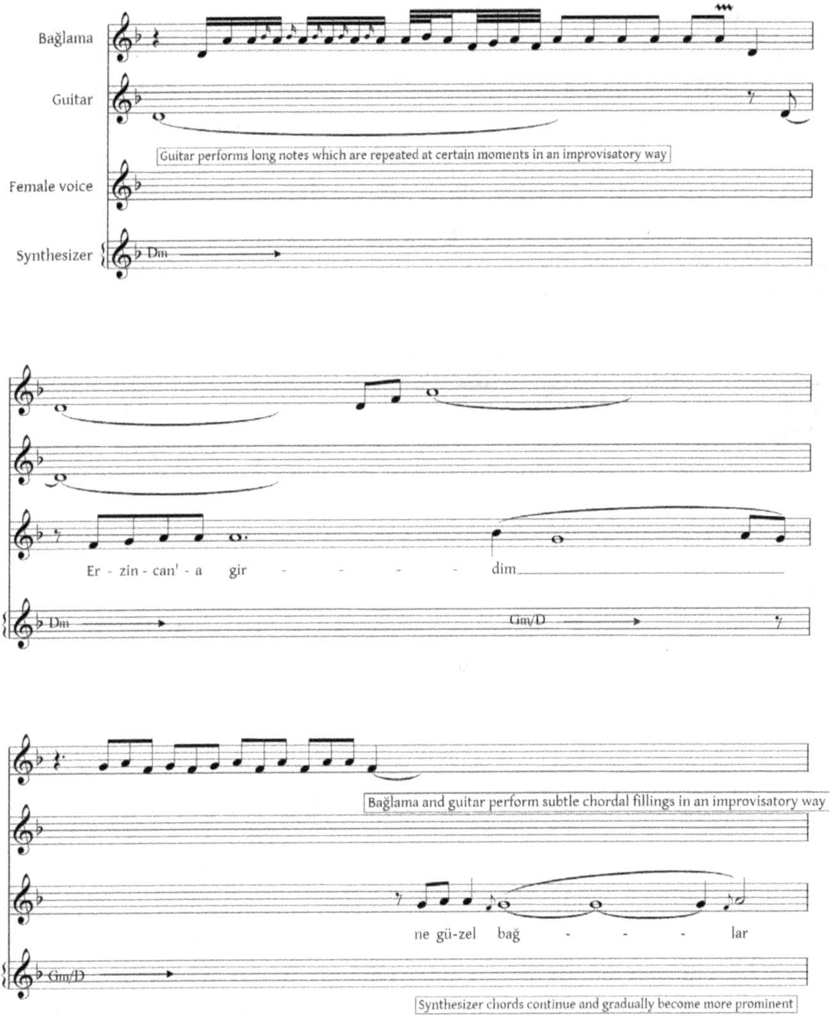

Figure 6.6: Example of a lightly popularized performance style (fragment) (transcription by the author)

A heavily popularized style displays a clear pop or rock sound involving strong beats, heavy bass, high amplification, distortion, and sound effects. Electr(on)ic instruments take over the role of acoustic instruments to a large degree; the *elektrosaz* is omnipresent (or even replaced by the electric guitar). Fast tempos and regular metres are idiomatic, as are repetition and the use of riffs. In general, a higher degree of standardization and simplification of the musical material occurs, involving a complete abandonment of *tavır/ağız*. Harmony is fully compatible with a pop or rock style. Possible elements defining this style are listed in Table 6.6.

Table 6.6: Elements defining a heavily popularized performance style

Standardization or elimination of "microtonal" intervals	Superstructural element: mode
Strong beats, heavy basses, high amplification, distortion, sound effects, prominence of electr(on)ic instruments and *elektrosaz*	Substructural element: instrumentation
Pop or rock harmonizations	Superstructural element: mode + Substructural element: texture
Simple, regular rhythmic-metrical structure, fast tempos	Substructural element: rhythm
Repetitions, riffs	Superstructural element: melody + Substructural elements: form and rhythm
Abandonment of *tavır* and *ağız*	Substructural elements: texture and rhythm

In Turkey, I observed this performance style at various parties and celebrations, festivals, and a *türkü* night. In Ghent, it was used in large-scale parties such as the benefit evening, the circumcision party, and the wedding party. An example of this style is provided in Figure 6.7, which represents a fragment of the musical performance during a wedding party of an *abdal* family in Emirdağ, involving a synthesizer that performs a programmed, heavy but simple, Arab-flavoured rhythm section [= substructural elements: instrumentation and rhythm], on which a melody is played in electronic imitation of a *zurna* [= substructural element: instrumentation], in alternation or co-existent with live performed clarinet melodies. The tempo, which is already fast in the traditional version of the song, is exaggerated in this version [= substructural element].

Figure 6.7: Example of a heavily popularized performance style (fragment) (transcription by the author)

Performance styles influenced by world music or other genres incorporate idiomatic elements belonging to the particular styles involved. Typical genres functioning as a source of inspiration are flamenco, *arabesk*, Balkan Gypsy music, Latin music, and so on. *Arabesk* influence expresses itself in, for example, characteristic accompaniments and interventions evoking a string orchestra on the keyboard. In the case of flamenco influence, typical flamenco harmonies, melodic phrases, rhythmic figures, or playing techniques are applied. In Turkey, *bağlama* techniques close to flamenco guitar techniques occurred during the *türkü* night in Izmir, while I observed influence from Balkan Gypsy music during a wedding party in Emirdağ. During the cultural festival in Ghent, influence from Latin music and Balkan Gypsy music was present.

Occurrence of the Styles

Table 6.7 gives an overview of the observed occurrence of the different performance styles of Turkish folk music, in relation to the kinds of attended events in Turkey and Belgium.

Table 6.7: Occurrence of the different performance styles

Performance style		Turkey	Diaspora
Mono-cultural	"Urban standardized"	Religious ceremony, artistic training, (café) concert, informal social gathering, dance education, festival, official opening	Festival, (café) concert, official opening
	"Rural traditional"	Informal social gathering, celebration of life-cycle event, festival	Festival, religious ceremony, celebration of life-cycle event
Poly-cultural	Classical-influenced	Celebration of life-cycle event	(Café) concert
	Jazz-influenced	[Not observed] [25]	Festival, (café) concert, celebration of specific event
	Lightly popularized	(Café) concert, formal social gathering, festival, celebration of life-cycle event, celebration of specific event, official opening, festival	(Café) concert, formal social gathering, festival, celebration of specific event
	Heavily popularized	(Café) concert, celebration of life-cycle event, celebration of specific event	Formal social gathering, celebration of life-cycle event
	World music-influenced	(Café) concert, celebration of life-cycle event	(Café) concert, celebration of life-cycle event, festival, formal social gathering

Conclusion: Aspects of Context and Musical Performance

The applied systematic, comparative approach succeeded in pointing out certain properties, commonalities, and differences of performances of Turkish folk music in the motherland and the diaspora with regards to contextual aspects (the kind of event or the use of the performance, the occasion, the set-up, financial aspects, aspects of time and place, the commissioners, the listeners, and the performers) and musical aspects (the performed music, the performed Turkish folk music, the used instruments, the way of creation, the performance quality, and the performance style). On the other hand, it should be clear that this essentially qualitative approach cannot involve any claims of conclusiveness, completeness, or representativeness.

Festivals and (café) concerts, formal and informal social gatherings, religious ceremonies, and celebrations of specific events (circumcisions, weddings, official openings, etc.) are shared between indigenous and diasporan contexts. Most events are planned in advance and commissioned by a third party. Spontaneously and/or self-initiated events happen more often in Turkey than in Ghent. Most events in Ghent are financed by authorities, mostly complemented by other financing channels (family celebrations being an obvious exception).

The preference for the weekend is pronounced in Ghent. Many events take place in the evening. Most observed events are recurrent, with rites of passage being the most typical non-recurrent events. Turkey and the diaspora display similar typical locations (public squares in cities, fields in rural environments, music cafés, and concert halls). In Turkey, the range of settings is broader, the difference between rural and urban environments is larger, and outdoor and private events are more common. The locations for religious ceremonies and for wedding and circumcision parties are clearly different in Turkey and in Ghent.

Commissioners are predominantly male in both contexts. Audiences often have an equal distribution of male and female listeners, and involve all ages, and mostly local people. Events such as open-air festivals involve a non-specific audience. Mixed Turkish and non-Turkish audiences are not exceptional. Elderly and exclusively male audiences are more often encountered in Turkey than in Ghent, as well as elderly performers. Most performers are young to middle-aged. Female performers seem to be more common in Ghent than in Turkey. While in Turkey, most performers belong to the region and are (semi-)professional, events in Ghent involve more diverse performers (e.g., transnational ad-hoc groups, mixed Turkish and non-Turkish groups, and mixed-level groups).

Regarding musical aspects, similar combinations of Turkish folk music with other genres and art forms occur in Turkey and the diaspora. In Ghent, more mixed programmes occur, contrary to Turkey, where programmes often consist solely of Turkish folk music. Weddings, certain kinds of festivals, and *cem* ceremonies exclusively feature Turkish folk music in both contexts. The popularity of Central Anatolian music is a constant, while in Turkey the local regional music is important as well. Although line-ups are diverse and variable, *bağlama* and synthesizer are omnipresent. *Davul* and *zurna* are more common in Turkey than in Ghent. In the diaspora, non-Turkish instruments are more often used. Most performances are semi-improvised; compositional aspects are rare. Similar mono- and poly-cultural performance styles exist, but mono-cultural performance styles are more often encountered in Turkey. The next chapter further illustrates these performance styles, alongside other musical and performance aspects, through transcriptions and comparative analysis of different versions of a particular song.

Chapter 7

Case Study of a Song: 'Hüdayda'

The different performance styles of the previous chapter become clearer by juxtaposing several performances of one particular Turkish folk song. 'Hüdayda' (also called 'Fidayda' or 'Bulguru kaynadırlar'[1]) is a popular dance song from the province of Ankara that is regularly performed throughout Turkey and in the diaspora, particularly at festive occasions. Originally, the song has a moderate tempo and is intended to be danced by two *seymens* (*zeybeks* of Central Anatolia) (Güler n.d.).

I encountered the song in diverse guises during my fieldwork in Turkey. During an informal social gathering in the small mountain town of Şavşat near the Georgian border, it was played on a flute in a style that could be characterized as mono-cultural and possibly as traditional. Another informal social gathering in a tea garden in Trabzon (Black Sea region) featured the piece performed with acoustic *bağlama* and voice in what could be described as a mono-cultural standardized or academic style. It was also performed in a popularized version as dance music during two festive occasions: a celebration of the end of the school year by teachers in Emirdağ, and a wedding party in Kırşehir. Both settings involved a synthesizer performing the rhythm section, a singer, and an amplified *bağlama* (Emirdağ) or *elektrosaz* (Kırşehir). While in Kırşehir the three parts were performed by the same musician, in Emirdağ a duo was involved, consisting of a *bağlama* player and a singer who also used the synthesizer. Both versions can be considered as poly-cultural and heavily popularized. In what follows, the performance styles and characteristics of the different versions of 'Hüdayda' are compared to each other and to the score published by the TRT.

The TRT Score (Hüdayda-0)

The "official" transcription by Turkish Radio and Television has a reference status and is, to some extent, used in the form of a musical "score"
by state and other musicians. The chapter on notation and the TRT archive,
however, has made clear that this allotted status is questionable and to be
put into perspective. The website www.repertukul.com[2] (from "*Repertuar
Türküleri Külliyatı*": "the complete repertoire of folksongs") gathers all folk
music included in the TRT repertoire, complemented by some other (composed or not yet archived) music, and a wealth of theoretical, organological,
and biographical information. The transcription or "score" of 'Hüdayda' as
prepared by the TRT and displayed on the website (see Figure 7.1) is provided with the usual meta-data including place, date, "source person", "collector", and "transcriber" (see Chapter 4), plus some extra information, such
as modal scale, first and final tone, and topic.

The musical scale of the score starts on D, and consists of the following
theoretical pitch classes (indicated in cents):

Table 7.1: Pitch classes of Hüdayda-0

0 (D)	Ca. 111 (E♭⁴)	300 (F)	500 (G)	700 (A)	800 (B♭)		1000 (C)	1200 (D)
		400 (F♯)			Ca. 856 (B♭²)			
					900 (B)			

The third and sixth scale degree are used in different forms (the ones from
the key signature and raised ones).

The musical form of the TRT version can be visualized as follows:

Table 7.2: Musical form of Hüdayda-0

A 8 bars	B 16 bars	(A) (1 bar)	C1: stanza 8 bars	C': chorus 8 bars	(A) (1 bar)	C2: stanza 8 bars	C': chorus 8 bars	D 12 bars
	B 16 bars	(A) (1 bar)	C3 8 bars	C' 8 bars	(A) (1 bar)	C4 8 bars	C' 8 bars	D 12 bars
A 8 bars	B 16 bars	D 12 bars	B 16 bars		A 8 bars			

T R T MÜZİK DAİRESİ YAYINLARI
T H M REPERTUAR No : 106
İNCELEME TARİHİ : 28. 1. 1973
2. İNCELEME TARİHİ : 1990
YÖRE
ANKARA
KAYNAK KİŞİ
SADIK ERGUN-BAYRAM ARACI
SÜRE :

BULGURU KAYNADIRLAR
(FİDAYDA-HÜDAYDA)

DERLEYEN
NİDA TÜFEKÇİ
DERLEME TARİHİ
1964
NOTALAYAN
NİDA TÜFEKÇİ

- 2 -
BULGURU KAYNADIRLAR
(FİDAYDA-HÜDAYDA)

NA   DIR   LAR   HAY   Dİ   BUL GU RU   KAY
BAŞ   A   ÇIK   HAY   Dİ   DA   MA ÇIK   MA

NA   DIR   LAR   (SAZ_ _ _ _ _ _ _ _)   SE Rİ NE YAY
BAŞ   A   ÇIK   AR PA LAR GA

LA DIR   LAR   A MAN   SE Rİ NE YAY
RA GIL   ÇIK   A MAN   AR PA LAR GA

LA DIR   LAR   (SAZ _ _ _ _ _ _ _ _ _ _ _ _ _ _)
RA GIL   ÇIK

BİZ DE   A   DET   BÖY   LE   DİR
E   ĞER GÖN   LÜN   VAR   İ

A   MANBİZ   DE   A   DET_ _ _ _ _ _   BÖ YÜ LE   DİR (SAZ _ _ _ _ _)
A   MAN   E   ĞER GÖN   LÜN   VA   Rİ   SE

· 3 ·

BULGURU KAYNADIRLAR
(FİDAYDA-HÜDAYDA)

GÜ ZE Lİ AĞ LA DIR LAR
GEY GA LU CU YO LA ÇIK

A MAN ÇİR Kİ Nİ SÖY LE DİR LER
A MAN GEY GA LU CU YO LA ÇIK

Fİ DAY DA DA AN KA RA LIM Fİ DAY DA

BEŞ YÜZ AL TIN YE DİR DİM Bİ RAY DA

GİT Tİ DE GEL ME Dİ NE FAY DA

BA ŞI NI DA YE SİN BU SEV DA

(SAZ -

- 4 -

BULGURU KAYNADIRLAR

(FİDAYDA-HÜDAYDA)

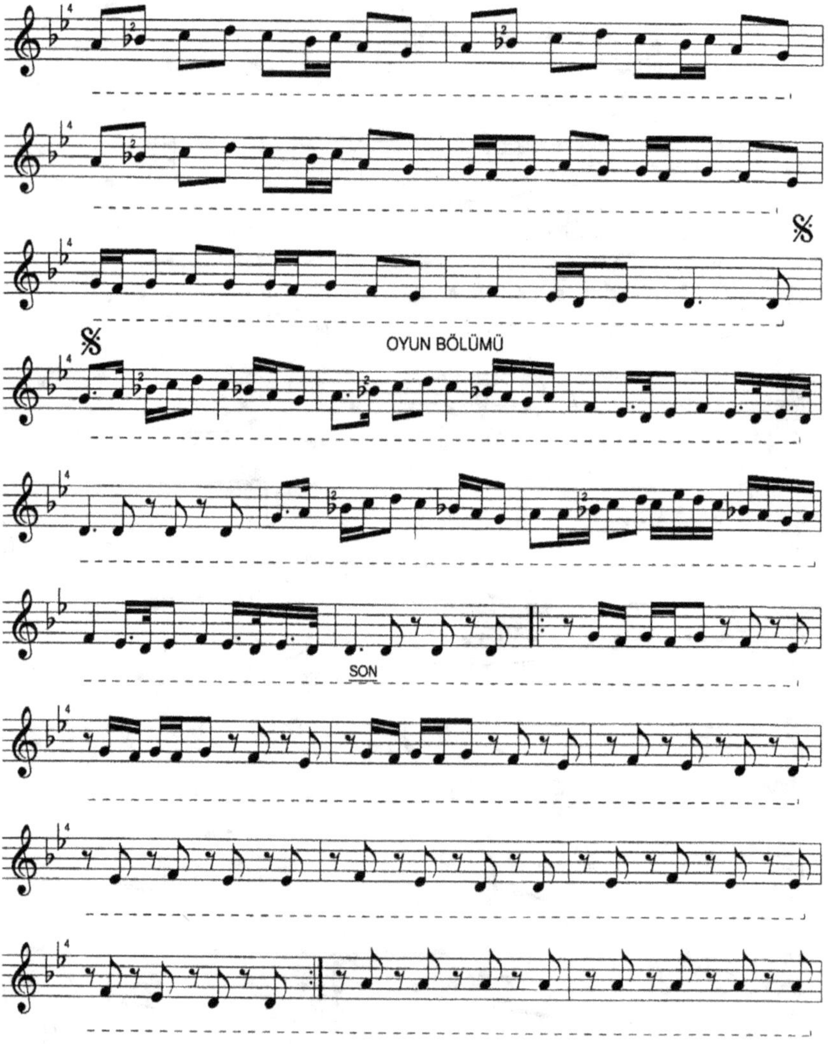

- 5 -
BULGURU KAYNADIRLAR
(FİDAYDA-HÜDAYDA)

(Aman) BULGURU KAYNADIRLAR
(Haydi) BULGURU KAYNADIRLAR
SERİNE YAYLADIRLAR
(Aman) SERİNE YAYLADIRLAR

BİZDE ADET BÖYLEDİR
(Aman) BİZDE ADET BÖYLEDİR
GÜZELİ AĞLADIRLAR
(Aman) ÇİRKİNİ SÖYLEDİRLER

BAĞLANTI :

FİDAYDA DA ANKARA'LIM FİDAYDA
BEŞ YÜZ ALTIN YEDİRDİM BİR AYDA
GİTTİ DE GELMEDİ NE FAYDA
BAŞINI DA YESİN BU SEVDA

(Aman) DAMA ÇIKMA BAŞ AÇIK
(Haydi) DAMA ÇIKMA BAŞ AÇIK
ARPALAR GARA GILÇIK
(Aman) ARPALAR GARA GILÇIK

EĞER GÖNLÜN VAR İSE
(Aman) EĞER GÖNLÜN VAR İSE
GEY GALUCU YOLA ÇIK
(Aman) GEY GALUCU YOLA ÇIK

BAĞLANTI

Figure 7.1: TRT score of 'Hüdayda' (www.repertukul.com/BULGURU-KAYNADIRLAR-Fidayda-Hudayda-106, reproduced with permission)

The musical themes, reduced to their essence, are presented in Figure 7.2.

Figure 7.2: Musical themes of 'Hüdayda' (Liselotte Sels)

"Traditional" Performance Style (Hüdayda-1)

A first performance of this song, encountered and recorded during my field-work, is a flute version performed in Şavşat near the Georgian border. This version can be characterized as mono-cultural and perhaps "traditional".

Figure 7.3: Transcription of a performance of 'Hüdayda' on flute (Liselotte Sels)

The scale used in this performance of 'Hüdayda' on flute (see Figure 7.3) consists of the following pitch classes (in cents):

Table 7.3: Pitch classes of Hüdayda-1

0 (G)	116 (A♭)	267 (B♭)	500 (C)	712 (D)	800 (E♭)	981 (F)	1200 (G)
	148=150 (A♯)	383 (B)					

The real pitch classes are detected by means of the TARSOS software, an open-source modular platform for precise pitch/scale analysis, designed by Joren Six and available through http://0110.be/Software (Six et al. 2013). The specific B♭ of this performance is a flat minor third on the first degree (a "septimal minor third" or "subminor third").

The musical form of this performance can be visualized as follows, in relation to the themes identified in the TRT score:

Table 7.4: Musical form of Hüdayda-1

B	D	B	C	C'	B	D
6 bars	7 bars	6 bars	8 bars	4 bars	6 bars	7 bars

Academic or Standardized Performance Style (Hüdayda-2)

A second version was recorded in Trabzon at the Black Sea. A music teacher sang and played 'Hüdayda' on acoustic *bağlama*, in a mono-cultural standardized or academic style.

Bul - gur - u kay - na - tır - lar
a - man bul - gur - u kay - - na - tır - lar
Ser - in - e yay - la - tır - - lar

a - man ser - in - e yay - - la - tır - - lar
Biz - de a - det böy - le - dir
a - man biz - de a - det böy - le - dir
Gü - zel - i ağ - la - tır - lar
a - man çir - kin - i söy - - le - dir - - ler

50
Hü - day - da da An - ka - ra - lım Hü - day - - da
52
Beş - yüz al - tın ye - dir - dim bir ay - - da
54
Git - ti de gel - me - di ne fay - - da
56
baş - ı - nı da ye - sin bu sev - - da
58
60
62

Figure 7.4: Transcription of a performance of 'Hüdayda' with acoustic *bağlama* and voice (Liselotte Sels)

The scale used in the performance of 'Hüdayda' with acoustic *bağlama* and voice (see Figure 7.4) consists of the following pitch classes (in cents):

Table 7.5: Pitch classes of Hüdayda-2

0 (E)	80 (F)	297=300 (G)	497=500 (A)	697=700 (B)	784 (C)	1000 (D)	1200 (E)
	148=150 (F♯)	350–400 (G♯)			878 (C♯³)		

The pitch corresponding to the major third is unclear and fluctuates between 350 and 400 cents.

The musical form of this performance can be visualized as follows:

Table 7.6: Musical form of Hüdayda-2

A	B	D	B	(A)	C1	C'	C2	C'	D
8 bars	8 bars	8 bars	6 bars	1 bar	8 bars	4 bars	8 bars	8 bars	10 bars

Heavily Popularized Performance Style (1) (Hüdayda-3)

A third version, poly-cultural and heavily popularized, was played during a celebration of the end of the school year by teachers in Emirdağ. It was performed by a *bağlama* player and a singer who also operated the synthesizer for the rhythm section.

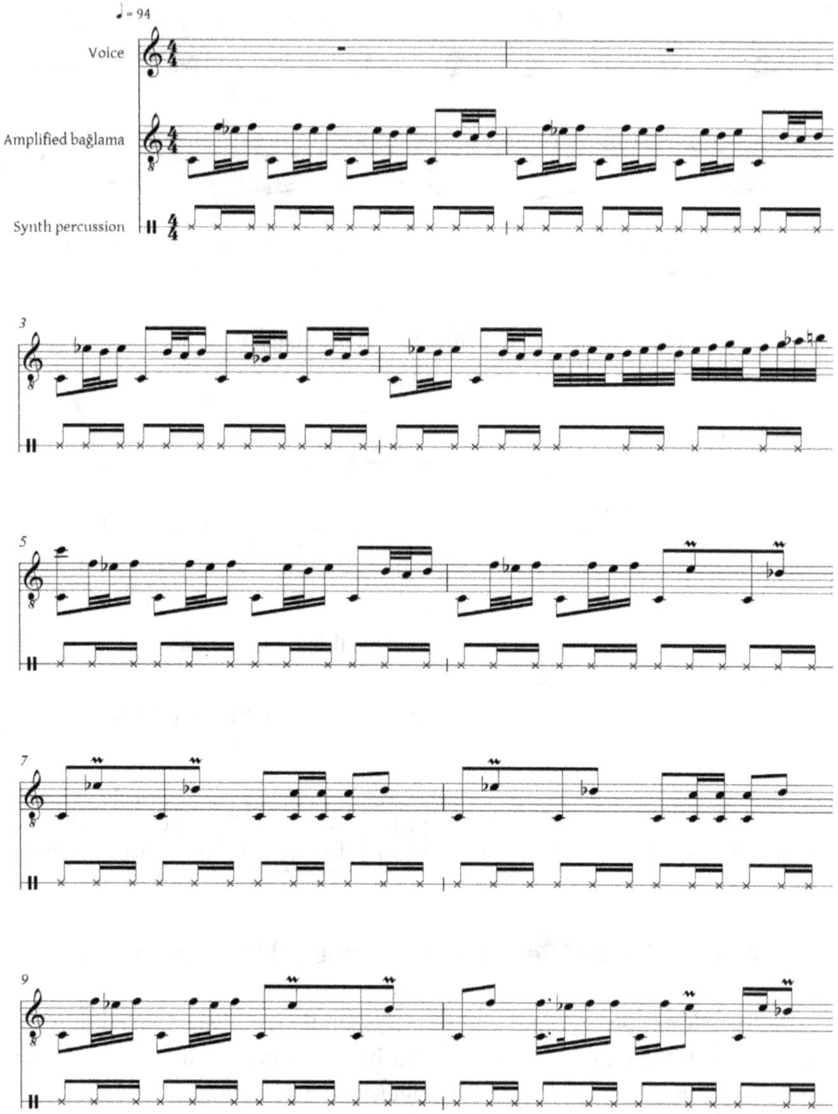
♩= 94
Voice
Amplified bağlama
Synth percussion
3
5
7
9

Bul-gur-u kay - - na - dır - lar
yav-rum bul-gur kay - na - dır - - lar
güz-el - i ağ - - - la - dır - lar
A-man çir-kin - i söy - - - le - dir - ler

22
24
a- man!
27
Biz - de a - det böy - le - dir
29
yav - rum biz - de a - det böy - le - dir
31
güz - el - i ağ - - - la - dır - lar

Figure 7.5: Transcription of a heavily popularized version of 'Hüdayda' (Emirdağ)
(Liselotte Sels)

The scale used in the performance of a heavily popularized version of 'Hüdayda' (Emirdağ) (see Figure 7.5) consists of the following pitch classes (in cents):

Table 7.7: Pitch classes of Hüdayda-3

0 (C)	93–115 (D♭)	300 (E♭)	491=500 (F)	702 (G)	793=800 (A♭)	986 (B♭)	1200 (C)
	125–225 (D♯–D)	410 (E)					

The pitch area between the minor and major second displays many peaks in TARSOS, without indicating one single, dominating pitch. The major second and the quarter-flat second only occur at the beginning of the performance and are later substituted by the minor second.

The musical form of this performance can be visualized as follows:

Table 7.8: Musical form of Hüdayda-3

B	C1	C2	C'	C2	C'
13 bars	4 bars	4 bars	5 bars	8 bars	8 bars

Heavily Popularized Performance Style (2) (Hüdayda-4)

The fourth, also poly-cultural and heavily popularized, version was performed during a wedding party in Central Anatolian Kırşehir. One musician played keyboard and *elektrosaz* and sang.

The scale used in the performance of a heavily popularized version of 'Hüdayda' (Kırşehir) (see Figure 7.6) consists of the following pitch classes (in cents):

Table 7.9: Pitch classes of Hüdayda-4

0 (C♯)	93 (D)	300 (E)	496=500 (F♯)	700 (G♯)	800 (A)	996=1000 (B)	1200 (C♯)
	144=150 (D♯)	375 (E♯)					

The musical form of this performance can be visualized as follows:

Table 7.10: Musical form of Hüdayda-4

B	D	B	C1	(X)	C	C'	C2	C'
5 bars	7 bars	4 bars	4 bars	(1 bar)	4 bars	4 bars	8 bars	6 bars
	D	B	C			C'	C	C'
	7 bars	4 bars	8 bars			4 bars	8 bars	8 bars

Between the two verses of the stanza, a transition or bridge based on thematic material is inserted.

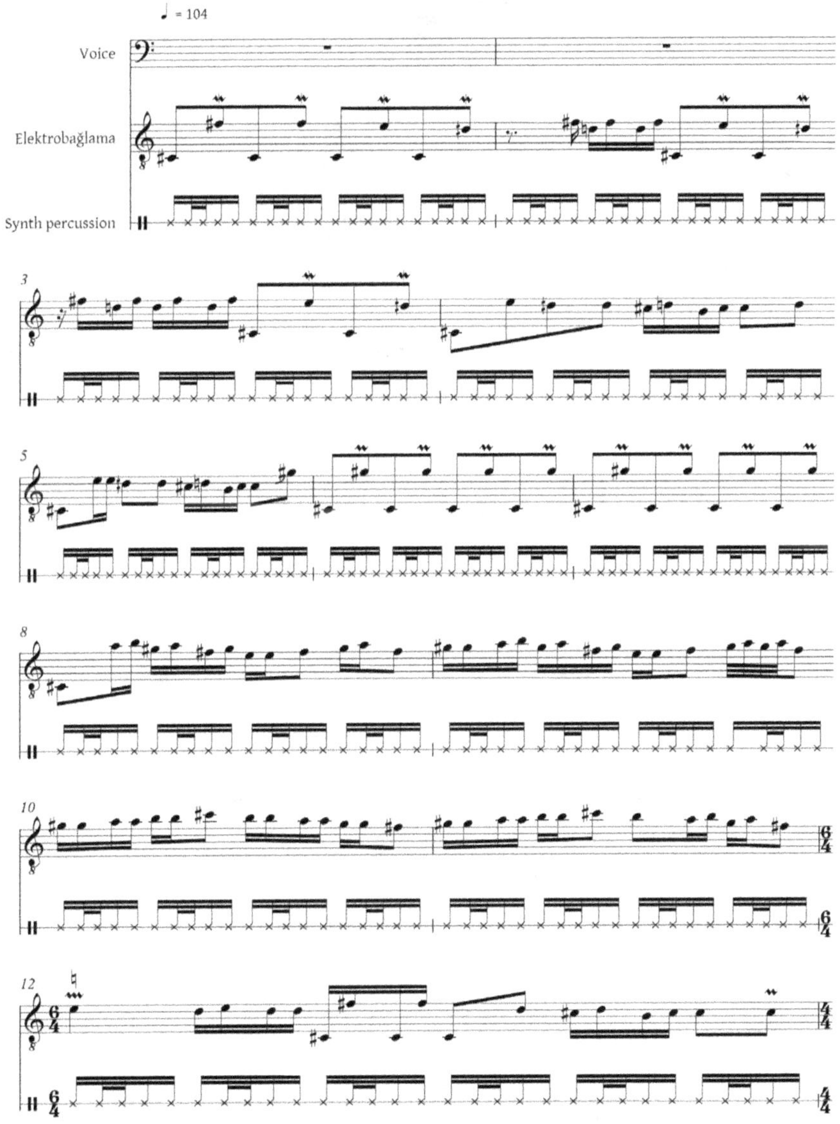

13
15
17
Bul - gur - u kay - na - dır - lar
19
yav-rum bul-gur-u kay - na - dır - lar
22
gliss.
(lyrics uncomprehensible - - - - - - - - -

24
)
26
gliss.
28
30
Biz - de a - det böy - le - dir
32
yav - rum biz - de a - det böy - le - dir

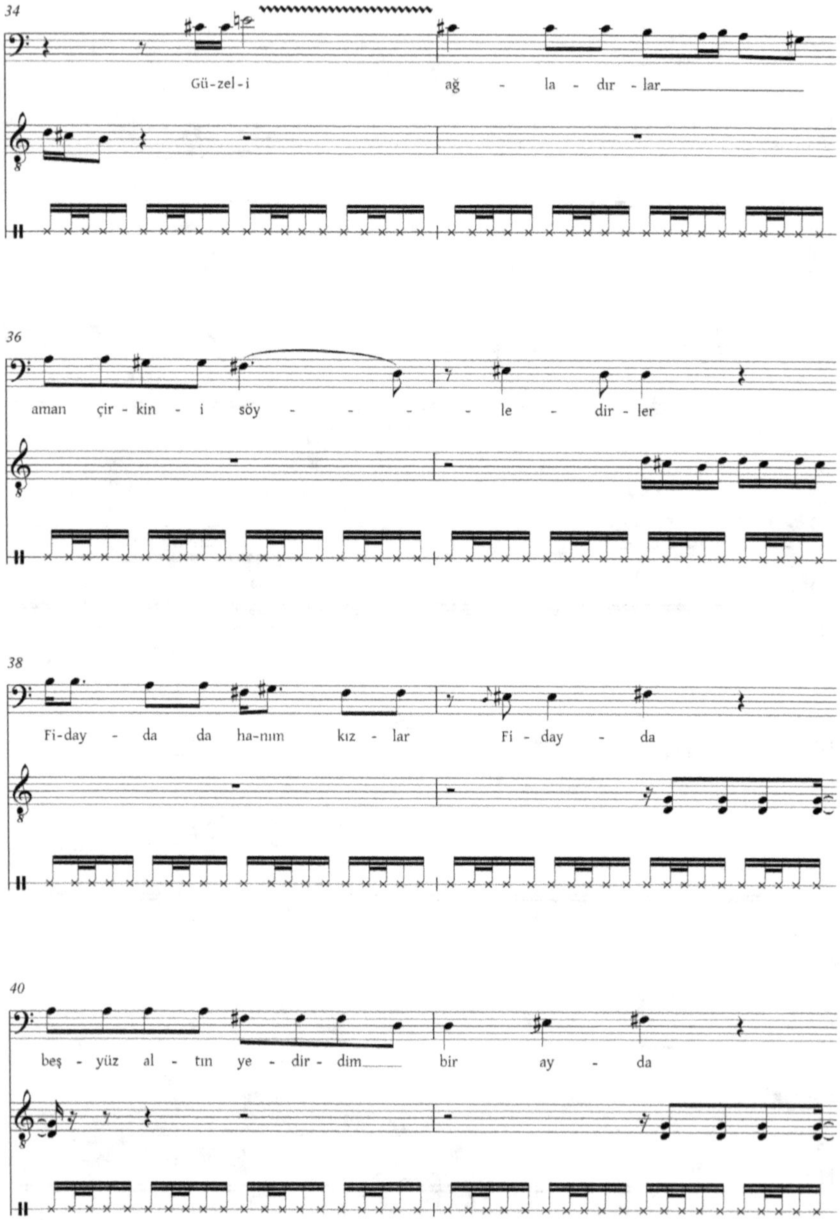
34
Gü-zel-i ağ - la - dır - lar
36
aman çir - kin - i söy - - - - le - dir - ler
38
Fi-day - da da ha-nım kız - lar Fi - day - da
40
beş - yüz al - tın ye - dir - dim bir ay - da

(lyrics   uncomprehensible   -   -   -   -   -   -   -   )

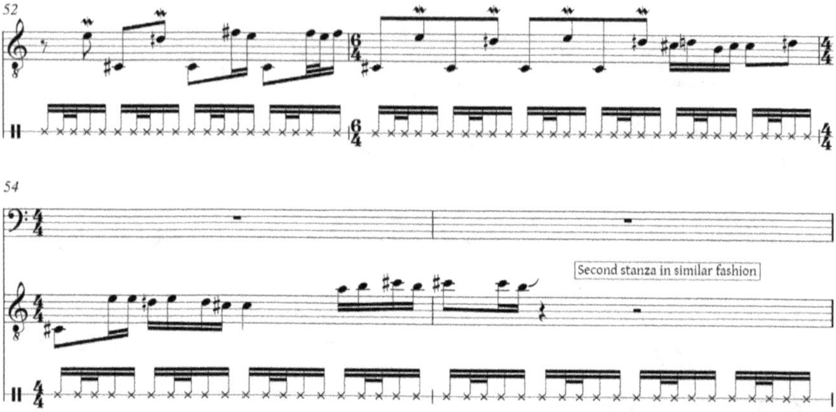

Figure 7.6: Transcription of a heavily popularized version of 'Hüdayda' (Kırşehir) (Liselotte Sels)

The Different Versions in Comparison

Tempo

The tempi of the four versions of 'Hüdayda' – aside from the slower introduction of the second version – are remarkably similar: between 94 and 104 beats (crotchets) per minute. The two popularized versions occupy the extremes, the *elektrosaz* typically rendering the fastest performance. The performance on flute is slightly slower than the performance with voice and *bağlama*, but gives a vivid impression because of the dense ornamentations. It may be believed that a common notion of the ideal tempo exists among musicians.

Intervallic Structure

Table 7.11 juxtaposes the intervallic structure as implied by the TRT score with those extracted from the four recorded performances.

A few observations can be made directly from this overview. While the TRT score uses only one pitch class for the second degree, the four performances switch between two different pitch classes for the second degree. On the other hand, the TRT score and the four performances use two different pitch classes for the third degree. For the sixth degree, besides the TRT score, only the second performance uses two different pitch classes. The different pitch classes per degree are bound to certain passages in the piece. Interestingly, the TRT score and the "academic" performance are the only two versions featuring musical theme A.

Table 7.11: Intervallic structure of the different versions of 'Hüdayda'

	1st	2nd	3rd	4th	5th	6th	7th degree
Hüdayda-0	0	Ca. 111	300 and 400	500	700	800, ca. 856 and 900	1000
Hüdayda-1	0	116 and 150	267 (septimal minor) and 383	500	712	800	981
Hüdayda-2	0	80 and 150	300 and 350–400	500	700	784 and 879	1000
Hüdayda-3	0	93–115 and 125–225	300 and 410	500	702 (perfect)	800	986
Hüdayda-4	0	93 and 150	300 and 375	500	700	800	1000

A detailed look at the figures reveals further findings. The most stable scale degrees are the fourth, fifth, seventh, quarter-flattened second, minor third (if present), and minor sixth degrees. The fourth degree corresponds with or approximates twelve-tone equal temperament. Only one version, the flute performance, displays a deviant fifth degree. This is possibly due to flute tuning issues, since the fifth is generally one of the most stable intervals. In most cases the fifth corresponds or approximates twelve-tone equal temperament, while in the third performance the natural perfect fifth prevails. The seventh degree to the octave is a whole tone in the TRT score as well as in the second and the fourth performance. The flute displays a deviant pitch again, almost one Pythagorean comma lower than usual. The third performance displays a smaller deviation.

The higher second degree is similar in all performances and equals or approximates a quarter-flattened second. This pitch class appears to be remarkably stable in Turkish folk music performances. The lower second degree varies considerably throughout the different versions. It ranges from 80 cents (second performance) over 93 cents (fourth performance) to 116 cents (first performance). The third performance is ambiguous in the lower and higher second degrees. The single pitch class indicated on the TRT score, a four-commas-flat second, occupies an intermediate position between the lower and higher second occurring in most performances.

The lower third degree is similar in all performances except one, and equals or approximates a minor third according to twelve-tone equal temperament. Only the flute displays an entirely different pitch class and involves a much lower "septimal minor third". The higher third degree is largely variable throughout the different versions. While the TRT score implies a 400-cents third corresponding with twelve-tone equal temperament, it ranges from 375 cents (fourth performance), over 383 cents, which approximates a pure major third (first performance), to 410 cents, approximating a Pythagorean ditone (third performance) in the musical performances. The second performance displays ambiguities for this degree.

In the versions without musical section A, and thus no need for an extra tone, the single sixth degree is similar and equals or approximates a minor sixth according to twelve-tone equal temperament. The TRT score and the second performance diverge in their two sixth degrees: in the performance, the lower sixth is lower and the higher sixth is higher than in the TRT score.

Form

The structure of the different versions is juxtaposed in Table 7.12 (vocal sections are italicized).

Theme A is omitted everywhere except in the second performance (acoustic *bağlama* and voice). Theme D is omitted in the third performance. All themes except A are versatile and occur in manifold guises across the different performances. The various manifestations of the themes are partially determined by the specific playing techniques and idioms of the different instruments used, but also a product of the personal taste, imagination, and abilities of the respective musicians.

Structurally, the official TRT version is the most complete version. It is divided into a song section consisting of two equal parts (except for the introductory section A which occurs only the first time), and a dance section. References to the introduction (A) punctuate the song section several times just before the stanza and chorus (C and C'), and the complete introduction is repeated at the beginning and the end of the dance section. In the song section as well as in the dance section, themes B and D occur in alternation with the introduction and the stanza and chorus. This complex and rich structure is not matched in the different performances.

Table 7.12: Formal structure of the different versions of 'Hüdayda'

Hüdayda-0	8 × A	16 × B	(1 × A)	8 × C1: *stanza*	8 × C': *chorus*	(1 × A)	8 × C2: *stanza*	8 × C': *chorus*	12 × D
		16 × B	(1 × A)	8 × C3	8 × C'	(1 × A)	8 × C4	8 × C'	12 × D
	8 × A	16 × B	12 × D	16 × B		8 × A			
Hüdayda-1	6 × B	7 × D	6 × B	8 × C		4 × C'	6 × B	7 × D	
Hüdayda-2	8 × A	8 × B	8 × D	6 × B	(1 × A)	8 × C1	4 × C'	8 × C2	8 × C'	10 × D
Hüdayda-3	13 × B	4 × C1		4 × C2	5 × C'		8 × C2	8 × C'	
Hüdayda-4	5 × B	7 × D	4 × B	4 × C1	1	4 × C³	4 × C'	8 × C2	6 × C'
		7 × D	4 × B	8 × C		4 × C'	8 × C	8 × C'	

The first performance (flute) playfully mixes the different themes to create a new version with a completely different sequence of themes. The only parallels with the TRT score are the sequence B – D – B (also occurring in the score's dance section), the sequence C – C' (stanza – chorus), and the ending on D (also occurring in the score's song section).

The second performance (acoustic *bağlama* and voice) is closest to the TRT score. This similitude is not incidental but originates in the context and purpose of the performance: the musician, a teacher and folk music expert in the company of his colleagues, aims at presenting a broad range of folk music of Turkey in a "learned" and exemplary way. The sequence A – B – D – B , part of the dance section of the score, occurs in this performance as well. The procedure of inserting one-bar references to the introductory theme (A) just before the stanza and chorus (C and C') is also adopted. Theme D ends the performance, as was the case in the first performance and in the song section of the TRT score.

After a long introduction elaborating on theme B, the third performance concentrates exclusively on the stanzas and choruses, which are rendered in multiple forms. Whereas the sequence of stanza and chorus occurred in an orderly fashion in the score and the first two performances (C1 – C' , C2 – C' , C3 – C' , C4 – C' in the score; C – C' in the first performance; C1 – C' – C2 – C' in the second performance), the third performance approaches the order more freely (C1 – C2 – C' – C2 – C'). This reduced version is intended for dancing and amusement, and its compact thematic structure serves this function well.

The fourth performance matches the TRT score in length, but is clearly not as thoughtfully constructed, which is completely logical given its improvisatory nature (as was the case for the third performance). As in the third performance, the emphasis is on the stanzas and choruses. The cluster B – D – B (taken from the dance section of the TRT score) and its reduced derivative D – B function as an introduction to the stanza-chorus sequences (C1 – C' – C' – C2 – C' and C – C' – C – C').

While the stanzas are always vocally rendered (except in the instrumental first version), the choruses occur in instrumental as well as in vocal form.

Performance Style

Regarding performance style, the first and second performances of 'Hüdayda' are mono-cultural and thus involve no extraneous, non-Turkish elements. The first performance on flute shows many characteristics specific to the playing techniques and musical idiom related to that instrument. Trills, turns, upper and lower mordents, and other ornamental figures (such as fast successive leaps of a fourth) abound. Important notes are accentuated.

The second performance displays typical *bağlama* techniques and motives, such as arpeggios, trills and mordents, hammer-on (*çarpma*), and pull-off (*çekme*). Trills and mordents are performed quickly and by the left-hand fingers only, without repeating the plectrum stroke with the right hand, in correspondence with the hammer-on technique. Other ornaments include rhythmic and melodic figurations of the themes. The tones of the sung and played melodies are discrete and easily discernible; the pronunciation of the sung parts is sufficiently clear and comprehensible. The singing style roughly matches the standardized "academic" way of performing Turkish folk music. The instrumental accompaniment follows the sung melodies closely.

The third and fourth performances of 'Hüdayda' are poly-cultural and strongly influenced by popular music. While both versions largely maintain the original modality-based texture of the piece and of Turkish music in general, extraneous elements are inserted into certain passages in the form of chordal accompaniment [= superstructural element: mode + substructural element: texture], guitar techniques [= substructural elements: texture and rhythm], and fast scale fillings [= substructural element]. Many of the original typical *bağlama* techniques and idioms are maintained in both popularized versions, such as trills, mordents, hammer-on, and pull-off. Vibrato on the string is added (third and fourth performance), as well as glissandi (fourth performance) [= substructural elements]. Both popularized versions make use of a synthetic drum section typical of Middle Eastern popular music [= substructural element: instrumentation]. While the *bağlama* sound is maintained in the third performance, albeit in a heavily amplified form, the fourth performance uses an *elektrosaz* and its typical sound effects (mainly reverb and phasing) [= substructural element: instrumentation]. The singing style differs greatly from the "academic" style of the second performance and is less controlled and less clear (tones and text are sometimes hardly discernible, and from time to time the music is shouted instead of sung).

Conclusion: A Folk Song's Different Versions

Popular dance songs such as 'Hüdayda' are performed throughout Turkey (and the diaspora) in all kinds of contexts and settings, and lend themselves to being performed in various musical styles. The four versions discussed above are not the only versions I encountered during my fieldwork in Turkey and in Ghent, but they provide a clear illustration of the great diversity of approaches and performance styles, from "traditional" (mono-cultural), to "academic" or "standardized" (also mono-cultural), to popularized (poly-cultural) renderings.

Remarkably, the song's tempo remains relatively stable throughout the performances. Different versions and the TRT score use different pitch classes for certain scale degrees. The second, third, and sixth degree often possess several forms. Perhaps surprisingly, the identified pitch classes point to the use of equal temperament for the *bağlama* (the flute displaying an alternative interval structure). Regarding musical form, the TRT score is the most intricate and varied. Its introductory section is omitted in all performed versions. The "academic" performance unsurprisingly matches the TRT version's structure most closely. While stanzas are always sung (except in the instrumental flute version), choruses can be rendered instrumentally or vocally.

It can be concluded that the TRT score – despite its status of official reference version – in practice does not function as a real performance model, except in purposively "faithful" renderings such as the one by the music teacher in Trabzon. The encountered versions are highly idiomatic for the specific instrument or instrument type on which they are performed (the flute, the acoustic *bağlama*, the amplified *bağlama*, and the *elektrosaz*), with a matching singing style. While much freedom is allowed in the treatment of the folk music repertoire, musicians operate within (implicit) stylistic boundaries which define the different performance styles.

Chapter 8

Musical Functions in Turkey and Ghent

Musical value and function represent a final perspective for the ethnographic study of musical events involving Turkish folk music performance. During all 46 events attended in Turkey and Ghent, I interviewed performers, listeners, and commissioners (if present) about what they thought to be the meaning, value, and function of the specific event, the music perfomed in it, and Turkish folk music in general. Although the responses were highly individual and very much related to the interviewees' background, experience, and expertise, qualitative analysis was able to bring out an array of musical functions, structured into personal, social, cultural, philosophical-spiritual, and ritual clusters.

Bruno Nettl discerns two scholarly approaches regarding musical function: the identification of multiple functions versus one principal function – the latter from the 1970s onwards often identified as identity-related (2005: 247). Many scholars have discussed the functions of music in general ways; compare the works by Merriam (1964) (see Chapter 6), DeNora (2000), Wade (2004), Nettl (2005) (see above), and Hesmondhalgh (2013), and from specific viewpoints, compare the works by Stokes (1994), Frith (1996), Hargreaves and North (1999), Born and Hesmondhalgh (2000), Sloboda, O'Neill and Ivaldi (2000), North, Hargreaves and Hargreaves (2004), and Street (2012). Recurring vantage points include identity, politics, and psychology.

Theatre scholar Hans van Maanen makes a major theoretical contribution in his book *How to Study Art Worlds*,[1] developing a theory around the concepts of "value" and "function" of art works. He regards these concepts as closely interrelated: "[T]he typical experiences art is able to generate in the act of reception" are called "value" (Maanen 2010: 149), while function is defined as "the use of the realized value": "value serves function" (2010: 150–51). Van Maanen identifies three kinds or levels of values and functions of arts: intrinsic, semi-intrinsic, and extrinsic. The intrinsic level is typical of and directly originates in the aesthetic experience. The extrinsic level, on the contrary, is not typical of the aesthetic experience, and can be realized indirectly. The semi-intrinsic level occupies a middle position, as it is not exclusively typical of the aesthetic experience, but if applied to this kind of experience, it directly originates in it. Van Maanen provides the following examples: "the capacity to evoke an aesthetic experience" is an intrinsic value of art (2010: 150); "the development of the power of the imagination" is an intrinsic function (2010: 151); "acquiring ... information ..., affecting the emotional system ... or ... social communication through common experience" are semi-intrinsic values; the development of knowledge, mental relief, or strengthening social cohesion are semi-intrinsic functions (2010: 150); the "economic value ... realized through trade" is an extrinsic value of an artwork; contributing to "an accumulation of capital" and experiencing a "relaxation value", "social value", or "informative value" are extrinsic functions (2010: 150–51, 195). The analytical framework is further elaborated by distinguishing three forms of aesthetic experience: decorative, comfortable, and challenging (artistic). The decorative form "does not seek a meaning", the comfortable form "can be understood by means of familiar perceptual schemata", and the challenging or artistic form "calls for a reassessment of one's perceptual schemata" (2010: 188). The combination of these three forms and the three mentioned levels produces a matrix displaying a whole range of possible values and functions of art(works) (2010: 193, 195). The combination of the intrinsic level and the comfortable, respectively challenging form of aesthetic communication involves the function of "confirmation of personal identity", respectively the function of "development of personal identity". On the semi-intrinsic level, the same combinations lead to the functions of "strengthening social identity" and "developing social identity" (2010: 195). A final dimension is added to the analytical framework by considering the societal level and the relation between the personal and the societal level (2010: 198–99).

The analysis of the functions of Turkish folk music presented in this chapter partly reflects the theoretical model of analysis proposed by van Maanen, but the view is more open as it is grounded in concrete data and involves an inductive approach. The conceptualizations and theorizations emerge from the discourse of the involved people as expressed in the interviews.[2] A "centrifugal movement" shifting from the very concrete and specific (the verbatim formulations and conceptualizations of the interviewees) towards the very abstract and general (interpretation and generalization of the input of the interviewees) takes place. As a result, the functions are categorized along different lines, distinguishable from but reminiscent of van Maanen's classification.

Turkish folk music still fulfils a diverse range of functions in contemporary society, in the motherland as well as in the diaspora. A culturally and nationally defined musical genre in a diaspora context turns out to have maintained rich values and functions related to the original context of the motherland, and to have acquired new ones rooted in the peculiarities of the diaspora context. It will become clear that the function of Turkish folk music is not confined to the construction or reinforcement of Turkish identity, which is often considered as a central function and put into the focus of research. However, "identity" is never an unambiguous concept but always multiple and in process, and it can also be constructed outside the cultural, ethnic, or national context. The importance of personal, psychological, and social functions of Turkish folk music in the diaspora points to a role which is for a large part "culture-independent".

Musical Functions in Turkey

One of the themes to come to the fore during my interviews with performers and listeners was the overall status of Turkish folk music in contemporary Turkey. Largely diverging and even contradictory views coexisted. An audience member of a *türkü* night in the student area in cosmopolitan Izmir deplored that, in contemporary Turkey, pop music has taken the place of folk music, and that listening to folk music is sometimes considered backward or "pre-modern". A similar view was expressed by a musician performing at a wedding party in the town of Milas. He estimated the share of people listening to folk music to be around 10 to 15 per cent, while the younger generations prefer rap, and the older generations favour "*sanat müziği*" (light classical music). Both interviewees considered folk music to be more important in the rural parts of Eastern Anatolia. A musician and owner of a *türkü* bar in Kırşehir regretted the deteriorating situation of folk music in Turkey and the disproportionate attention to Western music. Different musicians also recognized that folk music has a higher value for musicians (specialists) than for the general public.

The opposite view – a positive evaluation of the status of Turkish folk music – was expressed by an attendee of a three-day wedding ceremony in a district of Kırşehir, as well as by the *davul* and *zurna* players performing at a tradition-oriented circumcision party in the streets of Milas, and by the same kind of musicians performing at a large-scale *yayla* festival. They argued that "everyone loves [Turkish folk music]" and considered it "very important for the Turks" at present as well as in the future.

Several musicians mentioned the artistic value of Turkish folk music; they considered the folk music of Turkey as art or folk art. An important, recurrent conceptualization of Turkish folk music is its equation with a way of life ("*hayat tarzı*"), or even with life itself. A retired literature professor – at the same time a talented amateur musician – described Turkish folk music as "everything" and as an "excellent school" during an afternoon spent in the tea garden of the Teachers' House in Trabzon. However, some interviewees drew attention to the fact that not all folk songs have the same value and meaning. The owner of a *türkü* bar in Izmir named the songs with texts by Neşet Ertaş and Karacaoğlan as fine examples of meaningful music. The performance style and general approach towards the repertoire were also considered important factors determining the value of the music. The musicians playing at the wedding party in Milas called the popularized version of folk music they performed "bad" ("*kötü*") and did not consider it to be proper or real folk music.

The functions of Turkish folk music emerging from the interviews with performers, listeners, and commissioners can be grouped into a number of fairly distinct but interrelated fields of functioning: a personal, social, and cultural field – in between which are the intersecting personal-social and social-cultural fields – complemented by a philosophical-spiritual and a ritual field, the latter combining aspects from all other fields.

The personal field of functioning is grouped into two kinds of functions: an aesthetic and a psychological function. The cultural field involves the communication of emotional, cultural, or historical content, and the preservation or transmission of cultural heritage. The joint personal-social field encompasses different functions on the intersection of the personal and the social. The professional function, relating to the performers, is a particular case within this field. The social-cultural field relates to the expression of identity, whether (different "levels" of) cultural identity or other forms of identity. The social field integrates two levels: the creation or consolidation of social ties (micro-level), and a political function (macro-level). The philosophical-spiritual field can be divided into a mystical-religious pole and a philosophical-ethical pole. Although any religious doctrine also includes ethics, both poles can be clearly defined: ethics are oriented to the (immanent) fellowman, while religion and mysticism aim at unification with a (transcendent) higher order. The last field, the ritual field, concerns a specific type of event bridging all other fields: the ceremonial celebration of life-cycle events (rites of passage) or other important events. This domain, representing the core of a sociocultural system, occupies a central position.

Personal Functions

Overall, in the musical events I attended, the psychological function, a sub-function within the personal field, occupies the most important place. The most ubiquitous function is providing the opportunity to enjoy oneself and have fun. The expressions *"eğlenmek"* (having fun), *"eğlence"* (amusement), and *"eğlendirmek"* (to entertain) were very frequently used by performers and listeners alike in the context of diverse kinds of events (from wedding parties and other celebrations to *türkü* nights and informal social gatherings). Expressing one's own feelings and thoughts (in the case of the performer), and evoking feelings and thoughts (in the case of the performer and the listener) are also important psychological functions. The conservatoire student performing during the *türkü* night in a *türkü* bar in Izmir told me that "there [was] so much pain (*dert*) in [him] that [he] must perform". A musician accompanying a folk dance lesson for children in Kırşehir explained that he could "express [him]self and the feelings of the moment" by performing music. He gave the example of playing a fast piece when he was in love, or a slow piece when he was sad. The musicians playing on a musical evening in the soccer supporters club, also in Kırşehir, defined "moving people, letting them cry" as their main goal. A musician performing during a wedding considered "making the people happy with dance music, stirring feelings" as his task. In addition to facilitating joy and expressing or evoking feelings, Turkish folk music also appears to have a healing, therapeutic effect, and it was described as relieving the mind, being calming and relaxing, and providing the opportunity to find rest and forget problems. One of the *aşıks* in the *aşık* and folk dance association in Sivas explicitly compared participating in the tradition of *aşıklık* – be it as a performer or as a listener – to "music therapy", to being "far from all the stress" of everyday life. Interesting in this respect was the contribution of the retired literature teacher who played the *bağlama* in the tea garden of the Trabzon Teachers' House. He mentioned "reliving a trauma" as one of the effects of listening to Turkish folk music and argued that "finding pleasure in pain" (*acıdan lezzet almak*) is typical for the Black Sea culture and catalyses the creation of great art. Regarding the relaxing function of Turkish folk music, two audience members in the soccer supporters club indicated that the music made them "forget worries" and "disperse melancholy" (*efkar dağıtma*) and made their "minds rest" and their "thoughts lighter". An idiomatic expression stressing the importance of music (in this case Turkish folk music) for mental health, used by three different interviewees during different family celebrations, was "music is food for the soul" (*müzik ruhun gıdası*). The performance of Turkish folk music was also called a "motivation", something that gives energy. One final psychological function is the re-experiencing of past feelings or events, for example remembering childhood family life, or living conditions belonging to a nomadic existence such as passing time in the summer pastures.

The aesthetic function, also situated in the personal field, was most often mentioned in a rather implicit or moderate way, in terms of "loving the music", "wanting to listen to it", or "something that is pleasant for the ear". The *abdal* musicians playing *davul* and *zurna* at the wedding party in the small village of Çebişler in the province of Kırşehir called the music they played "something very beautiful".

Cultural Functions

The cultural field, occupying the second most important place after the personal field, can be divided in two sub-functions. The first is the communication of emotional, cultural, or historical content. This function was reflected in expressions such as "every türkü tells a story" (*türkü* night in Izmir), "every music has its own meaning, it tells the story of the people, the real story of the people" (musical evening in soccer supporters club in Kırşehir), "it tells the people itself, its sadness, its joy" (*türkü* night in Kırşehir), "from cradle to grave (*beşikten mezara*): all the things of life, traditions (*gelenekler*), customs (*görenekler*)" during an informal social gathering in a tea garden in Trabzon.

The preservation or transmission of cultural heritage, the second sub-function within the cultural field, explicitly and consciously aims at maintaining the practice of traditional folk music performance. The musicians performing at the celebration of the end of the school year in Emirdağ, articulated their aspirations as "perpetuating their music, performing the music of the Anatolian musicians, passing on the traditions to the younger generations". The *aşıks* in their association in Sivas also considered the transmission of the *aşık* tradition as their main task: "to tell our own culture to the people, to transmit it to the next generations, ... there are only a few people who can still perform this tradition". This task or responsibility towards cultural heritage was also expressed by other performers with various backgrounds and in divergent contexts, such as the *bağlama* player during the *cem* inaugurating the *cemevi* in the province of Sivas, the teachers in the tea garden in Trabzon, and the *zurna* player at the summer festival in the *yayla* of Trabzon.

Personal-social Functions

This joint field encompasses three sub-functions, of which the professional function, applicable to the performers, is the most important. In the discourse of the interviewees, the focus sometimes was on the aspect of earning a living, doing one's job, and sometimes on the aspect of self-realization, the development of one's talent. A second personal-social function is the communication of feelings and thoughts from performer to listener, articulated as "transferring the feelings of the inner self" (folk dance lesson in Kırşehir), or "sharing common feelings with the attendees" (*türkü* night in the same city). The induction of dance is another function with a personal and a social component. On the one hand, dancing has a psychological or even therapeutic effect; on the other hand, it also strengthens social ties. The importance of this function was pre-eminently expressed in the context of different wedding parties.

Social-cultural Functions

The function of the expression or construction of (cultural) identity can be situated in a joint social-cultural field. An individual's "identity" is not fixed or absolute but always "in process" and being negotiated (Hall 1996; 2003). Identification is multiple: it can occur on many different levels, and those levels can be interrelated or even contradictory. Different types of identification have emerged from the interviewees' discourses. Often, the level of identification was not made explicit. An important trope in those cases is the connection with childhood. An audience member of the *türkü* night in Izmir explained that she remembered her family, as she had heard the music frequently in her childhood years, and that she considered the "expression of identity the most important [function]" of Turkish folk music. Listening to *türküler* allowed her to "come closer to [her] own life", to become "more real, more serious".

More explicit identification processes occur in relation to the construction of "cultural identity" (Bayart 2005; Hall and Du Gay 1996). Identification with "Turkish culture" considered as a whole, which is an ideologically and politically coloured conceptualization, was rare and only implicitly mentioned by the interviewees. Identification with regional subcultures, on the other hand, was regularly and explicitly mentioned. The expression "music of the region" was used in a value-loaded sense by performers and listeners alike, in the context of various kinds of events. Identification with a religious subculture was expressed by an Alevi performer and listener in Izmir.

Social Functions

A first sub-function is the creation or reinforcement of social ties, which is situated on a "micro-level". This function is expressed in terms such as "sharing happiness with other people", "being together, being family, not letting each other down" (wedding party in Milas); "uniting people (*kaynaşmak*)", "friendship, companionship, brotherhood" (summer festival in the *yayla* of Trabzon); or "being together, sharing beautiful things, experiencing happiness" (informal social gathering in Şavşat). The second sub-function, expressing political views (the political function), is related to a social "macro-level". It was only explicitly mentioned by one interviewee, the performer during the *türkü* night in Kırşehir: "it can be political …, it can have a political meaning, in a closed audience of like-minded people".

Philosophical-spiritual Functions

The philosophical-spiritual field can be situated on a "higher" level than the previous fields but is also inextricably interconnected with them. It can be subdivided into a mystical-religious and a philosophical-ethical function. The mystical function (inducing a mystical experience) was rather insignificant and only mentioned implicitly by an attendee of the summer festival in the *yayla* of Trabzon: "all our music has a very beautiful meaning, for example love for each other, or for nature". The religious function (inducing a religious experience) occurred during the *cem* in the province of Sivas. The *bağlama* player during the ceremony described the function of the performance of a part of the Turkish folk music repertoire as "prayer, worship (*namaz, ibadet*)". The philosophical-ethical function, evoking feelings of solidarity, humanity, or philanthropy, was mentioned by (among others) an attendee in the *aşık* association in Sivas in terms of "tolerance, peace, brotherhood, love", and an attendee of the festival in the Trabzon *yayla*: "dancing together, making the same movement together, turning to the right, seeking the good". It was also expressed by the wish to transcend religious boundaries, to welcome Alevis and non-Alevis indiscriminately to the inauguration of the *cemevi* and the *cem* in the province of Sivas.

Ritual Functions

The last function, the ritual function, unifies aspects from all aforementioned fields (the personal, social, cultural, and philosophical-spiritual fields, and their intersections), and most often concerns the ritual accompaniment of life-cycle events (rites of passage). This function occupies a central role in society, and the music performed at such occasions is expected to obey particular rules connected with cultural, religious, and moral traditions. This function was mentioned in relation to different wedding and circumcision parties in various regional and social contexts. The grandfather of the boy celebrated during the circumcision party in Milas explicitly characterized the event as "of great importance, moral tradition (*maneviyat*), a kind of ritual, with religious rules". As well as accompanying life-cycle events, Turkish folk music can also play an important role in the ritual accompaniment of other important events, such as graduation or the inauguration of venues or associations.

Schematic Representation

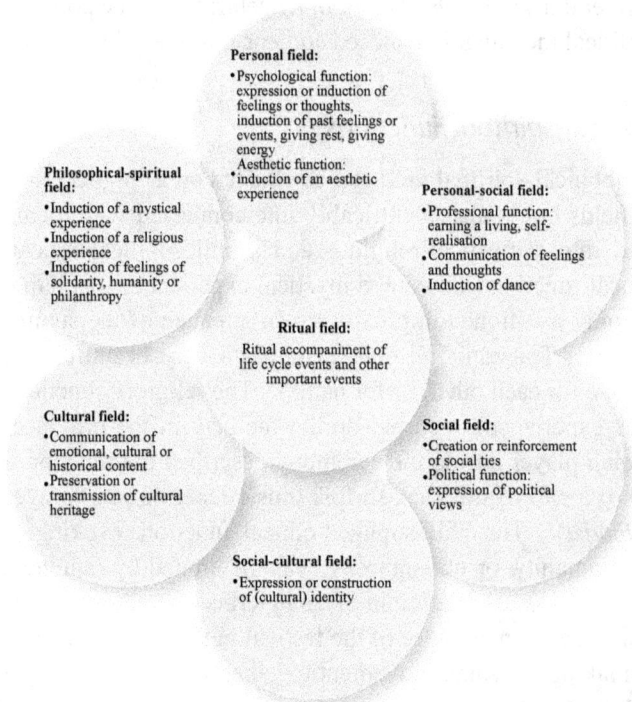

Personal field:
- Psychological function: expression or induction of feelings or thoughts, induction of past feelings or events, giving rest, giving energy
- Aesthetic function: induction of an aesthetic experience

Philosophical-spiritual field:
- Induction of a mystical experience
- Induction of a religious experience
- Induction of feelings of solidarity, humanity or philanthropy

Personal-social field:
- Professional function: earning a living, self-realisation
- Communication of feelings and thoughts
- Induction of dance

Ritual field:
Ritual accompaniment of life cycle events and other important events

Cultural field:
- Communication of emotional, cultural or historical content
- Preservation or transmission of cultural heritage

Social field:
- Creation or reinforcement of social ties
- Political function: expression of political views

Social-cultural field:
- Expression or construction of (cultural) identity

Figure 8.1: Functions of Turkish folk music in Turkey (Liselotte Sels)

Musical Functions in Ghent

Regarding the present-day status of Turkish folk music in the diaspora, a few interviewees expressed the opinion that Turkish folk music is somewhat dated and no longer plays a significant role in Belgium, even less so for the younger generations. A young musician performing Turkish folk music as an interlude during a karaoke night told me: "These are songs seldom listened to by the third generation", and "Unfortunately, I notice that there are many people listening less and less to Turkish folk music, even not recognizing this music anymore". A possible difference in meaning for different generations was mentioned by a Turkish musician from the Netherlands in Muzikantenhuis during a Turkish evening: "For the first (and second) generation it is nostalgia, looking back on old times; for the third generation it equals partying".

Many interviewed people, on the contrary, did consider folk music as relevant to the Turks living in Flanders, including the young generations. One of the musicians of the cultural festival in the city pointed out: "Young people who grew up here are still appreciating folk music, there is still a need for it". The commissioner of a *türkü* night in De Centrale underlined the importance of Turkish folk music in the diaspora. He linked this importance to a sense of nostalgia for the motherland, shared by many Turks in Europe, and even argued that Turkish folk music is more important in the diaspora than in Turkey: "In Turkey itself, it becomes less and less important, there is only little room for folk music in the media". A Belgian couple attending a *türkü* night at De Centrale describes the recognition by the Belgian audience of the importance of Turkish folk music for the Turks in Belgium: "For the second and third generation it is the music of their country, nostalgia. In this way they can keep in touch with their country".

All these nuances taken into account, the general tenor of the interviews recognized the importance of Turkish folk music in today's society, both in Turkey and in the diaspora, and across the different generations. Frequently recurring motives were the hope of a prosperous future, and the importance of transmission to the younger generations.

Several interviewees attributed general, broad meanings and values to Turkish folk music. A recurring motive was considering Turkish folk music as all-embracing: (metaphorically) equating the music with a way of life or with life itself. A performer at a cultural festival expressed this as follows: "Turkish folk music is a way of life … It also expresses everything, everything of Turkey". During a Turkish evening at Muzikantenhuis, this thought was formulated as "it is their life", or "it is life", by a listener and the commissioner, respectively.

In general, a deep, multi-layered value is attributed to Turkish folk music. A musician during the same Turkish evening at the Muzikantenhuis used the phrase: "different interpretations ..., different layers". Other musicians explicitly credited Turkish folk music with "much significance". On the other hand, other persons emphasized that certain types of Turkish folk are not profound at all.

The value of Turkish folk music is often perceived as very positive: "cheerful", "music with a positive meaning", "a positive atmosphere". The danceable aspect of the repertoire is frequently mentioned. Contrarily, the melancholic nature of many Turkish folk songs was also raised: "In all countries folk music equals cheerfulness (*neşe*) except among the Turks, there is a lot of sadness (*üzüntü*) ... 30% is lively, the rest is sad", as a musician of a *türkü* night at De Centrale explained.

Regarding the matter of universality of music, opinions differ somewhat. Some interviewees felt that music, and also Turkish folk music, is universal and can be understood by people of all cultures. This opinion is connected with the idea that the emotional value is contained in the music itself, and not in the text. Other people emphasized the connectedness to language and culture: "Belgians often do not feel addressed, they seldom attend Turkish concerts, they consider it boring", and "Above all Turkish people enjoy it", are considerations expressed by the (Belgian) commissioner and a Turkish performer of the open house at De Centrale. In general, however, the idea that Belgians can establish an emotional connection with Turkish folk music seems to prevail.

The fields of functioning identified in the diaspora are the same as those of the motherland. The personal field again involves an aesthetic and a psychological function. The social field functions on the lower societal level or micro-level within smaller social networks, and on the higher societal level or macro-level of society as a whole (political function). The joint personal-social field involves different functions with personal and social components, such as the communication of emotions and thoughts, and the induction of dance. The professional function, relating to the performers, is also situated in this field. The cultural field involves the communication of emotional, cultural, or historical content, and the preservation or transmission of cultural heritage. The joint social-cultural field relates to the expression of identity, whether culturally defined or not, and includes an intercultural function as well, which is typical for a diasporan context. The philosophical-spiritual field can be divided into a mystical-religious aspect and a philosophical-ethical aspect, similar to the Turkish case. The ritual field, which again occupies a central position, concerns the ceremonial celebration of life-cycle events (rites of passage) or other important events.

Personal Functions

The personal function, and more specifically the psychological function, emerged as the most important function from the qualitative analysis. It can involve superficial diversion as well as deep mental relaxation. The terms "ambiance", "entertainment", and "amusement" are recurrent in the discourses. The listeners attending a Turkish evening in Muzikantenhuis underlined the calming, comforting effect of listening to Turkish folk music: "[it] brings peace, it provides variation in the stressful and monotonous life in Belgium"; "[it gives] relief after a stressful week". Turkish folk music was also said to be able to bring "comfort in sorrow" and was often characterized with the expression "*müzik ruhun gıdası*" ("music is the food of the soul"). A young lady attending the *seyran* expressed her observations as follows: "With every song I remember an event or a period of my life", indicating the power of music to recall past events or feelings. Another function within the personal field is the aesthetic function: the induction of an aesthetic experience. This function was expressed (indirectly) by performers and listeners of diverse kinds of events with phrases such as "nice to hear", "enjoy the music", or "beautiful music".

Personal-social Functions

The personal-social field is the second most important field of functioning in Ghent, and involves three sub-functions. A first sub-function is the communication of feelings and thoughts by the performer to the listener. This function is reflected in the description by a *bağlama* player of the function of performances of Turkish folk music as "an expression of the mental state, the thoughts, in an artistic way". Inducing dance is a second sub-function of the personal-social field. This function was not often commented on in a thoughtful way; to be able or to be allowed to dance was mostly considered as a valuable purpose in itself. The longest account regarding this function was given by a family member participating in the circumcision party:

> The rhythm of the music puts us in a mood to dance. Turkish folk music can be compared with your [i.e., European or American] dance music … The first two people dance in a more interesting fashion than the next people. In the past, the tradition was the same as nowadays, the only difference might be that the songs have become faster now.

A third, frequently mentioned, sub-function within the personal-social field is the professional function, which concerns the performers. Within the professional function, different accents can be laid. The purely economic-financial function (earning a living) was mentioned by audience members as well as performers, but never as the sole motivation to perform Turkish folk music. Besides the economic-financial aspect, the professional function was interpreted as, on the one hand, promotion and publicity, and on the other hand, self-realization and professional development. Many musicians attached great importance to having a broad audience and were always looking for interesting opportunities to perform. This was also indicated by the commissioner of a *türkü* night in De Centrale: "[The musicians] like the infrastructure of De Centrale. Alevis usually play on evenings of associations in poor conditions. Here they get the chance to perform in good conditions", and by a female musician who took part in another similar evening: "[It was] spectacular, I have had a performance in Dortmund before, which was in front of strangers. At De Centrale it was in front of all my friends, family, and acquaintances. This made this evening enormously special". Several musicians evaluated their own "accomplishments" or that of their pupils as very positive: "It is an important event, some are for the first time in their life on stage, and their family is watching", is a statement by a teacher who gave a performance together with his pupils. A musician animating a wedding party articulated his professional function as follows: "[It was] a perfect evening; every time I play at a party, I become better". Other musicians considered each performance as "a kind of exam": "We are very critical of ourselves, we learn from it for the next time". A different accent within the professional field was expressed by the musician of the wedding party: "In my family no one plays music, I started to play after my father had instructed me to learn something in order to stay away from the streets and drugs and so on".

Social-cultural Functions

The social-cultural function of the expression or construction of cultural identity emerged as an important function. Cultural identity can play on different levels: the level of regional, ethnic, religious, or other subcultures, or the more general but imaginary-theoretical level of Turkish culture considered as a whole.

Identification with regional subcultures was often indirectly expressed: implicitly by means of spontaneous reactions during the musical event instead of explicitly during the interviews. People in the audience generally respond enthusiastically when music from their own region of origin is performed. Musicians know this and, if possible, adapt their programme to the specific composition of the audience. This phenomenon was sporadically referred to in the interviews: "The people were from Emirdağ and Ankara, the selection of the music was thus dependent on the public" versus "The audience can be from every region, so we chose music from everywhere; you don't know how the public will react". A particular case was the Suvermez night, which was entirely organized with the aim of the creation or reinforcement of a regional group identity. The organizer consciously had set himself this task; he described bringing together the *Suvermezliler* in order to get to know each other better as a kind of "education". As was the case in Turkey, reference to childhood was a significant trope regarding the function of identification. A performer expressed this as "memories, music of the own region, of childhood"; another one as "I have grown up with it, I have heard it from birth".

In the examined settings, identification with other kinds of (not region-specific) subcultures was mainly expressed as identification with the culturally and religiously specific Alevi identity. The organizer of a *türkü* night in De Centrale, although personally favouring the general, broadly oriented part of the programme than the part consisting solely of Alevi repertoire, found it logical that the musicians, being Alevi themselves, devoted such a large part of their programme to Alevi music. During the observed *cem*, particular emphasis was placed by the participants on the cultural aspect: "This is something cultural, this is our culture", and "It is really a special culture, not everyone does this". Yet the religious aspect has been expressed as well: "We are no ordinary Muslims, we do not go to the mosque".

Regarding the identification with Turkish culture considered as a whole, the expression or construction of "Turkishness", different emphases were laid. Generally, this aspect was described as: "[Turkish folk music] expresses … everything, everything of Turkey". The collective, common nature of

Turkish folk music was highlighted with statements such as "The music can be sung together, everyone knows it". In some cases, the historical aspect including its link with the past was emphasized: "I think Turkish folk music is our history", as a young female musician performing during a *türkü* night in De Centrale expressed it. Typical for a diaspora context, a component of nostalgia or longing for the motherland was often (openly or in a hidden way) present. A relative of the boy celebrated during the circumcision party expressed this component as follows: "Of course it does not feel the same as a party in Turkey, but we know that there is also something like this".

Remarkably, the identification with Turkish culture as a whole was also often mentioned by non-Turkish interviewees. While this illustrates the "autochthonous" recognition of the social-cultural function of musical performances in a diasporan context, it also makes clear that non-Turkish people often generalize about (post-)migrant culture without considering (or knowing) its internal diversity.

The expression or construction of identity without reference to (a) Turkish (sub-)cultural identity is also a socially and culturally embedded action. Turkish folk music is often identified with one's own personality, as was expressed by several performers: "It is your business card, your identity", or "Turkish folk music is what we ourselves are". This discourse was also used by commissioners and listeners.

A form of identity expression or construction typical of a diasporan context involves interaction with the broader society in which the Turkish population occupies a minority position. This is the intercultural function of music. Important here is the "visibility" of the Turkish musical expressions in wider society, possibly leading to a greater understanding and appreciation of and respect for this cultural minority. This function is reflected in the reflections of a performer about the cultural festival in which he participated: "Bringing cultures together. A beautiful day today at the Vrijdagmarkt. It is very important, it should happen more often. To get to know each other, to like each other. To transgress cultural boundaries". One of the commissioners of the festival used the following phrasing: "The emphasis is on knowledge of the Turkish culture. People recognize certain things. Mutual recognition, respect". This intercultural aspect was also confirmed on different occasions by non-Turkish interviewees, who evaluated it as something very positive, or even romanticized it: "In this way you can feel back in Turkey, another culture in your own city, nice to have it near you", or "Turkish music gives the feeling of being on a journey, which is very pleasant".

Social Functions

This important function has two aspects, situated on different levels: the creation or reinforcement of social ties on the one hand (micro-level), and the expression of political views on the other hand (macro-level). Regarding the creation or reinforcement of social ties, Turkish folk music appears to be an effective catalyst in bringing people together, as a commissioner of the Suvermez night confirmed: "The aim is to bring people together around music … Nothing can be as good as music to bring people together". The emphasis was often placed on sharing common experiences, by performers as well as by listeners and commissioners: "giving and receiving", "sharing with others, sharing friendship, love…", "sharing and being together in music, connectedness through *türküler*". As one commissioner put it: "[The musicians] do not come purely for profit, [for] a big concert, [with] great expectations, but to share something together", and "an audience that thinks like me, that is on the same wavelength". Other prevailing terms were "warmth", "conviviality", "trust", "feeling at home", "being themselves", and "intimate atmosphere".

The political function of the performance of Turkish folk music (the expression of political views) was referred to only once. In response to the question regarding the meaning of the music performed during an Alevi *türkü* night at De Centrale, the expression "protests of Anatolia" came forward, an explicit reference to the leftist, progressive political connotation of Alevism.

Cultural Functions

A central function belonging to the cultural field is the communication of emotional, cultural, or historical content. The emotions, thoughts, or events communicated through the music originally belonged to the creator or creating community of the song but can be subsequently appropriated by the "re-creators" of the music, or by the listeners. This cultural communication function is most often expressed by musicians in terms like "a true story, the more you sing it, the more you empathize", and "Turkish folk music narrates the events of life". Another performer indicated that his purpose is "to transfer as much as possible" while performing. An audience member stated that Turkish folk music "shows the feelings of the people", while a commissioner made clear that it is "about love, pain, sadness…" Some interviewees argued that contemporary Turkish folk music is superficial if compared to the old, traditional folk music: "Today's music is about love and separation, but the music of the past was also about other themes".

Another important function within the cultural field is the preservation or transmission of cultural heritage. The importance of preserving and passing on the traditions was highlighted by several people, such as a musician who described the task he set to himself as "presenting the traditional, unknown, forgotten songs to the people". A participant in the Alevi *cem* ceremony argued: "Normally this belongs to Turkey, but they are born here, and the tradition should be continued. The younger generations have not seen this often, they have to learn it too".

The cultural function also took shape in a pure form in the explicit inter-pretation of musical events as "cultural", as distinct from other possible functions of similar events. This interpretation manifested itself in the saying of a commissioner of a Turkish evening at Muzikantenhuis: "[This is] not a party, but a cultural happening", and in the view of the commissioner as well as a musician of the Alevi *türkü* night at De Centrale, who juxtaposed the nature of a "concert performance" with the nature of a performance in a religious context.

Philosophical-spiritual Functions

This field involves a philosophical-ethical and a religious-mystical com-ponent. The ethical function of evoking feelings of solidarity, humanity, or philanthropy is expressed in phrases such as "loving each other", "an open atmosphere, everyone is welcome", "no distinction between people", and in the fact that in Alevi-oriented concerts or other activities, non-Alevis are also welcome. An audience member of the official opening of the music café explained this function of music with the following words: "We are all together. When the sun shines, we all feel its warmth. It is beautiful when people can get on well with each other. Our people are connected. We are one people, the whole of Turkey: Kurdish, Turkish…"

The most explicit moral point of view was expressed by the participants of the *cem* ceremony: "The children should learn this too, for example, if some-body doesn't possess much, to help him. Not to do *haram*[3] things, for exam-ple moonlighting (*zwartwerk*), stealing…" Obviously, the religious function, inducing religious feelings, also came to the fore during the *cem*, verbally expressed with the powerful statement: "This is something else than folk music; it is praying!" The mystical function was most often mentioned by the musicians themselves. A young Turkish folk musician from Ghent declared: "The content is love. Not only being in love, but rather a connection with the world, mysticism". An internationally renowned Turkish folk musician performing at De Centrale described his mystical experience during performance as follows:

> I'm not really focused on the audience, I sometimes forget that I'm in the hall, we don't see the audience, it is as if we were alone. From the moment we start playing, offering music, everything changes ... The instrument is close to the body, it's a special feeling, a closeness, a good relationship.

Ritual Functions

The last function, the ritual function or the ritual accompaniment of life-cycle events and other important events, unites connotations of practically all other functions, and concerns different rites of passage. During the research in Ghent and its surroundings, two events involving the celebration of life-cycle events were studied: the circumcision party and the wedding party. The traditional folk music repertoire has played an important role during these kinds of events for many centuries. A relative of the boys being celebrated during the circumcision party explained it as follows:

> To be *sünnet* is the first step [towards manhood], and circumcision is very important for Muslim men, it is a tradition in our culture, and it is obligatory. This is a ritual ..., not only during this kind of party, but also at [other] special occasions, this kind of music is often performed.

Other events that could be considered as possessing ritual components are the official opening of the music café, and the celebration of 50 years of Turkish migration to Belgium.

Schematic Representation

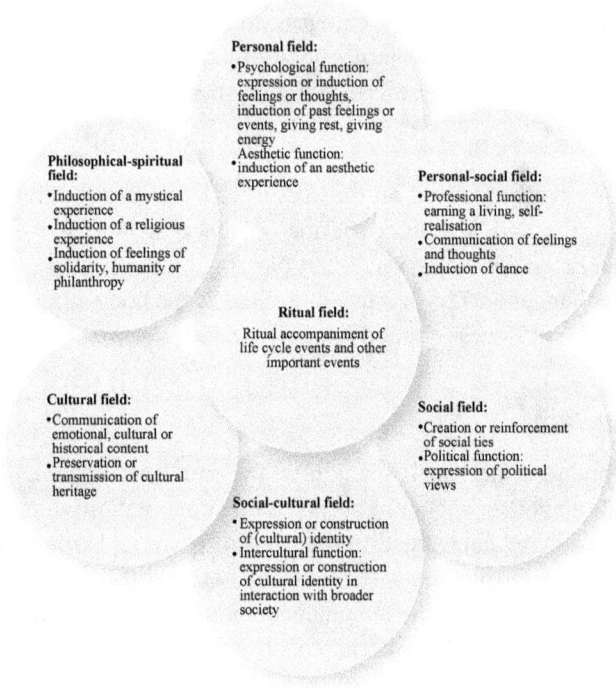

Personal field:
- Psychological function: expression or induction of feelings or thoughts, induction of past feelings or events, giving rest, giving energy
- Aesthetic function: induction of an aesthetic experience

Philosophical-spiritual field:
- Induction of a mystical experience
- Induction of a religious experience
- Induction of feelings of solidarity, humanity or philanthropy

Personal-social field:
- Professional function: earning a living, self-realisation
- Communication of feelings and thoughts
- Induction of dance

Ritual field:
Ritual accompaniment of life cycle events and other important events

Cultural field:
- Communication of emotional, cultural or historical content
- Preservation or transmission of cultural heritage

Social field:
- Creation or reinforcement of social ties
- Political function: expression of political views

Social-cultural field:
- Expression or construction of (cultural) identity
- Intercultural function: expression or construction of cultural identity in interaction with broader society

Figure 8.2: Functions of Turkish folk music (performances) in Ghent (Liselotte Sels)

Conclusion: Status, Value, and Function in Turkey and Ghent

The people I interviewed in Turkey and Belgium have largely convergent views on the overall status of Turkish folk music. Seemingly contradictory tendencies are found in Turkey as well as in Ghent: while certain respondents consider the importance of Turkish folk music as rapidly declining in Turkey and the diaspora (especially for young people and in urban milieus), other respondents consider Turkish folk music as still being highly important and relevant for people from all social classes, in the motherland and the diaspora. The omnipresence of pop music is often named as causing the decrease in importance, having taken over many functions of folk music. Regarding the relevance for the diasporan context, Turkish folk music is either viewed as less important or as more important than in Turkey itself.

These divergent and seemingly contradictory judgements can be related to determining factors such as personal and musical background, ideological views, and the definition of the concept "folk music". Respondents with a nationalistic ideology will often accentuate the importance of Turkish folk music (as a cultural product representing Turkishness – as such, they reflect official views on Turkish folk music). People with an urban background will likely attach higher importance to the manifestation of pop music than people with a rural background having experienced or still experiencing many performances of folk music on social occasions. The scope within which the folk music concept is placed also determines the share occupied by folk music, compared to pop music. If folk music is defined in the narrow sense of traditionally performed rural music forms, it is logically less important than if it is defined in the broad sense of all kinds of music based on the traditional folk repertoire, regardless of the performance style.

Respondents also largely agree upon the general values of Turkish folk music. The same tropes recur in both research contexts: Turkish folk music is often conceptualized as a way of life, or even life itself (more than an art form), and as possessing a strong moral value or deep meaning. The affective meaning of Turkish folk music is sometimes felt as positive (evoking or expressing feelings of happiness) and sometimes as negative (evoking or expressing feelings of sadness). In both contexts, the remark was made that not all kinds of Turkish folk music carry the same high moral, cultural, or aesthetic value. In the diasporan context, views diverged on the issue of universality: while some involved persons consider Turkish folk music as universally valuable (for Turks as well as non-Turks), other people doubt its ability to appeal to non-Turks. These different views are probably tied to personal experiences. The official discourses of the Turkish Republic regarding folk music are sometimes reflected in respondents' views.

A comparison of the identified functions in Turkey and in the diaspora reveals substantial similarities complemented by different accents and a few particularities bound to the specific motherland or diaspora context. Table 8.1 provides an overview with links to the concepts encountered in Van Maanen (2010).

Table 8.1: Functions of Turkish folk music (performances) in Turkey and the diaspora

Fields of functioning	Functions in Turkey	Functions in Ghent	Intrinsic, semi-intrinsic, extrinsic function (Van Maanen)
Personal field	Psychological function; aesthetic function		Semi-intrinsic; intrinsic
Personal-social field	Professional function; communication of feelings/thoughts; inducing dance		Extrinsic; semi-intrinsic; intrinsic
Social field	Creation/reinforcement of social ties; political function		Extrinsic; semi-intrinsic
Social-cultural field	Expression/ construction of (cultural) identity	Expression/construction of (cultural) identity (if in interaction with broader society: intercultural function)	Semi-intrinsic
Cultural field	Communication of emotional/cultural/ historical content; preservation/transmission of cultural heritage		Semi-intrinsic; semi-intrinsic
Philosophical-spiritual field	Inducing a mystical/religious experience; evoking feelings of solidarity/humanity/ philanthropy		Semi-intrinsic; semi-intrinsic
Ritual field	Ritual accompaniment of life-cycle events and other important events		Intrinsic

The similarity of functions in both contexts is striking. All seven identified fields of functioning occur in the motherland as well as in the diaspora. However, the specific interpretation of the functions can vary according to the concrete performance contexts, which are embedded in a larger motherland or diaspora context. The professional function, for example, will carry more weight in Turkey, since many of the performers are musicians by (primary) profession. The political function adopts a different content and focus in the diaspora compared to Turkey. Most clearly, functions related to the cultural field (the cultural, social-cultural, and ritual functions) are characterized by different interpretations in the motherland and the diaspora. This is a result of the different positions occupied by the Turkish culture or subcultures in both contexts, and the different power relationships between Turkish cultural fields and subfields, and non-Turkish cultural fields.

Conclusion: Looking Back and Forward

In this book, I have reviewed the history of Turkish migration and musical culture in Ghent and mapped out the actors and places constituting the Turkish folk music network in the city. I have attempted to sketch a picture of what Turkish folk music entails in the twentieth and twenty-first century, and to make clear the effects of notation and systematized archiving. To offer more insight into the general and specific ways in which Turkish folk music is employed, I have described traditional folk music occasions on the one hand, and transnationally shared folk music events, and events typical for the homeland or diaspora context, on the other. For this purpose, I have also analysed and compared contextual and musical aspects of Turkish folk music performances in both contexts and illustrated how one folk song can manifest itself in totally different guises. As a final ethnographic perspective, I have presented the genre's different functions for the people involved.

This concluding chapter recapitulates the main findings regarding the contemporary meaning, contexts, actors, characteristics, and functions of Turkish folk music in the studied transnational context, illustrates the ways in which these aspects interrelate with each other, and offers a general outlook on the past, present, and future of Turkish folk music "between Ghent and Turkey".

Contemporary Turkish Folk Music

The ways in which a tradition-based musical genre manifests itself in the twenty-first century in the context of migration, diaspora, and cosmopolitanism is a complex subject. During the previous century, Turkish folk music has been exposed to three top-down and bottom-up tendencies. The first tendency, from the 1920s onwards, involved the (top-down) processing of the folk repertoire of rural Anatolia with nationalist-motivated and Western-inspired methods and principles, according to the cultural policies of the newly established Turkish Republic. Similar developments had been occurring since the nineteenth century in Europe and globally, in the context of emerging nation states. The second tendency, from the 1960s onwards, involved a commercially motivated (bottom-up) synthesis of the Turkish folk music repertoire with popular music-derived elements. This evolution is to be considered in light of glocalized influences of Anglo-Saxon and Middle Eastern pop musics. It was accompanied by rural-urban migration flows within Turkey, and their cultural and musical implications. The third tendency, also from the 1960s onwards, involved further hybridization of the Turkish folk music repertoire in the context of the transnational (mainly Europe-directed) movement of Turkish people. The repositioning of Turkish music consumers and "producers" in a diasporan context entailed further interaction with other musical genres. These three major tendencies have affected the Turkish folk music repertoire in a cumulative and thorough way.

An attempt to define the subject and scope of Turkish folk music in the early twenty-first century should take all these developments into account. The concept of "folk music" (*halk müziği*) is highly ideologically and polit- ically charged in Turkey, since it has been put forward by Atatürk as the only musical repertoire capable of representing Turkish identity, and thus the Turkish nation. The state-directed folk music collection project and the estab- lishment of a folk music archive (consisting of recordings and scores) have been determining factors in defining what is considered the folk music of Turkey. This archive (the "TRT repertoire") has become the canon on which almost all folk music practice and discourse is based in urban contexts in and outside Turkey. In order to evaluate the scope and contents of this officially recognized "Turkish folk music repertoire", one should take into account its being a selection of pieces, belonging to rural and urban repertoires (in some cases influenced by classical musics), being either anonymous or authored (in some cases deliberately "anonymized"), either old or recent (in some cases influenced by popular music), and in some cases originating outside of Turkey. Pieces commonly known as authored (e.g., *aşık* music, or songs created by well-known folk singers) can be included in the repertoire if they are of "exceptional value" and/or sufficiently "non-personal" (i.e., fitting into a regional idiom). Furthermore, the selected pieces have been subjected to further processing in order to be transcribed, which involved the manipu- lation of lyrics (to bring them in accordance with, e.g., folk poetry "rules", Turkish constitution and laws, standardized regional Turkish dialects, and geographical names of modern Turkey), the creation of one final version out of different performed versions, the correction of mistakes made by the performers, and the construction of instrumental (*bağlama*) parts.

As a result of these processes, the concept of "Turkish folk music" covers a new reality. This "modern" folk music is canonized and standardized, is not orally transmitted, is not embedded in a rural context, and has lost its primary function. Furthermore, in everyday urban practice, boundaries between the tradition-grounded folk music repertoire – often performed in a somewhat popularized style – and pieces that could be classified as "contemporary folk music" (music created as imitation or interpretation of the tradition, or even music belonging to the categories of *özgün müzik* or related genres) are becoming increasingly blurred. Nevertheless, in spite of the influence of the TRT repertoire, and the conceptions and practices related to it, a "living tradition", grounded in rural (Turkish and non-Turkish) cultural practices of Anatolia, outside of this official canon, is still existing and further developing in present-day Turkey and (to a lesser extent) the Turkish diaspora.

Whichever definition of Turkish folk music is employed – an "exclusive" view with a limited scope, or an "inclusive" view with a broader scope – it is clear that the genre occupies an important position in today's Turkey and its diaspora. Partly a result of the cultural policy of the Turkish Republic, its presence and significance currently permeate not only the Turkish state system and its institutions, but also civil society and private life. This observation feeds back to Martin Stokes's 1992 proposition to investigate the ways in which and "[t]he extent to which [the folk music related] reforms have been absorbed, 'domesticated' and attained a degree of autonomy at local level" (1992a: 8–9). The inclusion of the diaspora context of Ghent – with its exceptionally high percentage of people of Turkish origin (up to 10% of the total population) – has enriched the study and broadened its scope.

Contemporary Musical Contexts

The kinds of events and occasions involving Turkish folk music in present-day Turkey and Ghent are diverse. Typical occasions involving folk music performance in traditional Turkish society, such as the nurturance of a small child, the circumcision of a boy, departure for military service of a young man, marriage, death, the signalling of sunrise during Ramadan, Alevi religious ceremonies, particular kinds of formal social gatherings, and the change of seasons, still persist in present-day Turkey, albeit sometimes in a modified form. The traditional gatherings with *aşıks* have disappeared and been replaced by modern *aşık* festivals. Singing work songs and playing *davul* and *zurna* at official welcomings are traditions that still occur but are gradually disappearing. The persisting tradition-grounded occasions are complemented by contemporary occasions, such as the end of the school year, or the official opening of a new organization – both occasions with a ritual component. Other musical events take place without a specific occasion, such as cultural activities organized by cultural organizations, and manifold formal and informal social gatherings. Many of these occasions are maintained in the diaspora, albeit sometimes on a less frequent basis. Circumcision and wedding parties are as important in the diaspora as in Turkey, and Turkish folk music is essential to them. *Cem* ceremonies are organized in Ghent as well, as are café concerts, concerts, and (summer) festivals. Formal and informal social gatherings are accompanied by folk music, as are certain kinds of celebrations with a ritual aspect, such as official openings. Typically occurring in a diaspora context are events celebrating Turkish migration, and benefit evenings to support a particular Turkish village. Typical events bound to the cultural context of Turkey, such as the celebration of departure for military service, *aşık* festivals and other *aşık* activities, folk dance lessons with live musical accompaniment, and the signalling function during Ramadan, have disappeared in the immigration country.

Most musical events, whether occurring in Turkey or in Ghent, appear to be planned in advance, and commissioned by a third party. However, in Turkey a larger number of events occur in a spontaneous way and/or are self-initiated (not commissioned). Except for private celebrations such as wedding or circumcision parties, most events in Ghent are partially financed by an authority, mostly complemented by other financing channels, such as an investment of the organizing body, sponsorship by (often Turkish) companies, or recuperation via the audience in the form of ticket sales or consumables. Investing associations or organizations can be situated on a local or supralocal level, in some cases even operating transnationally from Turkey. Supporting authorities can be local (e.g., the City of Ghent) or supralocal (e.g., the Flemish government). Subsidies can be provided directly to the organizing non-profit organizations, to umbrella self-organizations that distribute the funding to their member organizations, or to an intercultural centre such as De Centrale, which functions as a hub in the organization of Turkish folk music-related activities. The general picture of official recognition and funding, complemented by bottom-up initiatives, supported by sponsorship and solidarity, is paralleled in Turkey, although the context is fundamentally different. In Turkey, folk music is strongly promoted and supported by the state system and its cultural, social, and educational institutions, a situation grounded in the nationalist-motivated cultural policy of the (early) Turkish Republic.

Events involving Turkish folk music can take place at any time, although some events are preferably planned on the weekends. Typically, *türkü* nights are programmed on a daily basis in *türkü* bars in Turkey, while they are limited to the weekend in the diaspora. The summer is the preferred season for festivals, and circumcision and wedding parties. The duration of wedding parties is generally reduced considerably in urban Turkish and diasporic environments, compared to rural contexts in Turkey. The structure or order of the discerned stages of the ritual is equally flexible. While wedding and circumcision parties typically take place outdoors in Turkey, in Belgium often an alternative indoor location is employed, such as a party hall (typically exploited by Turks), or a Turkish restaurant. Traditionally conceived wedding parties in Turkey take place in two locations (belonging to the families of the bride and the groom) and display an interplay between private and public locations, as do circumcision parties. This is generally transformed to solely private parties in the diaspora, which are less strongly embedded in the larger social/societal context. While certain kinds of events take place in typical locations, similar in Turkey and the diaspora (such as public squares in city centres, open fields in rural environments, concert halls, or *türkü* bars), other kinds of events, such as Alevi *cem* ceremonies, lack adequate locations in the diaspora.

Contemporary Musical Actors

There are many parallels in the roles of commissioner, listener, and performer in the motherland and diasporan contexts. In Turkey as well as in Belgium, commissioning appears to be a male affair. The same types of private and institutional commissioners can be discerned in the motherland and the diaspora. Regarding audiences, both (equally) mixed male-female and exclusively male audiences are common in Turkey, the latter phenomenon being less common in the diaspora. Turkish folk music appeals to people of all age categories. While most audiences are specific in one way or another (e.g., consisting of people belonging to a specific religious or social group, or associated to the location or the other actors), certain events attract general audiences (in particular, festivals or concerts). Significantly, most events in Ghent attract an (almost) exclusively Turkish public; balanced constellations of Turkish and non-Turkish listeners less commonly occur. This points to the persisting "ethnic boundary" in Ghent. An example of the way in which this boundary is maintained by the members of the Turkish population themselves is that much publicity for Turkish events is in Turkish, and disseminated via Turkish channels.

The professional folk music performers in traditional Turkish society, including *aşıks*, *abdals* and Roma, still play an important musical role. In particular, the Alevi (Shiite) *abdals* and (mostly Sunni) Roma fulfil the role of professional musicians in many celebrations with a ritual component, such as wedding and circumcision parties, official openings, graduation parties, and so on. *Davul* and *zurna*, and in Central Anatolia also *bağlama* and other instruments, are typically employed. The original sociocultural function of *aşıks* has disappeared completely in Turkey and has been replaced by the purely cultural function of preserving and transmitting a historical art form. In the diaspora, Roma and *abdal* musicians are active as well. In Ghent, the title of *aşık* is borne by a few poet-musicians, but their activities are rather limited compared to what *aşıklık* means in Turkey. A large shift has occurred in the level of common people's musicking. While in traditional society opportunities to make music were limited, especially for Sunnites and even more for women than for men, the twentieth century has witnessed a movement towards greater openness. Amateur and even professional music-making have become socially accepted in almost all sections of society – a change in attitude that has been reflected in the diaspora as well. In Turkey, thorough multilevel professionalization of the folk music field has taken place. Contemporary folk music specialists are expected to master an extended repertoire consisting of music from all regions of Turkey, and to be able to perform it in the appropriate regional performance style (involving the proper *tavır*). In the diaspora, due to the limited opportunities for musical education, the level of theoretical knowledge and practical skills is generally lower than the average level of the folk musicians in Turkey. Regular music education is rarely attended by Turkish people in Ghent (cf. the aforementioned "ethnic boundary"). Mixed-level musical ensembles are more common in the diaspora than in Turkey. The number of performers varies greatly throughout the different kinds of events and contexts. A tendency for performers to be of younger age in the diaspora than in Turkey could be discerned – possibly a token of the diminished importance of hierarchy. Another tendency was the somewhat larger presence of female musicians in the diaspora, which could possibly signify a compliance with Western societal standards. As was the case for the audience, musical ensembles in the diaspora are generally mono-ethnic; collaborations between Turkish and non-Turkish musicians are still rather the exceptions proving the rule. Musician mobility is common in the motherland as well as in the diaspora. In Turkey, the employment of *abdals* migrating as "seasonal workers" to other provinces is a typical phenomenon, as is province-city mobility. In Ghent, often supralocal or international musicians are employed (from other diasporic centres in Europe or from Turkey). International mobility is two-way and often involves the aspiration to make a career in Turkey, by way of international recognition beyond the limited diaspora context.

Contemporary Musical Characteristics

The ways in which Turkish folk music is embedded in musical events are quite similar in the motherland and the diaspora. When Turkish folk music is combined with other musical genres and art forms, this is done in a similar fashion in Turkey and in Belgium. However, programmes exclusively consisting of folk music are more common in Turkey, often even confined to music of the region where the event takes place. In Ghent, Turkish folk music is often combined with other genres, and the combination of folk music from different regions of Turkey is standard. *Özgün müzik* and Alevi music are typical in the context of *türkü* bars, which are often left-wing in Turkey. Diasporic *türkü* bars appear to display more variation in musical genres. Music from Central Anatolia (more particularly Kırşehir and Ankara, and the music of Neşet Ertaş) is universally popular, featuring in festive settings in Turkey as well as in the diaspora. Typical for the specific diaspora context of Ghent is the popularity of the music of Emirdağ. Aşık Veysel's (Alevi) music is very popular as well. The largest part of the performed repertoire belongs to the official TRT archive, which is nevertheless approached in an unconstrained way, outside the context of academic or academically informed performances. Typical events (quasi) exclusively involving Turkish folk music are wedding parties, circumcision parties, *cem* ceremonies, and rural festivals.

Folk music events usually display a flexible line-up. The much propagated and standardized *bağlama*, and the "oriental" synthesizer are the preferred instruments to accompany the (largely vocal) Turkish folk music. In Turkey, this instrumental duo is often complemented by the fixed combination of *davul* and *zurna*, less common in Ghent, and if absent replaced by synthesizer samples. Non-Turkish instruments such as guitar and different kinds of percussion appear to be more commonly used in Ghent than in Turkey. The semi-electric *bağlama*, accompanied by other electr(on)ic instruments, has become the standard in many (non-academic and non-traditional) public performances – more than the real *elektrosaz*. The use of electr(on)ic instruments affects the musical idiom and belongs to lightly and heavily popularized poly-cultural performance styles. Other poly-cultural performance styles occurring in Turkey and the diaspora involve the adoption of elements from Western classical, jazz, or world music. Mono-cultural (either rural-traditional or urban-standardized) performance styles are more common in Turkey than in the diaspora. Certain events, such as rural festivals, typically involve a mixture of traditional and popularized performance styles. Throughout the diverse performance styles, the "superstructural" elements (mode, melody, text) are largely retained, while the "substructural" elements change. The use of quarter-tones is standard, despite the fact that official folk music theory and notation are based on a nine-comma system. Twelve-tone equal temperament has exerted significant influence on the tuning system of Turkish instruments. Folk music performance usually proceeds in a (more or less) improvisatory way; compositional aspects occur but are bound to certain kinds of events and settings.

The musical developments affecting Turkish folk music throughout the twentieth and twenty-first century correspond to larger global-glocal musical evolutions. The developments discussed by Shiloah and Cohen (1983) in the context of Jewish Middle Eastern music are fully applicable to Turkish folk music as well: loss of intimacy and introduction of the stage, introduction of new instruments, playing techniques and electronic amplification, introduction of large ensembles and their influence on the kind of music performed, introduction of notation and the Western education system, limitations on the length of musical pieces, and an increase in the importance of independent instrumental music. In terms of the conceptual framework developed by Nettl (1985), Turkish folk music has adopted the most typical Western traits (tonal harmony, large ensembles, notation, composition, and defined length), has experienced "consolidation" as well as "diversification" (which in this context are no longer contradictory), and has witnessed reduction/impoverishment, the reintroduction of non-Western elements in a new form, and peaceful coexistence of styles (also termed "compartmentalization" by Merriam in 1964). Referring to the framework of Shiloah and Cohen, the current types of Turkish folk music performance can be placed under the categories of "traditional", "neotraditional", and "popular" if intraculturally oriented, and "ethnic fine" and "fine" if transculturally oriented. The categories of "conserved" and "museumized" music are intraculturally oriented in the Turkish case.

Contemporary Musical Functions

The performance of Turkish folk music has constantly been acquiring new functions in connection with changing uses, contexts, and settings, and in relation to the diverging sociocultural contexts of the motherland and the diaspora. The original functions, in many cases reflected in the lyrics, are often replaced by new functions, anchored in the fundamental social changes occurring throughout the twentieth and twenty-first century.

The observed functions of (the performance of) Turkish folk music in the early twenty-first century are largely similar in the motherland and in the diaspora. They cover a broad spectrum and can be grouped into more or less distinct, but mutually interlinked, fields of functioning: a personal, social, cultural, philosophical-spiritual, and ritual field (the latter overlapping with all other fields), and the personal-social and social-cultural intersections. In reference to the framework developed by van Maanen, the different functions can be characterized as intrinsic, semi-intrinsic, or extrinsic.

The personal field concerns the semi-intrinsic psychological function (which can involve the expression or induction of feelings or thoughts, the induction of past feelings or events, and the induction of energy or rest) and the intrinsic aesthetic function (the induction of an aesthetic experience, which can be decorative, comfortable, or challenging, cf. van Maanen 2010). The social field involves the extrinsic function of the creation or reinforcement of social ties, and the semi-intrinsic political function (the expression of political views). The determination of the political function of music is a complex matter and should consider different levels and forms of "politics" (Street 2012). The cultural field involves the semi-intrinsic functions of the communication of emotional, cultural, or historical content, and the preservation or transmission of cultural heritage. The personal-social field involves the semi-intrinsic function of the communication of feelings or thoughts, the intrinsic function of the induction of dance, and the extrinsic professional function. The professional function, concerning the performers, involves the earning of a living and the realization of the self as a professional individual. The social-cultural field involves the semi-intrinsic function of the expression or construction of identity, whether culturally defined or not. This function receives an extra dimension in the diaspora; the expression or construction of identity in interaction with the new sociocultural context can be described as "intercultural" function. "Identity" is never definitive but always in motion and is actively constructed through "negotiation" with or "positioning" in the sociocultural context. Identification is multiple and possibly discordant; it can occur on many different levels, such as the virtual level of Turkish culture as a whole, or regional, religious, or ethnic-linguistic subcultures. A useful conceptualization is the juxtaposition of ("horizontal") affiliation and ("vertical") filiation (Said 1983), involving fluid boundaries. Identity expression or construction is not limited to individuals or groups, but can also be institutionalized: the specific identity of the Turkish associations in Germany (Greve 2006), and to a certain degree in Ghent, is reflected in their musical preference. Moreover, cultural or musical identification is closely linked to emancipation in society, and can easily acquire political dimensions, as in the case of Alevi or Kurdish music. The philosophical-spiritual field, finally, involves the semi-intrinsic functions of the induction of a mystical or religious experience, and the induction of feelings of solidarity, humanity, or philanthropy. The ritual field concerns the intrinsic or semi-intrinsic function of the ritual accompaniment of life-cycle events (rites of passage) and other important events. During such events, the ritual function can be alternated with personal-social, cultural, or other functions.

The identified functions of Turkish folk music in present-day Turkey and the diaspora show that many parallels exist between the two larger contexts. In many cases, musical performance adopts a culture-independent role, for example, when it functions on a personal or a social level. Although identity expression or construction is a typical musical function, it is not the most important one: a broad spectrum of functions is not identity-related, even when identification is recognized as multiple – involving even more layers in the diaspora than in the motherland. It becomes clear that in the diaspora, many original functions (originating in the sociocultural context of the motherland) are maintained, while new ones are added, or different accents are placed within existing ones, depending on the changed sociocultural context. This applies, for example, to the professional, political, and cultural field of functioning. Intercombinations of different functions are highly common and occurred in all observed events. The interrelation of the different combined functions can also vary according to the broader sociocultural context. An example is participation in a *cem* ceremony, which involves religious, social, and cultural functions (and reflects religious and cultural identities) in the diaspora, but additionally implies a political emancipative action in Turkey.

Interrelations

The study of contemporary manifestations of Turkish folk music in a transnational context has pointed towards certain interrelations between the different aspects of musical performances: the context, the actors involved, the performed music, and its functions. The identified interrelations belong to the time-bound (early twenty-first-century) picture presented in this book. They are not absolute or definitive but can be subject to changes and evolutions. Certain interrelations display differences in the diasporan context compared to the motherland. Two- and three-part sets of relations are abundant; four-part sets of relations are less easily identified and belong to well-defined types of musical events. Three examples are provided below:

1. The context, actors, music, and function pertaining to *cem* ceremonies are strongly interconnected, and their interrelation is relatively stable, even transnationally. *Cem* ceremonies take place in a protected environment (be it a specific *cem* house or a private home), preferably on a Thursday or Friday evening, and exclusively involve Alevis (usually belonging to a local community) in the roles of performer (*zakir/aşık*), commissioner (*dede*), and listener-participant. The performed music is well-defined and consists of traditional sung prayers and ritual dances accompanied on the *bağlama*. The function of the musical performance is mainly religious, with cultural and social – and (in Turkey) sometimes political – connotations. The interrelation is maintained in the diaspora, although the location (contextual aspect) sometimes differs, and the political connotation (functional aspect) is absent.

2. Musical performance during wedding and circumcision parties mainly fulfils a ritual function (ritual accompaniment of life-cycle events), alternated with personal, social, or cultural functions. The involved people are Turkish families on the one hand (adopting the role of commissioner-employer, and constituting a large part of the guests-listeners), and external professional musicians on the other hand (often but not exclusively belonging to a specific sociocultural group, such as the Roma or *abdals*). The music usually involves local and Central Anatolian folk dances, in a traditional *davul-zurna* version as well as in a popularized performance style. In the diaspora, the interrelation is largely maintained but approached in an undogmatic way, based on availability of the involved factors. Any

type of (semi-)professional performer can be employed, the sound of acoustic *davul* and *zurna* can be substituted by their synthetized variant, and the folk music repertoire can originate in all regions of Turkey and be complemented by (Western) popular music.

3.   So-called *türkü* nights involve a constellation of clearly interrelated aspects limited to the motherland context. This kind of musical event takes place in urban Turkey in specific venues known as *türkü* bars. The people involved (the barkeeper performing the role of commissioner, the invited musician(s), and the customers-listeners) often have leftist sympathies and/or adhere to Alevism. The performed music – slightly popularized Turkish folk songs (largely belonging to the Alevi repertoire) and *özgün müzik* – often conveys a political critical message. The function of the musical performance is thus political, as well as personal, cultural, and social. In the diaspora, this specific constellation is not parallelled: *türkü* bars and their public and music do not possess a clear political affiliation.

Other examples of interrelations include the transnationally similar events of a mother singing to her baby and a relative lamenting a deceased person (involving fixed contexts, actors, functions, and musical repertoires), and the motherland-bound event of sunrise *davul* playing during Ramadan (involving a fixed context, function, kind of music, target public, and musician type).

Past, Present, and Future of Turkish Folk Music "between Ghent and Turkey"

Turkish folk music – with all its diverse manifestations and conceptualizations – is still a vital part of Turkish culture, in its motherland as well as in the diaspora. The nationalist cultural project of the Turkish Republic, with folk music as one of its central foci, has fundamentally affected not only the ways in which folk music is conceived of and practised in contemporary Turkey, but also its societal resonance and position. This influence stretches to the Turkish diaspora in Belgium, which has been developing in constant and ever-increasing interaction with the motherland. In Turkey, a predisposition for the preservation, transmission, and further development of the folk music heritage can be found in all sections of society – the state and its institutions, as well as civil society and private associations. It has become clear throughout this book that parts of the cultural reforms have indeed been "absorbed" and "domesticated" at a local level in Turkey, and that this situation has been transferred (in a modified form) to the diaspora as well.

The Turkish diaspora in Ghent and Belgium mirrors the motherland "model" in many respects. This imitative tendency is situated on diverse levels, and involves among other things the structures of musical events (e.g., the length and course of programmes, the presence of hierarchy and officializing interventions in the form of speeches), musical aspects (e.g., repertoires, performance styles, instruments), behaviour and social relations of the involved people (performers, commissioners, listeners), and place-related contextual aspects (e.g., idiosyncratically decorated *türkü* bars and party halls, central city locations). Other aspects of the motherland's folk music production and consumption are either involuntarily or deliberately transformed into a diasporic variant. Examples of involuntary adaptations include the ad hoc transformation of a room in a cultural centre into a *cem* "house" and hiring a leisure park to accommodate the diasporic counterpart to a *yayla* festival. An example of deliberately or purposefully performed adaptations is the broadening of the musical programme and ideological orientation of diasporic *türkü* bars. Larger sociocultural developments with an impact on music occurring in Turkey during the past 50 years, such as a more positive assessment of music-making in general (by lay people and women), and of the music of ethnocultural minorities, have been paralleled in the diaspora as well.

Observable differences between indigenous and diasporic Turkish folk music manifestations reflect the social-societal, cultural, political, demographic, geographical, and even climatological conditions of the respective contexts. The creation and moulding of a context for musical production and consumption within the given circumstances of their new environment has been a constant undertaking of the Turkish (post-)migrants in Ghent. This process has led to the seemingly paradoxical combination of increased integration and interconnectedness with the Belgian context on the one hand, and increased self-sufficiency and independence on the other hand.

The strong diasporic focus on and reaction to the musical evolutions (and linked sociocultural developments) in Turkey have been facilitated by the development of diverse channels of transnational and global connectivity, such as international mobility of people and goods, and virtual contact via communication media (satellite TV, internet, etc.). The increased accessibility of devices for home recording is an additional catalyst. Musician mobility and exchange is significant in the context of the transnational relation between the Turkish diaspora in Ghent and the motherland. This phenomenon possesses bidirectional aspects. On the one hand, visits by professional singers and instrumentalists from Turkey to Belgium in the context of formally or informally organized performances or workshops create interesting opportunities for active (participative, collaborative) or passive learning by diasporic amateur or (semi-)professional musicians. On the other hand, visits by ambitious diasporic musicians to Turkey (in particular, Istanbul or Ankara) in order to give concerts, appear in TV contests or programmes, or attend professionalizing music courses, raise their status and possibly increase their opportunities in the home (i.e., diasporic) context. Some musicians even literally live in two countries. In this way, multi-sited and multi-layered translocal and transnational networks are created, and the concepts of "global homes" and "networks of homes" are realized.

Many musicians of the Turkish diaspora in Ghent seek transnational (or at least translocal) resonance. One way of characterizing or categorizing diasporic musicians is to position them in a multidimensional field defined by two distinct tendencies (axes or continua): intracultural versus transcultural, and local versus translocal reach. Turkish musicians in Ghent aim for translocal and transnational reach more often than for transcultural reach (be it on a local or translocal level). Only a minority of the Turkish folk musicians in Ghent has entered the "general" Belgian folk or world music circuit. This points to the aforementioned "ethnic boundary" between the Turkish and mainstream populations. This symbolic and social boundary influences the ways in which the Turks are socioculturally and musically incorporated in the Ghent context. In response to the still prevailing "othering" tendencies, various options are taken, ranging from consciously employing ethnic/oriental/exotic coding, over emphasizing multiculturalism, to refusing ethnic coding, or taking the intracultural turn by addressing their own group. These options are taken by Turkish (and other) individual actors and organizations and determine the ways in which Turkish folk music is integrated into the musical landscape of the city. The factual result is the coexistence of the various types of musical events examined in this book, featuring music situated somewhere on the continuum from Turkish to Western-cosmopolitan genres, and attended by audiences situated somewhere on the continuum from (quasi) exclusively Turkish to (quasi) exclusively Belgian composition.

The choices made by the Turkish actors are manifestations of the strategic (or potentially polemic) and reflexive character of the ways in which diasporic identities are created. Diasporic musicians – be it on an individual or collective basis – are challenged to find a position for themselves (and their groups) in the complex multilevel diasporic field of tension consisting of the Belgian/Flemish majority population, other present (ethnic-)cultural minority populations, (religious, political-ideological, regional, ethnic, generational, social…) subgroups within their own population, and the surrounding globalizing or cosmopolitanizing world context. Identification is always multiple, possibly contradictory, and in constant transformation, whether in an indigenous or a diasporan context. The heterogeneity and hybridity of Turkish people are not limited to diasporic subjects but apply equally yet differently to the people in Turkey. The repositioning of Turkish subjects into the Belgian context entails a shift in the way they can articulate their identities: levels related to the Turkish sociocultural context disappear and are replaced by new levels related to the diasporic sociocultural context. Subgroups within the population of Turkey with a sensitive relationship vis-à-vis identity expression and construction in the homeland, largely lose their relevance in Belgium, where the internal heterogeneity of the Turkish population is not recognized by the majority. Subgroup expression or emancipation is only functioning as an agency within a Turkish frame of reference, which recognizes the internal diversity. This has been illustrated in this book by the cases of the political or rather cultural-religious emancipation of Alevis, the leftist or rather neutral orientation of *türkü* bars, and the different conceptions of urban festivals in Turkey and in Ghent (*abdal*-oriented and featuring traditional local music in Turkey, or rather broadly oriented and featuring popularized music from all over Turkey in Belgium).

In my view, only from the moment the basic level of emancipation of the Turkish population "as a whole" is achieved in Belgium will room be created for more nuanced identity expression, and the "transcultural capital" of the Turkish musicians in Belgium will fully be put into action. Only under these conditions will the richness and diversity of the Turkish folk music repertoire – be it traditionally performed or interpreted in new and hybridizing ways – be revealed, and will meaningful openings towards artistic development and experimentation be created. As is the case in contemporary Turkey, where the performance of Turkish folk music, depending on the personal choices made by the musicians, is equally able to articulate all imaginable nuances of "self-conscious traditionality" (Bryant 2005) or "new modern Turkish identity" (Ustuner, Ger, and Holt 2000), Turkish folk music in its broadest sense has the potential to become a powerful medium for sociocultural incorporation. At the same time, the diaspora – with its sociocultural structure differing from the motherland context – has the capacity to develop further into an effective platform for the emancipation of minorities such as Kurds, Alevis, and other ethnic-linguistic, cultural, and religious subgroups. Kurdish- and

Laz-language music as well as the Alevi repertoire are already established components of Turkish concerts, parties, and other musical events in Ghent – albeit not always perceived (even by the Turkish public) as possessing identity-related or emancipative connotations. Further recognition and institutionalization of Turkish folk music, its genres, repertoires, and instruments, not only by the Belgian social and sociocultural establishment, but also – beyond that – by the cultural and (music-)educational establishment, is to be anticipated. Examples to follow and lessons to learn can be found in some neighbouring countries, with Germany as a dynamic and experienced case (Seidlitz 2017).

Outlook

Several of the gaps regarding music and musicking in Turkey, the Turkish diaspora, and the transnational field, identified in the Introduction, have been addressed in the chapters of this book. It represents an (at least partial) response to some propositions made by authoritative Turkish music scholars. Martin Stokes, in 1992, proposed to explore "[t]he extent to which [the state] reforms have been absorbed, 'domesticated' and attained a degree of autonomy at local level" (1992a: 8–9), while Martin Greve, 25 years later, has pointed to the lack of "serious debate in Turkey on [what he calls] an aesthetic crisis of Turkish music" (2017: 13), the need for unideological "research on musical styles and stylistic differences based on musical analysis", and the underdeveloped state of fields such as "the perception and reception of music, …, sociology of music, and … didactic of music" (2017: 13, 255, 265).

The Turkish presence in the city of Ghent is particular in its size (up to 10% of the population) as well as in its constitution (mostly originating in the West Anatolian town of Emirdağ). Notwithstanding Belgium's intense and fascinating migration history, this book pioneers as a published study of (post-)migrant music and musicking in the country. This paucity of interest and research stands out in contrast to the academic involvement in (post-)migrant and Turkish music in other countries, such as Germany. The music of Emirdağ is also an understudied area, treated in a subchapter of this book, and the subject of my video documentary *Emirdağ Vatanımız Elimiz – Emirdağ, onze thuis, ons volk* (available through https://youtu.be/nUwEL0-my-8). Other contributions to Turkish music scholarship include the evaluation of TRT discourses and practices, and the detailed transcription and analysis of musical examples and performance styles.

This book has explored, described, interpreted, and linked musical, contextual, and functional aspects of the manifestations of Turkish folk music in contemporary Turkey and a specific diasporan context in Belgium. Its unique multi-sited, transnational comparative outlook not only identifies "commonalities and 'universals'", but also "theoriz[es] about cultural differences and social transformations" (Testa 2019: 6). The inclusion of rural and small-town contexts, inextricably tied to the transnational realities of Turkish-Belgian migration and diasporization, generates important additional narratives. It is my hope that this study, anchored in detailed ethnographic reality, has contributed to the expansion of our views on what Turkish folk music signifies in the early twenty-first century, and it has added to the apprehension and appreciation of this broad, multifaceted, and topical musical genre.

Notes

Preface and Acknowledgements

1   This book grew out of a PhD project (2008–14), made possible by the financial support of the Research Fund of University College Ghent. The institutional support provided by Ghent University and University College Ghent was of great importance. I am very thankful for the team of supervisors and doctoral advisers whose guidance and feedback gave me direction and confidence. Especially, I would like to thank my Ghent University supervisor Prof. Francis Maes for his steady, supportive, and relaxed mentorship. Prof. Katia Segers and Prof. Emer. Rik Pinxten disclosed valuable sociological and anthropological perspectives relating to my subject. I am also indebted to my dissertation reading committee and doctoral examination board, presided by Prof. Marc Leman.

Introduction

1   The notion "Turkish" is defined by the Oxford English Dictionary Online as "of, pertaining or belonging to the Turks or to Turkey". The Turks are defined as "a ... family of the human race, occupying from prehistoric times large parts of central Asia, and speaking a language and dialects belonging to the Turkic ... branch of the Ural-Altaic ... linguistic family". The "contrast between how much the Turkic peoples have in common linguistically and how diverse they are in other ways" is a key issue in questions of unity and diversity (Findley 2005: 224). The heterogeneity of the Turkic people is equally valid for the population of the Republic of Turkey, which consists of a mix of ethnically or linguistically diverse "Turkish" and "non-Turkish" people. The Seljuk Turks conquered the territory of present-day Turkey (a part of the Byzantine Empire) in the eleventh century; Constantinople was taken by the Ottomans in 1453. The substratum of other diverse preceding peoples and civilizations is still present in Turkey's demography and culture. Claims of "pure Turkishness" in Turkey or the adherence to pan-Turkism in Central Asia are based on ideology rather than reality.

After the foundation of the Turkish Republic (1923), Atatürk's goal was to establish a strong national identity, breaking with the multinational nature of the former Ottoman Empire. This consciousness of Turkish nationhood was obtained through a purposive policy, aiming at the assimilation of ethnic, linguistic, religious, and cultural minorities. This process affected the society of Turkey in a profound way, but never succeeded completely. In present-day Turkey, Turkish is the lingua franca while other languages are more or less marginalized. After the Turkish language, Kurdish is the second most important language in Turkey, still persisting as the mother tongue of up to one-fifth of the total population (Ergil 2000). Religious minorities, such as (Orthodox) Christians, Jews, and the Shiite Alevis, are still in a relatively weak position. The hybrid nature of the society and culture of present-day Turkey makes it difficult to neatly distinguish between "Turkish" and "non-Turkish" people or cultural expressions. Therefore, in this book, the notion "Turkish" will be used to mean "belonging to Turkey", as such taking into account the hybridity of the cultural production grounded in diverse ethnic, linguistic, and cultural substrates.

2   Other terminology indicating the same repertoire includes *geleneksel halk müziği* ("traditional folk music"), *yöresel müzik* ("regional music"), or simply *türküler* ("folk songs").

3   The symbolic instrumentalization of the *bağlama* is by no means straightforward, but multidimensional and even ambivalent, as it is associated with different, sometimes conflictuous, groups and repertoires belonging to the Turkish/ Turkic cultural past and present (Seidlitz 2017; Varlı and Sari 2017: 303–4).

4   By way of comparison: ca. 4% of the population of Antwerp, and almost 5% of the population of Brussels has a Turkish origin ("Diversiteit in Alle Districten" 2014; "Portaal Vreemde Afkomst" 2014). Berlin, the city with the largest Turkish diaspora in the world, accommodates approximately 5% Turks ("Statistischer Bericht: Einwohnerinnen und Einwohner im Land Berlin am 31. Dezember 2013" 2014).

5   Ramnarine 2007; Levi and Scheding 2010; Kiwan and Meinhof 2011; Toynbee and Dueck 2011; Krüger and Trandafoiu 2014; Sardinha and Campos 2016.

6   Reinhard 1987; Uysal 2001; Kaya 2002; Greve 2006; Klebe 2008; Klebe 2009; Güney, Pekman, and Kabaş 2014; Güran Aydin 2016; Seidlitz 2017.

7   E.g., Agirdag, Van Avermaet, and Van Houtte 2013; Beirens and Fontaine 2011; Ben-Rafael and Ben-Rafael 2009; De Bock 2012; De Bock 2013; Goossens 2004; Keten 2002; Küçükcan 2007; Manço 2000; Schoonvaere 2013; Surkyn 1993; Swyngedouw, Delwit, and Rea 2005; Van Kerckem 2014; Van Kerckem, Van de Putte and Stevens 2013; Van Kerckem, Van der Bracht et al. 2013; Vanmeerhaeghe 2013; Vanparys 2002; Verhaeghe, Van der Bracht, and Van de Putte 2012; Yalçin et al. 2006.

8   Cocriamont 2016; Devos 1997; Van Hees 2000; Van Lancker et al. 2009; Van Maele 2008.

9   Martin Greve argues that "the state never succeeded in gaining control over the entire national music life, but rather only over state institutions" and emphasizes the importance of private and public actors and the influence of the media (2017: 246).

10   While English-language source material is still rather limited, Turkish-language sources sometimes consciously or unconsciously involve ideological or political (e.g., nationalistic) agendas, and contradictions are an inherent part of the literature.

11   Although the comparative perspective (motherland versus diaspora) applied in this book would also benefit from a quantitative approach, the qualitative method used in this study allows one to gain insight into the rich details and mechanisms of the ways in which Turkish folk music manifests itself musically, contextually, and functionally in both contexts.

12   In order to define the research contexts in Turkey that were relevant, from a comparative perspective, to the specific context and properties of the urban Turkish diaspora in Ghent, I used two different methods. The first consisted of identifying the regions to which the music performed in Ghent mainly belonged, first by asking the musicians and later by discerning this information from the performed repertoire based on experience. The second method was to ask musicians about the Turkish folk pieces or songs that they themselves or others most often performed.

13   The selection of Turkish folk music performances to be attended was made on the basis of purposive or selective sampling, a non-probability sampling technique. The type of purposive sampling applied here was maximum variation sampling (or diversity sampling or heterogeneity sampling). In this kind of approach, analysis and case selection typically happen simultaneously, and the selection of cases finishes when saturation is reached (when almost no new information is being added) (Lund Research 2012).

Chapter 1

1   A concentration of certain groups of people (e.g., ethnic minorities) into particular areas of a city is called an "enclave" if two conditions are met: (1) persistent socio-economic deprivation and genesis of an "ethnic economy", (2) strong institutional expansion and diversification of services (their own bars, places of worship, clubs, doctors, lawyers, brokers, media, retail, etc.) (Verhaeghe et al. 2012: 17–19).

2   Later editions only provide combined figures for Turkey and the Maghreb.

3   These figures include the people of whom the Turkish nationality is the oldest non-Belgian nationality, and the people still living with their parents of which the oldest non-Belgian nationality of the mother (or the father) is Turkish.

4   This information is derived from figures provided by the City of Ghent (2012).

5   This section is based on my article published in Dutch in *Brood en Rozen* (Sels 2014).

6   This form of support entails the risk of discontinuity, evident from the fact that several Turkish organizations only survived for a short period of time.

7   Based on Ateşli, i/v, 5 February 2014; Avşar, i/v, 12 February 2014; De Gendt, email to author, 8 February 2014; Demirkaya, i/v, 6 February 2014; Edeer, i/v, 6 February 2014; Sezer, email to author, 12 February 2014.

8   "Ibıdık" was the nickname given to the pater familias, Isa Demirkaya, during his childhood years in Emirdağ, and the name "Ibıdıklar" ("the Ibıdıks") graced the banner behind the music group during each of their performances.

9   Originally a mystical religious group settling in Anatolia from Khorasan (current Iran, Afghanistan, and Turkmenistan) during the twelfth century, which became associated with the Alevi-Bektashi form of Shiism.

10 The Gentse Feesten is a large-scale, ten-day annual festival supported by the city with concerts, theatre performances, and other activities in the streets and venues of Ghent. More details about the programming can be found at http://www.gentsefeesten.be.

11 Based on Audooren 1994: 23, 28–29, 31; Coşgun 2013; De Gendt, i/v, 6 December 2013; De Gendt 2014: 91, 124, 205; Avşar, i/v, 12 February 2014; Sezer, email to author, 12 February 2014; Alcı, i/v, 13 February 2014; Çırık, i/v, 24 February 2014; Ozan, i/v, 26 February 2014; Tapmaz, i/v, 26 February 2014; Ünal, i/v, 21 February 2014; Maréchal, i/v, 5 March 2014; De Leeuw, i/v, 10 March 2014; Wymeersch, i/v, 14 March 2014.

12 According to some informants, the Turkish musicians might have come from Turkey.

13 Flemish folk singer, sculptor, painter, and co-founder of the modern Gentse Feesten.

14 A short video report on one of the first large Turkish wedding parties in Ghent was made by Jean Daskalides in 1977, featuring Ozanlar as the band. It can be viewed on YouTube: https://youtu.be/BX-uBT6LqP0.

15 The mosque is situated in the Kazemattenstraat in a Turkish neighbourhood.

16 Based on Avşar, i/v, 12 February 2014; Çırık, i/v, 24 February 2014; Edeer, i/v, 6 February 2014; Yücesan, i/v, 5 February 2014.

17 Based on Çırık, i/v, 24 February 2014; Devreese 2014a, 2014b, 2014c; Toplar, i/v, 12 February 2014.

18 *Beraber* means "together".

19 Jong is a private youth welfare organization in Ghent, subsidized by the City of Ghent and other authorities.

20 Kom-Pas is a reception service for newcomers in Ghent, providing integration trajectories and other kinds of support to newcomers.

21 *Seda* means "voice".

22   Based on Dökmetaş, Facebook post, 17 December 2011; Lootens, i/v, 3 February 2014; Posman, i/v, 5 February 2014; Yücesan, i/v, 5 February 2014; Edeer, i/v, 6 February 2014; Toplar, i/v, 12 February 2014.

23   "Turkish Hearths" are Turkish nationalist cultural associations with a long history, which existed even before the foundation of the Turkish Republic in 1923. There are 77 departments in almost all provinces in Turkey. See http://www.turkocagi.org.tr.

24   Based on Vercoutere 2005; Beyaert 2010; Bakıroğlu, i/v, 23 March 2011, 5 February 2014; "Istanbul Ekspres Belçika Gent'te" 2013, "Istanbul Ekspres Gent Belçika" 2013, "Türk Konserleri – Turkse Concerten" 2014; Lootens, i/v, 3 February 2014; Posman, i/v, 5 February 2014; Yücesan, i/v, 5 February 2014; Maréchal, i/v, 5 March 2014.

25   Ottoman classical suite of vocal and instrumental pieces in a particular *makam*, or modern or popular derivative of this kind of suite.

26   Literally "unique, original, authentic music"; a kind of alternative music or left-ist protest music developed in the 1960s and 1970s, with a musical idiom close to that of traditional folk music.

27   The reason behind this closure was an unfortunate car accident in which the owner/president became paralysed.

28   Based on Avşar, i/v, 12 February 2014.

29   Based on Ateşli, i/v, 5 February 2014; Demirkaya, i/v, 6 February 2014; Edeer, i/v, 6 February 2014; Sezer, email to author, 12 February 2014; Çırık, i/v, 24 February 2014; Ozan, i/v, 26 February 2014.

30   Martin Greve provides more historical context (2017: 46).

31   The gender division was less important in certain subcultures, particularly in Alevi communities.

Chapter 2

1   The "hub" concept, as used by Kiwan and Meinhof, is an alternative conceptu-alization of this phenomenon (2011: 6–7).

2   Hannerz terms the totality of roles performed by an individual as the individual's "role repertoire", while the totality of roles performed in the studied community – e.g., the Turkish folk music network in Ghent – is called the "role inventory" (1980: 102).

3   The nuance between "organizer" and "employer" lies in the economic connota-tion of the role of "employer": providing some kind of remuneration. An "orga-nizer", on the other hand, is involved in the practical organization of a setting in which Turkish folk music can be performed and commissions the musician(s) to play. The term "patron" designates a person who supports an artist on a regular basis or for a long term and provides significant financial or material support, creating possibilities that would be otherwise nonexistent.

4   Lokeren is situated in the province of East-Flanders, 20km from Ghent. As of 2012, the city has a population of approximately 40,000 and accommodates almost 2,000 people of Turkish descent, representing ca. 5% of the population. Turks constitute the second largest ethnocultural minority after the Moroccans (Noppe 2014b).

5   Hıdırellez is a traditional, transculturally celebrated festival ritually marking the revival of nature and the arrival of summer. It celebrates the allegorical meeting of the prophets Hıdır and İliyas. The festival takes place on 23 April or 6 May, depending on the calendar used. It is also known as Saint-George's Day in Eastern Europe ("Nomination File No. 01006" 2013).

6   Historically, deaneries were official neighbourhood authorities dependent on the parishes. Nowadays they are transformed into secular associations of local shopkeepers and residents, their function being primarily social and cultural, and partly commercial ("Geschiedenis van de Dekenij Patershol" 2014; "Home" 2014).

7   *Hoca* was originally a religious title for spiritual masters, but its meaning has shifted towards the broader sense of "teacher" (religious or general). A tendency towards further trivialization of the term exists: nowadays it is often used in everyday language to address persons with (a little) more knowledge in a particular subject than average people. In the field of music, the level to be reached in order to be called a *hoca* is still lower in the diaspora than in Turkey.

8   The city of Sint-Niklaas is situated in the province of East-Flanders, 30km from Ghent, and has a population of approximately 73,000, of which around 2500 people have origins in EU candidate countries (almost exclusively Turkey). This represents approximately 3.4% of the total population. As was the case in Lokeren, the Moroccans are the largest ethnocultural minority in Sint-Niklaas, followed by the Turks (Noppe 2014c).

9   This reality is confirmed by the quantitative study conducted by Sabri Uysal among the Turks living in the German area of North Rhine-Westphalia. Only 14.3% of the interviewed individual musicians, and 11.8% of the members of musical ensembles, indicated musicianship as their main occupation (Uysal 2001: 51).

10 Based on Edeer, i/v, 7 May 2011; Edeer, i/v, 6 February 2014; Avşar, i/v, 12 February 2014; Sels 2011a; 2011b.

11 This distinction is paralleled by Slobin's conceptualization of "intra-community" versus "inter-community" (1992: 46), and that of Sağlam of "locals" ("intracultural" or "co-ethnic") versus "cosmopolitans" (interacting) (2008: 38–39).

12 This framework was developed in the context of my chapter "Mixing Multiple Tracks: Migration, Diaspora and Transcultural Music in Flanders" in the edited volume *Made in the Low Countries*, published by Routledge in 2017 (Sels 2017: 39–41).

13   See Klebe (2009: 300) for a definition of the three categories based on the framework provided by the European Commission and the UNESCO.

14   Description based on observations during participation in the *bağlama* beginners course taught by Iskender Arıcı in De Centrale (2008–2009).

15   Description based on observations during participation in the lessons led by Bekir Gürbüz, a *bağlama* player and singer, in Muzikantenhuis (2008–2009), and the observation of a lesson by Tuğrul Yücesan in the non-profit organization Özburun (2010).

16   Based on observations during private *bağlama* lessons with Tuğrul Yücesan in Muzikantenhuis (2008–2009).

17   TLS is a concept that originated in Irish folk music learning practices.

18   Kraankindersstraat 2, 9000 Ghent – www.decentrale.be.

19   An in-depth assessment of the phenomenon of *türkü* bars (and their older forms *türkü evleri*) can be found in Aslı Kayhan's article, "Musical Changes of Rural to Urban in Popular Culture. A Case Study: Türkü Bars in Istanbul" (2014).

20   This music café was located at Sleepstraat 141, 9000 Ghent. Currently, it has been turned into a gala and bridal clothing shop, run by the same owner, Fakı Edeer.

21   Dampoortstraat 50, 9000 Ghent – www.muzikantenhuis.be.

22   www.facebook.com/MizrapVzw.

Chapter 3

1   An illustration of the intensity of the debate is the congress organized by the Istanbul Technical University in 2008 on the subject, and the proceedings published afterwards: see Bayhan (2008).

2   Turkish folk music scholar, collector, educator, performer; central representative of the official institutionalized and professional folk music approach of the Turkish Republic.

3   Musicologist, educator and composer, educated in France and Germany.

4   Non-metrical music in Turkey does have metrical properties, only not in the Western sense of musical metre. It is related to the metrical structure of the text.

5   Teacher and head of the voice training department of the Turkish Music State Conservatory of Ege University in Izmir.

6   Notwithstanding the problems of a regionally-oriented approach, categorization of the folk music of Turkey along the lines of the seven larger geographical regions is still established on all levels of Turkish folk music discourse. The categories are maintained in scholarly as well as non-academic contexts, by musicians and theoreticians alike, in Turkey as well as the diaspora.

7   The *zeybek* is a dignified, gracious symbolic dance from the Aegean Sea region linked to a culture of resistance against the Ottoman authorities during periods of war or repression. The *efeler* (leaders) and the *zeybekler* (members) belonged

to a kind of guerrilla troop. The music is in slow or moderate tempo with a rhythm of nine beats.

8 At the same time, this distinction is relativized on the basis of two facts: cities in themselves unite people from different social classes who have their proper places in the city fabric, and there is and has been a lot of contact between the city and the villages (Emnalar 1998: 222).

9 According to Ayvas Başaran, representative of the *abdal* culture of Kırşehir, at present approximately 2000 musician-*abdals* are active in the province of Kırşehir, of which 500 dwell in the province capital itself (i/v, 27 July 2012).

10 Alevi rules of life are arranged into a system consisting of four "gates", each containing ten rules. The four gates, the "gate of the Sharia", the "gate of the religious order", the "gate of merit", and the "gate of truth" lead to offices situated in the fields (levels) of "friendship", "leadership", "mentorship", and "love" (Ayışıt Onatça 2007: 25–27).

11 This adds to the paradoxicality of the *bağlama*'s "place within the republic": the instrument "is supposed to represent a religion that is regarded with mistrust by a nation which also claims to be represented by this same instrument" (Seidlitz 2017: 397).

12 In 2014, I made the documentary movie *Emirdağ Vatanımız Elimiz* about the music from Emirdağ and its villages, which can be viewed on YouTube: https://youtu.be/nUwEL0-my-8.

13 More information about the Byzantine city Amorium/Amorion and its present-day archaeological site can be found at https://amoriumexcavations.org/site/.

14 The Alevi population in the town itself consists largely of the *abdal* families.

15 In Emirdağ, the *abdals* are usually referred to by the name *ede*, originally meaning "big brother".

16 I interviewed 11 musicians (presenting themselves and functioning primarily as artists) in March 2010, using a semi-structured survey. The group consisted of one Belgian and nine Turkish musicians primarily involved with Turkish folk music, and one Turkish musician chiefly focusing on Turkish classical music.

17 The common designation of "quarter-tones" is at odds with the official Turkish music theory, which rejects the equally tempered quarter-tone scale, a system (partly) adopted by official Arab music theory since the 1932 conference on Arab music in Cairo (Thomas 2007), in favour of the nine-comma system.

Chapter 4

1 The *Halkevleri* (People's Houses), established in 1932, were local-level official institutions with an important function in promoting public interest in the arts, sports, social help, and other fields, and in providing adult education on different levels. These urban institutions fulfilled a significant role in the construction of a national music, by collecting, processing, and teaching regional folk songs and

music. Their rural counterparts were the smaller-scale *Halkodaları* (People's Rooms) in the villages. An extensive overview and analysis of the activities and principles of the *Halkevleri* and *Halkodaları* can be found in Öztürkmen's dissertation (1993: 96–162).

2   In his discussion of Ottoman music life in Edirne (Thrace), Onur Güneş Ayas makes clear the extent to which boundaries between "art" and "folk" music, musicians, audiences, and contexts were blurred (Ayas 2016).

3   The other provinces of Turkey also have a radio house, but a smaller one without its own choir.

4   Literally "course, route": the melodic structure or development particular to a specific mode – *makam* in Ottoman classical music or (by extension) *ayak* in Turkish folk music.

5   Literally, "manner, style"; a broader concept than *tavır*, denoting the general stylistic characteristics of a region.

6   Literally, "manner, attitude"; specific stylistic features and playing techniques belonging to a particular region (or by extension: to a particular singer or group).

7   Literally, "mouth"; the typical dialect, accent, or way of singing belonging to a particular region (or by extension: to a particular singer or group).

8   *Halk aşığı* (plural *halk aşıkları*): "folk *aşık*"; an *aşık* belonging to the common people.

9   Artistic advisor and head of the broadcasting department of the TRT General Management.

10   Turkish folk music expert and member of the repertoire committee of the TRT General Management (deceased in 2015).

11   According to a study by Hasan Tahsin Sümbüllü, around 5% of the TRT repertoire consists of songs collected from *aşıks* (functioning as "source persons"). Sümbüllü does not assess whether those songs could be authored by them (Sümbüllü 2016: 43).

12   Producer and transcriber at the Ankara TRT Radio House.

13   Musicologist, composer, and performer of Turkish classical music.

14   Composer and musicologist.

15   Composer, musicologist, and educator.

16   Composer and musicologist.

17   Turkish folk music scholar, collector, educator, and performer.

18   "Prescriptive" scores, for example, do not reproduce regional plectrum techniques and ornamentations, known as *tavır*.

19   This would be contrary to the official TRT policy to reject pieces from individuals who are still alive, in order to avoid issues of copyright and financial profit (Stokes 1992a: 56). Possibly, this principle has not been maintained or has changed over the years.

20   "Individual" here means that the author is known (the opposite of "anonymous"); "authentic" means that it is based on and appreciated as folk culture

and bears regionally defined characteristics (the opposite of "populist", denoting commercial interests and based on and appreciated as urban culture).

21 According to Emnalar at the time of his writing, 25 songs by Neşet Ertaş have been included in the TRT repertoire (out of a total of 4500 folk songs and pieces). Twenty-nine songs have been included from his father Muharrem Ertaş – for whom the situation was the same except for the fact that he died in 1984 and that a large part of his music was included after his death (Emnalar 1998: 744).

22 The word *yakmak* (literally, "to light, to turn on") is the standard expression used in the creation of folk songs (*türküler*). It is a somewhat "weaker" and rather ambiguous term for "creation", approximating the sense of "ignorant" creation. The term has been brought into use to create a strong distinction with the learned and urban act of "composition" (*beste yapmak* or *bestelemek*).

23 Bowed lute with three strings tuned in fourths, typical of the Black Sea region. It is played vertically, whether sitting or standing.

Chapter 5

1 See the Introduction and Appendix 3 for more details on the methodology and for a list of the attended events.

2 Although many other parallel events could be described, for example informal social gatherings (recall the jam session and the tea house scene of the Prologue), I believe that the selected events will provide a sufficiently rich and broad basis for ethnographic description, comparison, and analysis.

3 Other examples of events in which Turkish folk music performances occupy a central place in Turkey but not in the diaspora are celebrations of the end of the school year and graduation, musical evenings of clubs (such as soccer supporters clubs), and certain kinds of official openings. In parallel events in the diaspora, other kinds of music – belonging to the cultural sphere of the Belgian majority – would replace the folk music used in Turkey.

4 The identification of the functions of Turkish lullabies has been the subject of several studies (e.g., Emeksiz 2011; Çıblak Coşkun 2013).

5 According to an article in the newspaper *Milliyet*, circumcision can be performed when the boy is 6 to 15 months, 2 to 4 years, or 7 to 10 years old (*Milliyet* 2013).

6 Today, *sünnet* refers to circumcision, but the original, broader meaning of this Arabic word (سنة) embraces the notions "tradition" and "custom". *Düğün* usually means "wedding party", but can also be used for other kinds of family celebrations, particularly circumcision parties.

7 This difference is illustrated by the examples of Emirdağ and Kırşehir: while in Emirdağ the *abdals* play at the *seher*, this is not the case for the city of Kırşehir and its town of Kaman (Başaran, i/v, 27 July 2012; Göçer, i/v, 27 July 2012; Karademir, i/v, 31 July 2012).

8   This derogatory view originates in Alevis's "freer" attitude towards Islam and its strict rules and orders: they often do not fast during Ramadan, do not pray five times a day, and they drink alcohol and attach a positive value to music.

9   This does not mean that this is the only option in the diaspora; circumcision parties with a public component celebrated on the streets occur as well.

10   Pir Sultan Abdal was a sixteenth-century mystical poet of Turkmen origin, born in Banaz in the province of Sivas. He was the prototype of Alevi *aşıks*, accompanying himself on a long-necked lute. His poems were also politically charged, criticizing the Ottoman rule. He was executed by the authorities and became a martyr and a symbol for the Alevis. His poems belong to the core repertoire of the Alevi poetic and musical tradition.

11   Literally, "he who remembers (God)" (Arabic); *bağlama* player during the Alevi *cem.*

12   Zazas, like Kurds, belong to the Indo-European people, and the Zazaki language, like Kurdish, belongs to the Iranian language family.

13   In total, 12 symbolic roles or duties (*oniki hizmet*) are performed during *cem* ceremonies. Besides the aforementioned *dede*, *zakir*, *süpürgeci* and *bekçi* or *gözcü*, are the functions of *rehber* (assistant of the *dede*), *çerağcı* (person in charge of the candles), *ibrikçi* (person in charge of water), *kapıcı* (doorkeeper), *kurbancı* (person in charge of the offerings), *semahcı* (ritual dancer), *iznikçi* (guard of the shoes), and *peyik* (announcer of the *cem*) (Sökefeld 2008: 148). A slightly different set of functions is provided by Neşe Ayışıt Onatça: *rehber*, *gözcü*, *çerağcı*, *zakir*, *süpürgeci*, *dolucu* (person who offers sorbet to the elderly members), *pervane* (person who performs the *semah*), *bekçi*, *kurbancı*, *kuyucu* (person who cleans the remnants of the offered food), *ibrikçi* (person who cleans the hands of the members) (Ayışıt Onatça 2007: 33–35).

14   The current, reinforced Justice and Development Party (AK Parti) regime has started a countermovement disciplining the Alevis by, e.g., impeding the construction of *cemevis* and building unwanted mosques in Alevi villages (Özkul 2015).

15   Mehmet Somuncu and Serdar Ceylan give an assessment of substantial changes in festivals in the Black Sea region, effected by tourism and popular culture. The festivals, now being "labelled as cultural events" and instrumentalized "to sustain the regional economy", are "occasions that (re)interpret various symbolic elements of the social existence of a group or community, with the effect of recreating social relations and the symbolic foundations underpinning everyday life" (Somuncu and Ceylan 2015: 90). By way of comparison to the observed events, on another level, Daniela Ivanova-Nyberg analyses the annual, privately organized, commercial Balkan Fest in San Diego – an American evocation of generalized Balkan village life – in terms of transnationality and ethnicity, transculturality, an "out-of-time experience", and a "bridge building and family bonding experience" (Ivanova-Nyberg 2019).

16 This tension is the subject of the doctoral dissertation by Klaartje Van Kerckem (2014).

Chapter 6

1 The base of the pyramid matches Merriam's definition: it concerns "overt uses of music, the activities that music accompanies". The middle involves an "increased abstraction of these uses", while Nettl discerns a "single, overriding, major function for any one society" near the top, and a "single, overriding function of music for all humanity" at the top (2005: 248–49).

2 In a "Response to Alan P. Merriam", Nettl argues that it is not always possible to maintain the clear distinction between use and function, and that Merriam's list of ten functions is not specific to music, but can be applied to all the arts (2005: 246). As a response to Merriam's suggestion that musical functions are not readily available for the researched culture's members, Nettl explicitly states that uses as well as functions can be analysed from both perspectives (2005: 249–51).

3 The designation "not observed" means that the kind of event has not been observed during the systematic phase of the fieldwork (2011–12) and does not imply that the category is non-existent in that context.

4 The categories of "concert", "café concert" and "festival" are different types of aesthetic activities in front of a more or less formalized audience. "Festival" differs from "concert" in being a festive setting in which a varied programme is completed and the music is only part of a larger whole, while the distinction between "café concert" and "concert" lies in the fact that a café concert is more small-scale (smaller space and audience) and that the atmosphere is more informal: the audience is situated closer to the musicians and is allowed to have a drink and sometimes to chat during the performance.

5 During the specific period of systematic fieldwork (which was carried out during the summer months, after the closing of the concert season), I did not attend any formal concerts, which of course does not imply that this kind of event would be rare.

6 Festivals not being observed during the systematic fieldwork phase are camel wrestling festivals (*deve güreşleri*), which take place during winter in the Aegean region, and *aşık* festivals (*aşık bayramları*).

7 A third rite of passage, important in Turkey but not occurring in the diaspora, is the farewell ceremony for a young man departing for military service (*asker düğünü*). Although this kind of event has been encountered during the systematic fieldwork phase, no permission could be obtained to attend the private celebration.

8   Another event related to religious ritual not observed during the systematic field-work is the signalling of the moment of sunrise during the Ramadan. It was encountered during the complementary phase.

9   This aspect was not taken into consideration during my fieldwork in Turkey.

10   These authorities can be situated in Belgium as well as in Turkey; if in Turkey, operating transnationally. This applies to associations as well.

11   The weekend is defined as the period from Friday afternoon or evening to Sunday evening.

12   Morning is defined as before noon, afternoon as between 1 and 6 pm, evening as between 6 pm and midnight, and night as after midnight.

13   The duration could not always be exactly determined; if this was the case an estimation was made.

14   Of course, the appearance of children in folk music performances is by no means bound to the diaspora context; on the contrary, in urban and rural Turkey, many children are involved at a young age in learning and performing Turkish folk music.

15   Erkan Oğur is a famous Turkish composer, singer, and performer on the fretless guitar and other plucked instruments. Derya Türkan plays the classical *kemençe* (a pear-shaped bowed instrument).

16   The analysis of the performed Turkish folk music repertoire displays certain shortcomings, since it was practically impossible to record and name in an exact way all the pieces performed during the 46 attended musical events. The analy-sis is based on a sample of the folk music pieces which could be identified, be it exactly or in a general way (as belonging to a certain regional or transregional style).

17   The musical idioms of the adjacent provinces of Kırşehir and Ankara are closely related to each other.

18   The formerly Ottoman regions of the Balkans are indicated by the term "Rumeli" (literally, "lands of the Byzantanine Empire").

19   Examples of synthesizers encountered during the fieldwork are Yamaha PSR A1000 Original, Roland E40 Oriental, Korg PA55TR, Korg PA80, and Korg PA800.

20   Fishman is a brand of pickup for amplifying acoustic instruments that is very popular in Turkey (Murer, email to author, 24 July 2014).

21   Klebe's third category, "the complexes of pop music and hip-hop; new creations in both areas and fusion styles" (2008: 69), belongs to another musical realm which I consider as separate from the folk music domain.

22   These elements all belong to a rather comfortable aesthetic idiom. A more chal-lenging (experimental, abstract) idiom, closer to Western modernist/contempo-rary classical music, could be applied as well.

23   This stylistic parameter does not fit properly in the conceptualization by Karahasanoğlu and Skoog. The insertion of the mentioned elements does not affect the melody fundamentally, but rather on a superficial level.

24 The lyrics of the song could not be discerned but are of little relevance in this context.
25 This style was not observed during the systematic fieldwork in Turkey, which obviously does not imply that it does not occur in Turkey.

Chapter 7

1 The woman's name Hüdayda/Fidayda (a corruption of Hüdai/Hüdaiye) possibly refers to a legendary dancer from Ankara. "*Bulguru kaynadırlar*" ("they cook the bulgur") are the first words of the lyrics of the song ("Hüdayda Türküsünün (1.Varyant) Notası" n.d.).
2 This website is prepared by Savaş Akbıyık, who is a musician employed by the Ministry of Culture, aided by many contributors from inside and outside the TRT.
3 Theme C without qualifier (number or accent) is an undefined stanza of which the lyrics could not be discerned.

Chapter 8

1 Although the discourse of this work can predominantly be associated with the visual arts, music-related examples are also provided, and the overall approach and general conclusions are largely applicable to music.
2 During the interviews it became clear that not all interviewees (even not all musicians) had an opinion on the subject or were able to articulate it. Furthermore, not all interviewees attached a particular meaning to Turkish folk music. A girl attending a *türkü* night in Ghent, for example, characterized Turkish folk music as "beautiful, normal, not special". A board member of a student club organizing a karaoke evening in Ghent considered Turkish folk music as just one of many musical genres to which one can listen: "I listen to all kinds of music, without preference. Turkish folk music does not have any special meaning". A considerable amount of information elicited by the respondents during the interviews was only indirectly related to the actual research question. Several people formulated attributes or criteria for the definition of Turkish folk music, instead of mentioning values or functions, such as regional diversity, a long history, diverse influences, oral transmission, importance of the text, performance by amateurs, anonymity, creation by the people, property of the people, and creation by *aşıks*.
3 *Haram*: forbidden by Islamic law.

Appendix 3

1   Folk music events in Turkey not being studied during the systematic phase of the fieldwork include ceremonies prior to departure for military service (*asker düğünleri*), camel wrestling festivals (*deve güreşleri*), aşık festivals (*aşık bayramları*), and the signalling of the moment of sunrise (*seher* or *sahur*) during the Ramadan by *davulcular* (*davul* players).

2   "Family-in-law", part of the wedding ceremony involving mutual visits by the families of the bride and groom.

Bibliography

Abadan-Unat, Nermin. 2011. *Turks in Europe: From Guest Worker to Transnational Citizen*. New York: Berghahn Books.

Agirdag, Orhan, Piet Van Avermaet, and Mieke Van Houtte. 2013. "School Segregation and Math Achievement: A Mixed-Method Study on the Role of Self-Fulfilling Prophecies". *Teachers College Record* 115(3): 1–50.

Ágoston, Gábor, and Alan Bruce. 2009. *Encyclopedia of the Ottoman Empire*. New York: Infobase Publishing.

Akbıyık, Savaş. 2016. "Repertükül – Repertuar Türküleri Külliyatı" [Repertkül: Complete Repertoire Folk Songs]. http://www.repertukul.com/ (accessed August 12, 2020).

Akdoğu, Onur. 1996. *Türk Müziğinde Türler ve Biçimler* [Genres and Forms in Turkish Music]. İzmir: Ege Üniversitesi Basımevi.

Amsab-ISG, Sound and Image Collection. n.d.a. "Benefiet Turkije" [Benefit Turkey].

Amsab-ISG, Sound and Image Collection. n.d.b. "Vreemd Op de Planken" [Foreigners on Stage].

Artun, Erman. 2009. *Aşıklık Geleneği ve Aşık Edebiyatı* [The Bardic Tradition and Bardic Literature]. 4th ed. Istanbul: Kitabevi.

"Âşıklık (Minstrelsy) Tradition". 2009. UNESCO. http://www.unesco.org/culture/ich/en/RL/00179 (accessed August 12, 2020).

"Asker Uğurlama" [Soldier's Sendoff]. n.d. Müşküle Köyü. http://www.muskulekoyu.com/muskule-askerugurlama (accessed August 12, 2020).

Ataman, Adnan. 2009. *Bu Toprağın Sesi: Halk Musikimiz* [The Sound of This Soil: Our Turkish Folk Music]. Edited by Süleyman Şenel. 2nd ed. Türk Edebiyatı Vakfı Yayınları 128. Istanbul: Türk Edebiyatı Vakfı.

Audooren, Fabien, ed. 1994. *Het Vuur Aan de Lont: Biografie van 25 Jaar Gentse Feesten Bij Sint-Jacobs* [The Fire on the Match: Biography of 25 Years of Ghent's Summer Festival at Sint-Jacobs]. Gent: Sintjoris.

Ayas, Onur Güneş. 2016. "Observations on the Blurred Boundaries between Classes, Social Groups and Genres in the Musical Life of Ottoman Edirne". In *Music and Music Education from Ottoman Empire to Modern Turkey*, edited by Hasan Tahsin Sümbüllü and William Sayers, 7–14. London and Istanbul: AGP.

Aydemir, Adem. 2013. "Türk Dünyasında Bazı Düğün Terimleri ve 'Al Duvak' Geleneği Üzerine" [About Some Wedding Terms in the Turkish World and the "Red Veil" Tradition]. *Turkish Studies* 8(9): 619–55.
https://doi.org/10.7827/TurkishStudies.3715

Ayışıt Onatça, Neşe. 2007. *Alevi-Bektaşi Kültüründe Kırklar Semahı: Müzikal Analiz Çalışması* [The Semah of the Forty in the Alevi-Bektashi Culture: A Musical Analysis]. Müzik Bilimleri 8. Istanbul: Bağlam.

Balkılıç, Özgür. 2005. "Kemalist Views and Works on Turkish Folk Music during the Early Republican Period". Ankara: Middle East Technical University. http://etd.lib.metu.edu.tr/upload/12606528/index.pdf (accessed August 20, 2020).

Başgöz, İlhan. 2008. *Türkü* [Folk Song]. Istanbul: Pan Yayıncılık.

Bates, Eliot. 2011. *Music in Turkey: Experiencing Music, Expressing Culture*. Oxford University Press.

Bauböck, Rainer, and Thomas Faist. 2010. *Diaspora and Transnationalism: Concepts, Theories and Methods*. Amsterdam University Press.
https://doi.org/10.5117/9789089642387

Bayart, Jean-François. 2005. *The Illusion of Cultural Identity*. London: Hurst & Company.

Bayhan, N. 2008. Problems and Solutions for Practice and Theory in Turkish Music: International Invited Congress Proceedings. İTÜ Turkish Music State Conservatory. Istanbul: Istanbul Metropolitan Municipality Culture Co. Publications.

Beirens, Koen, and Johnny Fontaine. 2011. "Somatic and Emotional Well-Being among Turkish Immigrants in Belgium: Acculturation or Culture?" *Journal of Cross-Cultural Psychology* 42(1): 56–74.

Beken, Münir Nurettin. 2008. "Turkfest and Music Making among the Diaspora Cultures in Seattle". In *Music from Turkey in the Diaspora*, edited by Hande Sağlam and Ursula Hemetek, 139–50. Klanglese 5. Vienna: Institut für Volksmusikforschung und Ethnomusikologie.

Ben-Rafael, Miriam, and Eliezer Ben-Rafael. 2009. "The Linguistic Landscape of Transnationalism: The Divided Heart of Europe". In *Transnationalism: Diasporas and the Advent of a New (Dis)Order*, edited by Eliezer Ben-Rafael and Yitzhak Sternberg, 399–416. Leiden: Brill.

Beyaert, Ellen. 2010. "De Centrale Staat Onder Stroom: Spetterend Feest voor 15-Jarig Bestaan Intercultureel Centrum" [De Centrale Powered: Glittering Celebration for the Intercultural Centre's 15-year Existence]. *Gent: Stadsmagazine*, March 2010.

Beyhom, Amine. 2011. "Exploring the Concept of Mode". In *La Modalité, Un Pont Entre Orient et Occident: Les Actes*, 101–3. Brest: Spectacle vivant en Bretagne & Drom.

Bider, Emma Ruth. 2018. "The Sound of Home: Tuareg Women's Tendé Drumming in France and Belgium". Master's thesis. Ottawa: Carleton University. https://curve.carleton.ca/49267c83-2eff-42ad-a375-425ffa80255f (accessed August 12, 2020).

Bohlman, Philip V. 1988. *The Study of Folk Music in the Modern World*. Bloomington and Indianapolis: Indiana University Press.

Born, Georgina, and David Hesmondhalgh. 2000. "Introduction: On Difference, Representation, and Appropriation in Music". In *Western Music and Its Others: Difference, Representation, and Appropriation in Music*, edited by Georgina Born and David Hesmondhalgh, 1–58. Berkeley and Los Angeles: University of California Press.

Bryant, Rebecca. 2005. "The Soul Danced into the Body: Nation and Improvisation in Istanbul". *American Ethnologist* 32(2): 222–38.
https://doi.org/10.1525/ae.2005.32.2.222

Büyükyıldız, H. Zeki. 2009. *Türk Halk Müzigi: Ulusal Türk Müziği* [Turkish Folk Music: National Turkish Music]. Istanbul: Papatya Yayıncılık.

Çelebioğlu, Âmil. 1982. *Türk Ninniler Hazinesi* [Turkish Lullabies Treasure]. Istanbul: Ülker Yayınları.

Çıblak Coşkun, N. 2013. "Türk ninnilerine işlevsel yaklaşım". *Turkish Studies* 8(4): 499–513.

City of Ghent. 2012. "Geboorteplaats_Turken" [Place of Birth Turks]. Excel file.

Cocriamont, Marie. 2016. "Opleiding Ud: Een Verkennend Vergelijkend Onderzoek Tussen de Methodiek van De Centrale in Gent, de Kunstbrug in Gent En 'Beit El-Ud' in Caïro" [Ud Education: An Exploratory Comparative Study of the Methodology of De Centrale in Ghent, De Kunstbrug in Ghent and 'Beit El-Ud' in Cairo]. Master's thesis. Ghent: Ghent University.

Coşgun, Meryem. 2013. "Fototentoonstelling 'Tussen Krijt En Tablet' van Recep Cirik in Het Pand" [Photo Exhibition "Between Chalk and Tablet" by Recep Cirik at Het Pand]. *Het Nieuwsblad*, May 4, 2013.
http://www.nieuwsblad.be/article/detail.aspx?articleid=BLMCO_20130504_002 (accessed August 12, 2020).

De Bock, Jozefien. 2012. "'Alle Wegen Leiden Naar Gent': Trajecten van Mediterrane Migranten Naar de Arteveldestad, 1960–1980" ["All Roads Lead to Ghent": Trajectories of Mediterranean Migrants to Artevelde's City, 1960–1980]. *Brood En Rozen* 3: 47–75.

De Bock, Jozefien. 2013. "'We Have Made Our Whole Lives Here': Immigration, Settlement and Integration Processes of Mediterranean Immigrants in Ghent, 1960–1980". Doctoral dissertation. Florence: European University Institute.

De Clerck, Jan. 1999. "Concert 'Belkis Akkale' in Gent". *Nieuwsbank*. http://www.nieuwsbank.nl/inp/1999/12/1205E001.htm (accessed August 12, 2020).

De Gendt, Tina. 2014. *Turkije Aan de Leie: 50 Jaar Migratie in Gent* [Turkey at the Lys: Fifty Years of Migration in Ghent]. Tielt: Lannoo.

Değirmenci, Koray. 2006. "On the Pursuit of a Nation: The Construction of Folk and Folk Music in the Founding Decades of the Turkish Republic". *International Review of the Aesthetics and Sociology of Music* 37(1): 47–65.

Demir, Sertan. 2013. *Türk Halk Müziğinde Türler* [Forms in Turkish Folk Music]. Istanbul: Usar.

DeNora, Tia. 2000. *Music in Everyday Life*. Cambridge: Cambridge University Press. https://doi.org/10.1017/CBO9780511489433

De Schepper, Ronny. 2011. "Stekelbees Voor Kinderen" [Stekelbees for Children]. *Dagelijks Iets Degelijks* (blog). May 29, 2011. http://ronnydeschepper.com/2011/05/29/stekelbees-voor-kinderen/ (accessed August 12, 2020).

Devos, Veerle. 1997. "Interculturaliteit in de Populaire Muziek: Onderzoek naar de Muziekvoorkeur van Marokkaanse en Turkse Jongeren tussen 12 en 18 Jaar in Vlaanderen" [Interculturality in Popular Music: Research into the Music Preference of Moroccan and Turkish Young People between 12 and 18 in Flanders]. Master's thesis. Leuven: Katholieke Universiteit Leuven.

Devreese, Johan. 1991. "Werkingsverslag 1991" [Report 1991]. Ghent: De Poort-Beraber.

Devreese, Johan. 1992. "Werkingsverslag 1992" [Report 1992]. Ghent: De Poort-Beraber.

Devreese, Johan. 1993. "Werkingsverslag 1993" [Report 1993]. Ghent: De Poort-Beraber.

Devreese, Johan. 2014a. "Turkse Muziek & De Poort-Beraber" [Turkish Music and De Poort-Beraber], email communication, February 11, 2014.

Devreese, Johan. 2014b. "Tekstje over De Poort-Beraber Ter Controle" [Text about De Poort-Beraber], email communication, March 4, 2014.

Devreese, Johan. 2014c. "Tekstje over De Poort-Beraber Ter Controle" [Text about De Poort-Beraber], email communication, March 6, 2014.

"Diversiteit in Alle Districten" [Diversity in All Districts]. 2014. Antwerp: City of Antwerp.

Dökmetaş, Kubilay. 2011. "Dr. Recai Özdil". Facebook, December 17, 2012. https://www.facebook.com/Dokmetas.Kubilay/posts/337474652933916

Duygulu, Melih. 2006a. *Anadolu Ninnileri – Anatolian Lullabies*. Istanbul: Kalan.

Duygulu, Melih. 2006b. *Türkiye'de Çingene Müziği – Batı Grubu Romanlarında Müzik Kültürü* [Gypsy Music in Turkey: The Music Culture of the West Group of Roma]. Istanbul: Pan Yayıncılık.

Duygulu, Melih. 2012. *Emirdağ Türküleri: Emirdağ'a Bir Gitmeyle Yol Olamaz* [Folk Songs from Emirdağ: One Person Going to Emirdağ Doesn't Make a Road]. Istanbul: Kalan.

Emeksiz, A. 2011. "Are Lullabies to Sleep?" *Trakya Üniversitesi Edebiyat Fakültesi Dergisi* 1(2): 143–56.

"Emirdağ". 2018. In *Vikipedi*. https://tr.wikipedia.org/w/index.php?title=Emirda%C4%9F&oldid=19892310 (accessed August 12, 2020).

"Emirdağ Da Bu Ramazan Davul Yok". n.d. [No Davul in Emirdağ During this Ramadan]. *Emirdağ.tr.com* (blog). https://www.afyonhaber.com/emirdag-amp-8217-da-bu-ramazan-davul-yok/26989/

Emnalar, Atınç. 1998. *Tüm Yönleriyle Türk Halk Müziği ve Nazariyatı* [Turkish Folk Music in All its Aspects and its Theory]. İzmir: Ege Üniversitesi Basımevi.

Ergil, Dogu. 2000. "The Kurdish Question in Turkey". *Journal of Democracy* 11(3): 122–35. https://doi.org/10.1353/jod.2000.0054

Erol, Ayhan. 2008. "Reconstructing Cultural Identity in Diaspora: Musical Practices of the Toronto Alevi Community". In *Music from Turkey in the Diaspora*, edited by Hande Sağlam and Ursula Hemetek, 151–61. Klanglese 5. Vienna: Institut für Volksmusikforschung und Ethnomusikologie.

Erol, Ayhan. 2009. "Marketing the Alevi Musical Revival". In *Muslim Societies in the Age of Mass Consumption: Politics, Culture and Identity between the Local and the Global*, edited by Johanna Pink, 165–84. Newcastle: Cambridge Scholars Publishing.

Findley, Carter Vaughn. 2005. *The Turks in World History*. New York: Oxford University Press.

Frith, Simon. 1996. "Music and Identity". In *Questions of Cultural Identity*, edited by Stuart Hall and Paul Du Gay, 108–27. London: Sage.
https://doi.org/10.4135/9781446221907.n7

Furniere, Andy. 2014. "Flanders Celebrates 50 Years of Migration". *Flanders Today*. January 2014.
http://www.flanderstoday.eu/living/flanders-celebrates-50-years-migration (accessed August 12, 2020).

"Geschiedenis van de Dekenij Patershol" [History of Deanery Patershol]. 2014. Koninklijke Dekenij Patershol v.z.w. 2014.
http://www.patershol.org/dekenij/geschiedenis-dekenij (accessed August 12, 2020).

Gill, Denise. 2018. "Listening, *Muhabbet*, and the Practice of Masculinity". *Ethnomusicology* 62(2): 171–205.
https://doi.org/10.5406/ethnomusicology.62.2.0171

Gök, Şaban. 2011. "Belçika Türk Dernekler Birliği Tarafından Belçika'da 'Halk Hikayeleri Günleri' Gerçekleştiriliyor" ["Turkish Storytelling Days" are Organized in Belgium by the Belgian Union of Turkish Associations]. *Yologlu Yollarda Medya* (blog). February 9, 2011. http://www.yologluyollarda.com/2011/02/belcika-turk-dernekler-birligi-tarafindan-belcika%e2%80%99da-%e2%80%9chalk-hikayeleri-gunleri%e2%80%9d-gerceklestiriliyor/ (accessed March 1, 2014).

Goossens, Ann. 2004. "Een Turkse Droom die Geschiedenis Werd: De Historische Ervaring van Turkse Arbeidsmigranten in Antwerpen" [A Turkish Dream That Became History: The Historical Experience of Turkish Migrant Workers in Antwerp]. Ghent: Ghent University.

Greve, Martin. 2006. *Almanya'da "Hayali Türkiye"nin Müziği* [The Music of "Imaginary Turkey" in Germany]. Istanbul: Bilgi Üniversitesi Yayınları.

Greve, Martin. 2008. "Turkish Music in European Institutions". In *Music from Turkey in the Diaspora*, edited by Ursula Hemetek and Hande Sağlam, 89–95. Klanglese 5. Vienna: Institut für Volksmusikforschung und Ethnomusikologie.

Greve, Martin. 2009. "Music in the European-Turkish Diaspora". In *Music in Motion: Diversity and Dialogue in Europe*, edited by Bernd Clausen, Ursula Hemetek, and Eva Saether. Bielefeld: transcript.

Greve, Martin. 2017. *Makamsız: Individualization of Traditional Music on the Eve of Kemalist Turkey*. Istanbuler Texte und Studien 39. Würzburg: Ergon Verlag.

Güler, Yalçın. n.d. "Ankara'nın Milli Marşı (Hüdayda) [The National Anthem of Ankara (Hüdayda)]". *Yalçın Güler Blog* (blog). https://www.yalcinguler.net/ankaranin-milli-marsi-hudayda/ (accessed August 12, 2020).

Güney, Serhat, Cem Pekman, and Bülent Kabaş. 2014. "Diasporic Music in Transition: Turkish Immigrant Performers on the Stage of 'Multikulti' Berlin". *Popular Music and Society* 37(2): 132–51. https://doi.org/10.1080/03007766.2012.736288

Güran Aydın, Pınar. 2016. "Drawing a Homeland on the Staff: Music of Turkey in Berlin". In *Transglobal Sounds: Music, Youth and Migration*, edited by João Sardinha and Ricardo Campos, 201–20. London: Bloomsbury Academic. https://doi.org/10.5040/9781501311994.ch-010

Hall, Stuart. 1996. "Introduction: Who Needs 'Identity'?" In *Questions of Cultural Identity*, edited by Stuart Hall and Paul Du Gay, 1–17. London: Sage. https://doi.org/10.4135/9781446221907.n1

Hall, Stuart. 2003. "Cultural Identity and Diaspora". In *Theorizing Diaspora: A Reader*, edited by Jana Evans Braziel and Anita Mannur, 233–46. Oxford: Blackwell.

Hall, Stuart, and Paul Du Gay, eds. 1996. *Questions of Cultural Identity*. London: Sage.

Halman, Talat Sait. 1991. "Anniversary: Yunus Emre". *The Unesco Courier*, December. https://unesdoc.unesco.org/ark:/48223/pf0000090316

Hanáková, Martina, Itzana Dobbelaere, and Hélène Sechehaye. 2016. "The Sersera of the Guembri: Anthropological Approach to the Device in the Context of Gnawa Diasporas in Brussels and Morocco". *Kwartalnik Młodych Muzykologów UJ* 30(3): 7–27. https://doi.org/10.4467/23537094KMMUJ.16.012.8051

Hannerz, Ulf. 1980. *Exploring the City: Inquiries toward an Urban Anthropology*. New York: Columbia University Press. https://doi.org/10.7312/hann91086

Hargreaves, D. J., and A. C. North. 1999. "The Functions of Music in Everyday Life: Redefining the Social in Music Psychology". *Psychology of Music* 27(1): 71–83. https://doi.org/10.1177/0305735699271007

Heck, Özge Girit. 2011. "Representing Turkish National Culture and Turkish-American Identity in Chicago's Turkish Festivals". Doctoral dissertation, Iowa: University of Iowa.

Hecker, Pierre. 2006. "Country Profile: Turkey". Focus Migration. http://focus-migration.hwwi.de/Turkey.1234.0.html?&L=1 (accessed August 12, 2020).

Hesmondhalgh, David. 2013. *Why Music Matters*. West Sussex: Wiley Blackwell.

"Home". 2014. Koninklijk Verbond der Gebuurtedekenijen van de Stad Gent. http://www.dekenijen.be/ (accessed August 12, 2020).

Huber, Harald, and Martin Sigmund. 2008. "Oriental House in Vienna". In *Music from Turkey in the Diaspora*, edited by Hande Sağlam and Ursula Hemetek, 49–59. Klanglese 5. Vienna: Institut für Volksmusikforschung und Ethnomusikologie.

"Hüdayda Türküsünün (1.Varyant) Notası". n.d. Türkü Dostları. https://www.turkudostlari.net/nota.asp?turku=479 (accessed August 12, 2020).

Hutchison, Robert, and Andrew Feist. 1991. *Amateur Arts in the UK*. London: Policy Studies Institute.

"Istanbul Ekspres Belçika Gent'te" [Istanbul Ekspres in Ghent, Belgium]. 2013. Intercultureel centrum De Centrale.

"Istanbul Ekspres Gent Belçika" [Istanbul Ekspres, Ghent, Belgium]. 2013. Intercultureel centrum De Centrale.

İstanbullu, Serenat. 2017. "Kimlik ve Müzik Özelinde Emirdağ Karacalar Köyü Bacı Sultan Vuslat Yıldönümü Etkinlikleri" [The Activities for the Bacı Sultan Anniversary Meeting about Identiy and Music in the Karacalar Village of Emirdağ]. *Journal of International Social Research* 10(54): 571–84.

Ivanova-Nyberg, Daniela. 2019. "Transnationality, Transculturality and Ethnicity: A Look at Balkan Fest, San Diego, California". *Musicologist* 3(1): 1–36. https://doi.org/10.33906/musicologist.563206

"Izmir, Turkije: Fascinerend Veelzijdig" [Izmir, Turkey: Fascinatingly Versatile]. 2009. Accenta. http://www.gent.be/docs/Departement%20Stafdiensten/Dienst%20 Stedenbeleid%20en%20Internationale%20Betrekkingen/47644a-magazine6-9%20FINAAL.pdf (accessed June 20, 2014).

"Jeugdhuis Posküder: Gent Posof Culturele Vereniging" [Youth Centre Posküder: Ghent Posof Cultural Association]. 2013. http://poskuder.be/ (accessed June 20, 2014).

Karahasanoğlu Ata, Songül. 2002. "The Collection of Turkish Folk Music and Its Current Situation". *Acta Ethnographica Hungarica* 47(1): 255–62. http://acta.bibl.u-szeged.hu/70301/1/szegedi_vallasi_010_255-262.pdf

Karahasanoğlu, Songül, and Gabriel Skoog. 2009. "Synthesizing Identity: Gestures of Filiation and Affiliation in Turkish Popular Music". *Asian Music* 40(2): 52–71. https://doi.org/10.1353/amu.0.0031

Karakaya, Oğuz. 2012. "Musical Note Writing Systems Developed between 17th and 19th Century". In *International Proceedings of Economics Development and Research*, 34: 47–51. Singapore: IACSIT Press.

Kaya, Ayhan. 2002. "Aesthetics of Diaspora: Contemporary Minstrels in Turkish Berlin". *Journal of Ethnic and Migration Studies* 28(1): 43–62. https://doi.org/10.1080/13691830120103921

Kaya, Doğan. n.d.a. "Türkü". Türkü Sitesi: Türküler Internette. http://www.turkuler.com/thm/turkuler2.asp (accessed August 12, 2020).

Kaya, Doğan. n.d.b. "Türkü". Türkü Sitesi: Türküler Internette. http://www.turkuler.com/thm/turkuler3.asp (accessed August 12, 2020).

Kaya, Gazi Erdener. 1995. "Bağlamada Tavırlar" [*Tavır* on *Bağlama*]. Türkü Sitesi: Türküler Internette. http://www.turkuler.com/baglama/tavir.asp (accessed August 12, 2020).

Kayhan, Aslı. 2014. "Musical Changes of Rural to Urban in Popular Culture. A Case Study: Türkü Bars in Istanbul". *International Review of the Aesthetics and Sociology of Music* 45(1): 149–66.

Keten, Yeter. 2002. "Zorgvraag en Zorgaanbod Bij Turkse Ouderen. Ouder Worden in den Vreemde" [Care Demand and Care Supply among Turkish Older People: Growing Older Abroad]. Final thesis. Ghent: Vormingsleergang voor Sociaal en Pedagogisch Werk.

Kiwan, Nadia, and Ulrike Hanna Meinhof. 2011. "Music and Migration: A Transnational Approach". *Music and Arts in Action* 3(3): 3–20.

Klebe, Dorit. 2008. "The Türkgünü [Turkish Day] in Berlin and Its Musical Forms of Expression". In *Music from Turkey in the Diaspora*, edited by Ursula Hemetek and Hande Sağlam, 61–76. Klanglese 5. Vienna: Institut für Volksmusikforschung und Ethnomusikologie.

Klebe, Dorit. 2009. "Music in the Immigrant Communities from Turkey in Germany: Aspects of Formal and Informal Transmission". In *Music in Motion: Diversity and Dialogue in Europe*, edited by Bernd Clausen, Ursula Hemetek, and Eva Saether, 299–326. Bielefeld: transcript. https://doi.org/10.14361/9783839410745-018

Kor, Gamze. 2018. "Afyonkarahisar, Emirdağ Karacalar Köyünde Gerçekleştirilen Ritüellerde Gelenekler ve Musikinin Kullanımı" [Tradition and the Use of Music in the Rituals of the Karacalar Villaga of Emirdağ, Afyonkarahisar]. Master's thesis. Afyonkarahisar: Afyon Kocatepe Üniversitesi.

"Kosten Concert Intercultureel Ontmoetingscentrum (19/01/1998)" [Expenses Concert Intercultural Meeting Centre (19/01/1998)]. 1997. 150. Bulletin Vragen en Antwoorden. Ghent: City of Ghent. http://www.gent.be/eCache/THE/34/409.cmVjPTExMzExNQ.html (accessed March 1, 2014).

Krüger, Simone, and Ruxandra Trandafoiu, eds. 2014. "Introduction: Touristic and Migrating Musics in Transit". In *The Globalization of Musics in Transit: Music Migration and Tourism*, 1–26. Routledge Studies in Ethnomusicology. New York: Routledge. https://doi.org/10.4324/9780203082911

Küçükcan, Talip. 2007. "Bridging the European Union and Turkey: The Turkish Diaspora in Europe". *Insight Turkey* 9(4): 85–99. https://doi.org/10.2139/ssrn.2498541

"Kültür-Sanat: Belçika'dan Aşıklar Geçti / 03/11/2010" [Culture-Art: *Aşıks* Have Passed through Belgium]. 2010. *Belçika Haber* (blog). November 2010. http://www.belcikahaber.be/?act=show&code=page&id=5&id_page=7345&resume=0 (accessed March 1, 2014).

Kumartaşlıoğlu, Satı. 2018. "Geography and Place Elements in Emirdağ". *PALIMPSEST / ПАЛИМПСЕСТ* 3(5): 99–113.

Levi, Erik, and Florian Scheding, eds. 2010. *Music and Displacement: Diasporas, Mobilities, and Dislocations in Europe and Beyond.* Lanham, MD: Scarecrow Press.

Lund Research Ltd. 2012. "Sampling Strategy". *Lærd Dissertation.* https://dissertation.laerd.com/sampling-strategy.php (accessed April 8, 2021).

Maanen, Hans van. 2010. *How to Study Art Worlds: On the Societal Functioning of Aesthetic Values.* Amsterdam: Amsterdam University Press.

Manço, Ural. 2000. "Turks in Europe: From a Garbled Image to the Complexity of Migrant Reality". In *The Image of Turks in Europe from the Declaration of the Republic in 1923 to the 1990s*, edited by N. K. Burçoğlu, 21–35. Istanbul: The Isis Press.

Markoff, Irene. 1986. "Musical Theory, Performance and the Contemporary Bağlama Specialist in Turkey". Doctoral dissertation. Washington: University of Washington.

Markoff, Irene. 2002a. "Alevi Identity and Expressive Culture". In *The Garland Encyclopedia of World Music*, edited by Scott Marcus, Virginia Danielson, and Dwight Reynolds. Volume 6: The Middle East: 793–800. New York: Routledge.

Markoff, Irene. 2002b. "Aspects of Turkish Folk Music Theory". In *The Middle East*, edited by Virginia Danielson, Scott Marcus, and Dwight Reynolds, 77–88. The Garland Encyclopedia of World Music 6. New York and London: Routledge.

Markoff, Irene. 2008. "Sustaining Traditional Music in Toronto's Turkish Community: Textured Identities/Communitas in Flux". In *Music from Turkey in the Diaspora*, 163–73. Klanglese 5. Vienna: Institut für Volksmusikforschung und Ethnomusikologie.

Martiniello, Marco, and Andrea Rea. 2003. "Belgium's Immigration Policy Brings Renewal and Challenges". Country Profiles. Washington: Migration Policy Institute. http://www.migrationpolicy.org/article/belgiums-immigration-policy-brings-renewal-and-challenges/ (accessed August 12, 2020).

Merriam, Alan P. 1964. *The Anthropology of Music.* Evanston, IL: Northwestern University Press.

Milliyet. 2013. "Sünnet İçin İdeal Yaş Nedir?" [What is the Ideal Age for Circumcision?], April 2013. http://www.milliyet.com.tr/sunnet-icin-ideal-yas-nedir--haberpanosu-1689726/ (accessed August 12, 2020).

Myers, Helen, ed. 1992. *Ethnomusicology: An Introduction.* New Grove Handbooks in Music. London: Macmillan.

Nekka-Nacht 2012 / Mustafa Avsar & Willem Vermandere. 2012. http://www.youtube.com/watch?v=_HmAF__EBzM (accessed August 12, 2020).

Nettl, Bruno. 1985. *The Western Impact on World Music: Change, Adaptation, and Survival.* New York: Schirmer Books.

Nettl, Bruno. 2005. *The Study of Ethnomusicology: Thirty-One Issues and Concepts*. New edn. Urbana and Chicago: University of Illinois Press.

Nketia, J. H. Kwabena. 1990. "Contextual Strategies of Inquiry and Systematization". *Ethnomusicology* 34(1): 75–97. https://doi.org/10.2307/852357

"Nomination File No. 00384 for Inscription on the Representative List of the Intangible Cultural Heritage of Humanity in 2010". 2010. United Nations – Intangible Cultural Heritage. https://ich.unesco.org/doc/src/07482-EN.pdf (accessed August 12, 2020).

"Nomination File No. 00385 for Inscription on the Representative List of the Intangible Cultural Heritage of Humanity in 2010". 2010. United Nations – Intangible Cultural Heritage. https://ich.unesco.org/doc/src/07483-EN.pdf (accessed August 12, 2020).

"Nomination File No. 01006 for Inscription on the Representative List of the Intangible Cultural Heritage of Humanity in 2014". 2013. United Nations – Intangible Cultural Heritage.
https://ich.unesco.org/doc/download.php?versionID=30321 (accessed August 12, 2020).

"Nomination for Inscription on the Representative List in 2009 (Reference No. 00179)". 2009. United Nations – Intangible Cultural Heritage.
https://ich.unesco.org/en/RL/asklk-minstrelsy-tradition-00179 (accessed April 4, 2021).

Noppe, Jo. 2014a. "Lokale Inburgerings- En Integratiemonitor Editie 2013: Gent". Lokale Inburgerings- En Integratiemonitor.
http://aps.vlaanderen.be/lokaal/pdf/integratiemonitor/Gent.pdf (accessed June 20, 2014).

Noppe, Jo. 2014b. "Lokale Inburgerings- En Integratiemonitor Editie 2013: Lokeren". Lokale Inburgerings- En Integratiemonitor.
http://aps.vlaanderen.be/lokaal/pdf/integratiemonitor/Lokeren.pdf (accessed June 20, 2014).

Noppe, Jo. 2014c. "Lokale Inburgerings- En Integratiemonitor Editie 2013: Sint-Niklaas". Lokale Inburgerings- En Integratiemonitor.
http://aps.vlaanderen.be/lokaal/pdf/integratiemonitor/Sint-Niklaas.pdf (accessed June 20, 2014).

Noppe, Jo. 2014d. "Cijfers Personen van Turkse Herkomst Gent", email communication, 21 February 2014.

Noppe, Jo, and Edith Lodewijckx. 2012. "De Gekleurde Samenleving: Personen van Vreemde Herkomst in Vlaanderen" [The Coloured Society: People of Foreign Origin in Flanders]. SVR – Webartikel D/2012/3241/061. Brussel: Studiedienst van de Vlaamse Regering.
http://www.vlaanderen.be/nl/publicaties/detail/de-gekleurde-samenleving-personen-van-vreemde-herkomst-in-vlaanderen (accessed August 12, 2020).

Noppe, Jo, Myriam Vanweddingen, Gerlinde Doyen, Karen Stuyck, Yinthe Feys, and Philippe Buysschaert. 2018. "Vlaamse migratie- en integratiemonitor 2018"

[Flemish Migration and Integration Monitor]. Agentschap Binnenlands Bestuur. https://www.vlaanderen.be/publicaties/vlaamse-migratie-en-integratiemonitor-2018 (accessed August 12, 2020).

North, Adrian C., David J. Hargreaves, and Jon J. Hargreaves. 2004. "Uses of Music in Everyday Life". *Music Perception: An Interdisciplinary Journal* 22(1): 41–77. https://doi.org/10.1525/mp.2004.22.1.41

Okan, Sungu. n.d. "Collections". Turkish Music Portal. http://www.turkishmusicportal.org/page.php?id=51 (accessed August 12, 2020).

Özdemir, Erdem. 2008. "Emirdağ Musiki Geleneğinde Abdallar ve Yeni Onaltı Türkü" [*Abdals* and 11 New Folk Songs in the Emirdağ Music Tradition]. Master's thesis. Sakarya: Sakarya Üniversitesi.

Özdemir, Ulaş. 2018. "Between Debate and Sources: Defining Alevi Music". In *Alevism between Standardisation and Plurality: Negotiating Texts, Sources and Cultural Heritage*, edited by Benjamin Weineck and Johannes Zimmermann, 165–93. Geschichte und Kultur des Modernen Vorderen Orients. Bern: Peter Lang.

Özkul, Derya. 2015. "Alevi 'Openings' and the Politicisation of the 'Alevi Issue' during the AKP Rule". *Turkish Studies* 16(1): 80–96. https://doi.org/10.1080/14683849.2015.1022722

Öztürk, Okan Murat. 2016. "Halk Mûsikîsi Repertuar Incelemelerinin Makam Nazariyesi Araştırmalarına Yapabileceği Katkılar" [The Possible Contributions of Turkish Folk Music Repertoire Studies to the Research in Makam Theory]. *EÜ Devlet Türk Musikisi Konservatuvarı Dergisi* 2015(7): 1–27.

Öztürkmen, Arzu. 1993. "Folklore and Nationalism in Turkey". Doctoral dissertation, University of Pennsylvania.

"Paspoort (televisieprogramma)". 2014. In *Wikipedia*. http://nl.wikipedia.org/w/index.php?title=Paspoort_ (televisieprogramma)&oldid=33469813 (accessed August 12, 2020).

Pegg, Carole, Philip V. Bohlman, Helen Myers and Martin Stokes. n.d. "Ethnomusicology". In *Grove Music Online*, edited by Carole Pegg, Helen Myers, and Philip V. Bohlman. Oxford University Press. https://doi.org/10.1093/gmo/9781561592630.article.52178

Picken, Laurence. 1975. *Folk Musical Instruments of Turkey*. London: Oxford University Press.

"Portaal Vreemde Afkomst" [Portal Foreign Origin]. 2014. Non-Profit DATA. 2014. http://www.npdata.be/Data/Vreemdelingen/Vreemde-afkomst/1990-2008/ tabellen/Portaal/index.html (accessed August 12, 2020).

Powers, Harold S., Frans Wiering, James Porter, James Cowdery, Richard Widdess, Ruth Davis, Marc Perlman, Stephen Jones, and Allan Marett. n.d. "Mode". In *Grove Music Online*. Oxford University Press. https://doi.org/10.1093/gmo/9781561592630.article.43718

"Public Space". 2014. In *Wikipedia*. http://en.wikipedia.org/w/index.php?title=Public_space&oldid=605506220 (accessed August 12, 2020).

Ramnarine, Tina K., ed. 2007. *Musical Performance in the Diaspora*. New York: Routledge.

Reinhard, Kurt, Martin Stokes, and Ursula Reinhard. n.d. "Turkey". In *Grove Music Online*. Oxford University Press. http://www.oxfordmusiconline.com/subscriber/article/grove/music/44912 (accessed August 12, 2020).

Reinhard, Ursula. 1987. "Türkische Musik: Ihre Interpreten in West-Berlin und in der Heimat. Ein Vergleich" [Turkish Music: Its Performers in West-Berlin and the Homeland. A Comparison]. *Jahrbuch für Volksliedforschung* 32: 81–92. https://doi.org/10.2307/849414

Reinhard, Ursula. 2002. "Turkey: An Overview". In *The Middle East*, edited by Virginia Danielson, Scott Marcus, and Dwight Reynolds, 759–77. The Garland Encyclopedia of World Music 6. New York and London: Routledge.

Reinhard, Ursula, and Tiago de Oliveira Pinto. 1989. *Sänger ndu Poeten mit der Laute – Türkische Âşık und Ozan* [Singers and Poets with the Lute: Turkish *Aşıks* and *Ozans*]. Veroffentlichungen des Museums für Völkerkunde Berlin. Berlin: Staatliche Museen Preussischer Kulturbesitz / Dietrich Reimer Verlag.

Rice, Timothy. 2010. "Ethnomusicological Theory". *Yearbook for Traditional Music* 42: 100–34.

Sabuncu, Sabri. n.d. "Türk Halk Müziği Nazariyat" [Turkish Folk Music Theory]. Document.

Sağlam, Hande. 2008. "Cosmopolitans and Locals: Music Production of the Turkish Diaspora in Vienna". In *Music from Turkey in the Diaspora*, edited by Hande Sağlam and Ursula Hemetek, 37–48. Klanglese 5. Vienna: Institut für Volksmusikforschung und Ethnomusikologie.

Sağlam, Hande. 2009. "Transmission of Music in the Immigrant Communities from Turkey in Vienna, Austria". In *Music in Motion: Diversity and Dialogue in Europe*, edited by Bernd Clausen, Ursula Hemetek, and Eva Saether, 327–43. Bielefeld: transcript. https://doi.org/10.14361/9783839410745-019

Said, Edward W. 1983. *The World, the Text, and the Critic*. Cambridge, MA: Harvard University Press.

Sardinha, João, and Ricardo Campos, eds. 2016. *Transglobal Sounds: Music, Youth and Migration*. London: Bloomsbury Academic. https://doi.org/10.5040/9781501311994

Schoonvaere, Quentin. 2013. "Demografische Studie over de Populatie van Turkse Herkomst in België" [Demographic Study on the Population of Turkish Origin in Belgium]. Brussels: Centrum voor gelijkheid van kansen en racismebestrijding.

Sechehaye, Hélène, and Stéphanie Weisser. 2015. "The Gnawa Musicians in Brussels: A Cultural Reorganisation". *Brussels Studies* 90. https://doi.org/10.4000/brussels.1294

Seidlitz, Kirsten. 2017. "The Bağlama – Whose Instrument? Traditions and Changes in Playing Bağlama among Musicians from Turkey in Germany". In *Studia Instrumentorum Musicae Popularis V (New Series)*, edited by Gisa Jähnichen.

Series of the ICTM Study Group on Musical Instruments 5. Münster: readbox unipress.

Sels, Liselotte. 2011a. "Turkse Volksmuziek in Gent: Casestudie van Een Muzikant: Fakı Edeer" [Turkish Folk Music in Ghent: Case Study of a Musician: Fakı Edeer]. *Intercultureel Centrum De Centrale*, 2011.

Sels, Liselotte. 2011b. "Turkse Volksmuziek in Gent: Een Overzicht" [Turkish Folk Music in Ghent: An Overview]. *Intercultureel Centrum De Centrale*, 2011.

Sels, Liselotte. 2014. "Vijftig Jaar Migratie, Veertig Jaar Muziek: Een Reconstructie van de Geschiedenis van de Turkse Muziek in Gent" [Fifty Years of Migration, Forty Years of Music: A Reconstruction of the History of Turkish Music in Ghent]. *Brood en Rozen* 19(2): 4–35. https://doi.org/10.21825/br.v19i2.3556

Sels, Liselotte. 2017. "Mixing Multiple Tracks: Migration, Diaspora and Transcultural Music in Flanders". In *Made in the Low Countries: Studies in Popular Music*, edited by Lutgard Mutsaers and Gert Keunen, 37–47. Routledge Global Popular Music Series. New York: Routledge.

Shiloah, Amnon, and Erik Cohen. 1983. "The Dynamics of Change in Jewish Oriental Ethnic Music in Israel". *Ethnomusicology* 27(2): 227–52. https://doi.org/10.2307/851076

Signell, Karl L. 1977. *Makam: Modal Practice in Turkish Art Music*. Seattle: Asian Music Publications.

Six, Joren, Olmo Cornelis, and Marc Leman. 2013. "Tarsos, a Modular Platform for Precise Pitch Analysis of Western and Non-Western Music". *Journal of New Music Research* 42(2): 113–29. https://doi.org/10.1080/09298215.2013.797999

Slobin, Mark. 1992. "Micromusics of the West: A Comparative Approach". *Ethnomusicology* 36(1): 1–87. https://doi.org/10.2307/852085

Sloboda, John A., Susan A. O'Neill, and Antonia Ivaldi. 2000. "Everyday Experience of Music: An Experience-Sampling Study". In *Proceedings*. Keele University. http://www.escom.org/proceedings/ICMPC2000/Tue/Sloboda.htm (accessed August 12, 2020).

Sökefeld, Martin. 2008. *Struggling for Recognition: The Alevi Movement in Germany and in Transnational Space*. New York: Berghahn Books.

Somuncu, Mehmet, and Serdar Ceylan. 2015. "Folk Music, Local Dances and Summer Pasture Festivals in Rural Areas of the Eastern Black Sea Region, Turkey". *Coğrafi Bilimler Dergisi* 13(2): 79–92. https://doi.org/10.1501/Cogbil_0000000165

"Statistischer Bericht: Einwohnerinnen und Einwohner im Land Berlin am 31. Dezember 2013" [Statistical Report: Residents in the State of Berlin on December 31, 2013]. 2014. Berlin: Amt für Statistik Berlin-Brandenburg. https://www.statistik-berlin-brandenburg.de/Publikationen/Stat_Berichte/2014/SB_A01-05-00_2013h02_BE.pdf (accessed August 12, 2020).

Stekelbees – Ondersteboven (4/4) [Stekelbees – Upside Down]. 2008. Vol. 4. 4 vols. http://www.youtube.com/watch?v=DbqSFukY50s&feature=youtube_gdata_player (accessed August 12, 2020).

"Stekelbees Ondersteboven". n.d. Muziekarchief. http://www.muziekarchief.be/albumdetails.php?ID=44478 (accessed August 12, 2020).

Stirling, Paul. 1994. "Chapter Nine: Marriage". Turkish Village. http://era.anthropology.ac.uk/Era_Resources/Era/Stirling/Pages/Page_178.html (accessed August 12, 2020).

Stokes, Martin. 1992a. *The Arabesk Debate: Music and Musicians in Modern Turkey*. Oxford Studies in Social and Cultural Anthropology. Oxford: Clarendon Press.

Stokes, Martin. 1992b. "The Media and Reform: The Saz and Elektrosaz in Urban Turkish Folk Music". *British Journal of Ethnomusicology* 1(1) (January): 89–102. https://doi.org/10.1080/09681229208567201

Stokes, Martin. 1994. "Introduction: Ethnicity, Identity and Music". In *Ethnicity, Identity, and Music: The Musical Construction of Place*, edited by Martin Stokes, Jonathan Webber, and Shirley Ardener, 1–27. Oxford: Berg.

Stone, Ruth M. 1982. *Let the Inside Be Sweet: The Interpretation of Music Event among the Kpelle of Liberia*. Bloomington: Indiana University Press.

Street, John. 2012. *Music and Politics*. Cambridge: Polity Press.

Sümbüllü, Hasan Tahsin. 2016. "Melody Characteristics of Today's Minstrel (Âşık) Music". In *Music and Music Education from Ottoman Empire to Modern Turkey*, edited by Hasan Tahsin Sümbüllü and William Sayers, 42–46. London and Istanbul: AGP Academic Research.

Surkyn, Johan. 1993. "Migratiegeschiedenis en Regionale Herkomstverschillen bij Turkse Vrouwen in Vlaanderen en Brussel" [Migration History and Regional Origin Differences among Turkish Women in Flanders and Brussels]. Working paper. Brussels: Vrije Universiteit Brussel. http://interfacedemography.be/wp-content/uploads/2016/02/wpem1993-3.pdf (accessed April 8, 2021).

Swyngedouw, Marc, Pascal Delwit, and Andrea Rea. 2005. *Culturele diversiteit en samenleven in Brussel en België* [Cultural Diversity and Coexistence]. Leuven: ACCO.

Tekelioğlu, Orhan. 1996. "The Rise of a Spontaneous Synthesis: The Historical Background of Turkish Popular Music". *Middle Eastern Studies* 32(2): 194–215. https://doi.org/10.1080/00263209608701111

Tekelioğlu, Orhan. 2001. "Modernizing Reforms and Turkish Music in the 1930s". *Turkish Studies* 2(1): 93–108. https://doi.org/10.1080/14683849.2001.11009175

Testa, Alessandro. 2019. "Doing Research on Festivals: Cui Bono?" *Journal of Festive Studies* 1(1): 5–10. https://doi.org/10.33823/jfs.2019.1.1.23

Thomas, Anne Elise. 2007. "Intervention and Reform of Arab Music in 1932 and Beyond". Conference on Music in the World of Islam. Asilah.

Toprak, Ergülen. 2012. "Amerikalı Doktora Öğrencisinden Elektro-Saz Belgeseli" [The *Elektrosaz* Documentary of the American Doctoral Student]. TurkishNY: Leading Turkish-American Web Portal. 2012. http://www.turkishny.com/headline-news/2-headline-news/95390-amerikali-doktora-ogrencisinden-elektro-saz-belgeseli (accessed June 20, 2014).

Toynbee, Jason, and Byron Dueck, eds. 2011. *Migrating Music*. New York: Routledge. https://doi.org/10.4324/9780203841754

Tuna, Sibel Turhan. 2006. "Türk Dünyasındaki Düğünlerde Koltuklama ve Kırmızı Kuşak Bağlama Geleneği" [The Tradition of Fetching the Bride and the Red Girdle Wearing at Weddings in the Turkish World]. *Türk Dünyası Sosyal Bilimler Dergisi* 38: 149–60.

Türk Halk Müziği Repertuar Kurulu. n.d. "Değerlendirme Kriterleri" [Evaluation Criteria]. Turkish Radio and Television.

"Türk Konserleri – Turkse Concerten" [Turkish Concerts]. 2014. Intercultureel centrum De Centrale.

Turkish Cultural Foundation. 2014a. "Circumcision". Turkish Cultural Foundation. http://www.turkishculture.org/lifestyles/ceremonies/circumcision/tradition-of-circumcision-541.htm?type=1 (accessed August 12, 2020).

Turkish Cultural Foundation. 2014b. "Henna Party". Turkish Cultural Foundation. http://www.turkishculture.org/lifestyles/ceremonies/henna-party-539. htm?type=1 (accessed August 12, 2020).

Turkish Cultural Foundation. 2014c. "Landmarks in Life". Turkish Cultural Foundation. http://www.turkishculture.org/lifestyles/turkish-culture-portal/customs/landmarks-in-life-513.htm?type=1 (accessed August 12, 2020).

Turkish Cultural Foundation. 2014d. "Military Service and Leaving Home". Turkish Cultural Foundation. http://www.turkishculture.org/lifestyles/turkish-culture-portal/the-army/military-service-508.htm?type=1 (accessed August 12, 2020).

Turkish Cultural Foundation. 2014e. "Wedding Tradition". Turkish Cultural Foundation. http://www.turkishculture.org/lifestyles/ceremonies-536.htm (accessed August 12, 2020).

Uğurlu, Nurer. 2009. *Halk Türkülerimiz: Folklor ve Etnografya* [Our Folk Song: Folklore and Ethnography]. Cağaoğlu, İstanbul: Orgun Yayınları.

Ustuner, Tuba, Guliz Ger, and Douglas B. Holt. 2000. "Consuming Ritual: Reframing the Turkish Henna-Night Ceremony". *Advances in Consumer Research* 27: 209–14.

Uysal, Sabri. 2001. *Zum Musikleben der Türken in Nordrhein-Westfalen* [On the Musical Life of the Turks in North Rhine-Westphalia]. Gräfelfing: BuchVerlag Gräfelfing.

Van Hees, Kathleen. 2000. "Marokko En Turkije: Een Kans Om Bruggen Te Slaan". [Morocco and Turkey: An Opportunity to Build Bridges]. Thesis. Leuven: Hogeschool voor Wetenschap en Kunst.

Van Herreweghe, Arnold. 2014. "Vorig Weekend" [Last Weekend]. *Gentblogt.Be* (blog). July 25, 2014. https://gentblogt-archief.stad.gent/2014/06/25/vorig-weekend.html (accessed August 12, 2020).

Vanherwegen, Dries. 2008. "'Alleen Elvis Blijft Bestaan?' Een Beschrijvend Onderzoek Naar de Carrières van Vlaamse Professionele Popmuzikanten" [Only

Elvis Remains? A Descriptive Study of the Careers of Flemish Professional Pop Musicians]. Master's thesis. Leuven: Katholieke Universiteit Leuven.

Van Kerckem, Klaartje. 2014. "Bridging the Gap: How Ethnic Boundary Dynamics Shape Socio-Cultural Incorporation. A Case Study among Turkish Belgians". Doctoral dissertation. Ghent: Ghent University. https://biblio.ugent.be/publication/7008210

Van Kerckem, Klaartje, Bart Van de Putte, and Peter Stevens. 2013. "On Becoming 'Too Belgian': A Comparative Study of Ethnic Conformity Pressure through the City-as-Context Approach". *City & Community* 12(4): 335–60. https://doi.org/10.1111/cico.12041

Van Kerckem, Klaartje, Koen Van der Bracht, Peter Stevens, and Bart Van de Putte. 2013. "Transnational Marriages on the Decline: Explaining Changing Trends in Partner Choice among Turkish Belgians". *International Migration Review* 47(4): 1006–38. https://doi.org/10.1111/imre.12053

Van Lancker, An, Aurore Werniers, Carla Defrancq, Daisy Vandecaetsbeeck, Dieter Pollier, Elien Vernackt, Jolien De Ridder et al. 2009. "Diversiteit en Muziekonderwijs in Gent: Een Uitstekende Combinatie? Verslag van een Beleidsgericht Onderzoek" [Diversity and Music Education in Ghent: An Excellent Combination? Report of a Policy-oriented Study]. Ghent: Ghent University. https://demos.be/sites/default/files/diversiteit_en_muziekonderwijs_in_gent_0. pdf (accessed April 8, 2021).

Van Maele, Nele. 2008. "Onderwijsbeleid en Niet-Westerse Muziek" [Educational Policy and Non-Western Music]. Master's thesis. Brussels: Vrije Universiteit Brussel.

Vanmeerhaeghe, Maaike. 2013. "'Gastarbeiders, Welkom te Gent?': De Ontwikkeling van het Stedelijk Migrantenbeleid in de Stad Gent (1971–1988)" ["Guest Workers, Welcome in Ghent?": The Development of the Urban Migrant Policy in the City of Ghent (1971–1988)]. Ghent: Ghent University. http://lib.ugent.be/fulltxt/RUG01/002/060/216/RUG01-002060216_2013_0001_ AC.pdf (accessed April 8, 2021).

Vanparys, Wouter. 2002. "Het Turkse Verenigingsleven in Gent: Een Casestudy" [Turkish Club Life in Ghent: A Case Study]. Gent: Universiteit Gent. http:// lib.ugent.be/fulltxt/RUG01/000/825/259/RUG01-000825259_2010_0001_ AC.pdf (accessed August 12, 2020).

Varlı, Özlem Doğuş, and Mahmut Cemal Sari. 2017. "The Re-Construction of Music Text on the Turkish Instrument Bağlama". In *Studia Instrumentorum Musicae Popularis V (New Series)*, edited by Gisa Jähnichen, 299–312. Series of the ICTM Study Group on Musical Instruments 5. Münster: readbox unipress.

Vercoutere, Marc. 2005. "De Problematiek van de Multiculturele Samenleving Vanuit Stedelijk Perspectief: Casus Gent" [The Problems of the Multicultural Society from an Urban Perspective: The Ghent Case]. Master's thesis. Ghent: Ghent University.

Verhaeghe, Pieter-Paul, Koen Van der Bracht, and Bart Van de Putte. 2012. *Migrant Zkt Toekomst: Gent op een Keerpunt Tussen oude en Nieuwe Migratie* [Migrant Seeks Future: Ghent at a Turning Point between Old and New Migration]. Antwerpen: Garant.

Volkan. 2011. "Erkin Koray ve Elektro Bağlama" [Erkin Koray and the *Elektrosaz*]. *Dipsahaf Plak Deposu* (blog). http://www.dipsahaf.com/erkin-koray-ve-elektro-baglama/ (accessed August 12, 2020).

Vzw Mızrap. 1999. "Subsidieaanvraag" [Grant Application].

Wade, Bonnie C. 2004. *Thinking Musically: Experiencing Music, Expressing Culture.* Global Music Series. New York: Oxford University Press.

Yalçin, Hilâl, Ina Lodewijckx, Rudy Marynissen, and Rut Van Caudenberg. 2006. *Verliefd, Verloofd... Gemigreerd: Een Onderzoek Naar Turkse Huwelijksmigratie in Vlaanderen* [In Love, Engaged... Migrated: A Study on Turkish Marriage Migration in Flanders]. Steunpunt Gelijkekansenbeleid. https://www.steunpuntgelijkekansen.be/wp-content/uploads/33.-Verliefd-verloofd-gemigreerd-H.-Yalcin.pdf (accessed April 8, 2021).

Yaldızkaya, Ömer Faruk. 1990. "Emirdağ Yöresi Ağıtları" [Lamentations from the Emirdağ Region]. In *Ömer Faruk Yaldızkaya.* Afyonkarahisar. http://www.omerfarukyaldizkaya.com/emirdag_yoresi_agitlari.htm (accessed June 20, 2014).

Yaldızkaya, Ömer Faruk. 1995. "Emirdağ Türküleri" [Folk Songs from Emirdağ]. In *Ömer Faruk Yaldızkaya.* Afyonkarahisar. http://www.omerfarukyaldizkaya.com/emird_turkuleri.htm (accessed June 20, 2014).

Yaldızkaya, Ömer Faruk. 2006. *Emirdağ Türküleri* [Folk Songs from Emirdağ]. 2nd ed. İzmir: Analiz Matbaacılık.

Yaldızkaya, Ömer Faruk. 2018. *Emirdağ Yöresi Türkmen Ağıtları* [Turkmen Lamentations from the Emirdağ Region]. 2nd ed. Emirdağ Belediyesi Kültür Yayınları 5. İzmir: Kanyılmaz Matbaacılık Kağıt.

Yang, Xi. 2018. "History and Organization of the Anatolian Ašuł/Âşık/Aşıq Bardic Traditions". In *Diversity and Contact among Singer-Poet Traditions in Eastern Anatolia*, edited by Ulaş Özdemir, Martin Greve, and Wendelmoet Hamelink, 15–36. Istanbuler Texte und Studien 40. Baden-Baden: Ergon Verlag. https://doi.org/10.5771/9783956504815-15

Yöre, Seyit. 2012. "Kırşehir Yöresi Halk Müziği Kültürünün Kodları ve Temsiliyeti" [The Codes and Representations of the Kırşehir Region Folk Music Culture]. *Uluslararası İnsan Bilimleri Dergisi* 9(1): 563–84.

Appendix 1: Remarks on the Turkish Language

Table 1: Pronunciation of the Turkish letters

A	a	short "a", close to the "u" in "**but**"
C	c	like in "**John**"
Ç	ç	like in "**change**"
E	e	short "e", like in "**end**"
G	g	like in "**good**"
Ğ	ğ	pronounced as "y" ("**year**") between front vowels (e, i, ö, ü) pronunciation close to the French "r" between back vowels (a, ı, o, u)
I	ı	close to the *schwa* like in "**open**"
İ	i	short "i" like in "**winter**"
J	j	like in "**pleasure**"
O	o	short "o" like in "**not**"
Ö	ö	German "ö", close to the "u" in "**turn**"
R	r	rolled r
Ş	ş	like in "**shine**"
U	u	like in "**zoo**"
Ü	ü	German "ü"
V	v	like in "**voice**"
Y	y	like in "**you**"

Table 2: Turkish suffixes

-ler, -lar	Plural	*Adam* (man) → *adamlar* (men) *Türk* (Turk) → *Türkler* (Turks)
-(s)i, -(s)ı, -(s)ü, -(s)u	Compound nouns	*Kına gecesi* (henna night) *Türkü akşamı* (song evening)
-li, -lı, -lü, -lu	Place of origin	*Istanbullu*: born/living in Istanbul
-ci, -cı, -cü, -cu, -çi, -çı, -çü, -çu	Occupation (profes- sionally or temporarily)	*Davul* (drum) → *davulcu* (drummer) *Sanat* (art) → *sanatçı* (artist)
-lik, -lık, -lük, -luk	Forms a noun from adjective or noun (e.g., -ness, -hood, -ship)	*Aşık* (minstrel) → *aşıklık* (minstrelsy)

Appendix 2: Glossary of Turkish Terms

Abdal: Originally a mystical religious group settling in Anatolia from Khorasan (current Iran, Afghanistan, and Turkmenistan) during the twelfth century, which became associated with the Alevi-Bektashi form of Shiism. Historically as well as currently, they fulfil(ed) the social function of professional musicians.

Ağıt: Lamentation, often improvised and created for a specific mourning occasion.

Ağız: Literally "mouth"; the typical dialect, accent, timbre, singing style of a particular region (or by extension: of a particular singer or group).

Alevi: Literally "follower of Ali"; belonging to Alevism. Alevism is the main form of Shiism in the Ottoman Empire and contemporary Turkey. It is based on the teachings of the thirteenth-century mystic Haji Bektash Veli. The distinction between Shiism and Sunnism originates in a different vision on the succession of the Prophet.

Anadolu rock: Popular genre developing in the late 1960s and 1970s, drawing on the repertoire of Anatolian folk music, but displaying a musical idiom borrowed from Western rock and roll and pop music. The instrumentation involves a combination of Turkish and Western instruments, and the lyrics are often politically engaged.

Arabesk: Hybrid melancholic-nostalgic genre with a strong influence from Arab music, particularly popular in the 1980s.

Aşık: Literally "in love"; itinerant poet-singer accompanying himself on the *bağlama*, prevailing in Eastern Anatolia, the Southern Caucasus, Iran, and Perso-Turkic Central Asia. The *aşık* repertoire consists of an ancient corpus of poetry and epics, and personal corpora of new poems created through improvisation. Most *aşıks* adhere to Alevism, although Sunni *aşıks* exist as well. Their historical social role involved the transmission of religious-mystical and moral traditions, as well as social criticism.

Asker uğurlama or asker düğünü: Ceremonial send-off party for young men leaving for military service, involving visits, presents or pocket money, a banquet, (traditional) music and dancing, and sometimes a parade through the village or neighbourhood.

Ayak: Literally "foot, base"; the folk music counterpart to the classical *makam* concept, developed in the context of Republican scholarly folk music research.

Bağlama (*saz*): Literally "binding"; long-necked folk lute existing in different sizes and with a shorter (*kısa sap*) or longer (*uzun sap*) neck. It possesses three double or triple strings which can be tuned in different ways, and 17 movable frets per octave.

Bendir: Frame drum with snare or jingles.

Bozlak: Literally "shouting out, crying out"; Central Anatolian, highly expressive *uzun hava* lamentation of Turkmen origins.

Cem: Literally "gathering" (Arabic); an Alevi (Shiite) religious ceremony.

Cemevi: "*Cem* house"; specific venue where Alevi *cems* take place, to be discerned from Sunni mosques.

Damat: Groom.

Davul: Large double-headed drum, played with a thick stick and a thin reed. Forms a fixed duo with *zurna*, played outdoors on traditional festivities in all regions of Turkey.

Dede: Spiritual guide in the Alevi community, who also leads the *cem* ceremonies.

Def: Frame drum.

Düğün: Wedding party. Also used for other kinds of ritual celebrations, especially the *sünnet düğünü* (circumcision party).

Elektrosaz: Modified *bağlama* with built-in pickup, developed during the 1960s and 1970s, and modelled upon the electric guitar.

Fasıl: Literally "division, chapter, season"; Ottoman classical suite of vocal and instrumental pieces in a particular *makam*, or modern or popular derivative of this kind of suite.

Gece: "Night"; used in compositions such as *türkü gecesi*, *sıra gecesi* or *Suvermez gecesi*.

Gelin: Bride.

Gelin alma: "Taking the bride"; the last part of a Turkish wedding ceremony, during which the bride is fetched by the groom's family to her new home.

Halay: Fast line dance occurring in Central, East, and Southeast Anatolia, accompanied by *davul* and *zurna*.

Halk: Folk, people.

Halk aşığı: "Folk *aşık*"; an *aşık* belonging to the social stratum of the "common people".

Halk müziği: Folk music.

Halk ozanı: "Folk *ozan*"; an *ozan* belonging to the social stratum of the "common people".

Haram: Forbidden by Islamic law.

Hoca: Originally a religious-spiritual master; also "teacher" (religious or general), or specialist.

Horon: Folk dance of the Black Sea region, danced in lines or circles, and characterized by a fast tempo.

Kaşık: Musical instrument (idiophone); wooden spoon used in pairs to create a percussive sound.

Kayın: "Family-in-law"; used to indicate a part of a wedding ceremony, during which mutual visits are paid by the families of the bride and groom.

Kemençe (Karadeniz kemençesi): Literally "small bow" (Persian); a bowed lute with three strings tuned in fourths, typical of the Black Sea region. It is played vertically, whether sitting or standing.

Kına gecesi: "Henna night"; a fixed part of a wedding ceremony, taking place at the bride's home the night before the wedding, traditionally representing the farewell of the bride to her female relatives and friends.

Kırık hava: Literally "broken air"; metrical folk song. Used in contrast with *uzun hava*.

Kısa sap: Short neck (*bağlama*).

Makam: Concept belonging to Ottoman classical music. Literally "site, locality"; musical mode characterized by a specific intervallic structure, tonal hierarchy, and melodic development (*seyir*, "course, route").

Muhtar: Elected head of a village or of a town or city district.

Nişan töreni: "Engagement ceremony"; a fixed part of a wedding ceremony, taking place at the bride's home, originally celebrated a certain period before the actual wedding, but in contemporary society often integrated into the wedding party.

Oyun havası: Dance tune (literally "dance air"). Can be purely instrumental (*sözsüz*: "without words") or vocal-instrumental (*sözlü*: "with words").

Ozan: Poet-singer, accompanying himself on the *saz* (or its predecessor the *kopuz*). Central Asian concept related to the concept of *aşık*. Contemporary usage of the term usually refers to composing poet-singers, in contrast with improvising *aşıks*.

Özgün müzik: Literally "unique, original, authentic music"; a kind of alternative music or leftist protest music developed in the 1960s and 1970s, with a musical idiom close to that of traditional folk music.

Saz: "Musical instrument" (Persian); also used to indicate the most common folk instrument: the *bağlama*.

Semah: Literally "listening" (Arabic); a ritual dance performed during the Alevi *cem* ceremonies, characterized by turning movements. It is related to the *semah* of the Sufi lodge of the "whirling dervishes".

Seyran: Literally "promenade" or "picnic"; in contemporary usage an open-air festival involving live music performances.

Sıra gecesi: Literally "turn night"; originally a traditional social event in the city of Urfa in the southeast of Turkey, involving live music and poetry, and characterized by an intimate atmosphere and participation from the audience.

Sünnet: Literally "tradition, custom" (Arabic); nowadays referring to Islamic circumcision.

Sünnet düğünü: "Circumcision party"; a large-scale family celebration, usually taking place several months or even years after the actual circumcision.

Şenlik: Festivity, party.

Şölen: Feast, banquet.

Tavır: Literally "manner", "attitude"; specific stylistic features and playing techniques belonging to a particular region (or by extension: to a particular singer or group).

Türkü: Literally "belonging to the Turks" (originally "Türki"); generic and specific denotation for (a kind of) Turkish folk poem or song. The general form of a *türkü* is syllabic, metrical, and consisting of stanzas (*bent*) and choruses (*bağlama* or *kavuştak*).

Türkü bar (türkübar) or türkü evi (türküevi): "Folk song bar" or "folk song house"; a specific type of music café becoming popular in the 1990s in

Istanbul and other major cities in Turkey, which was later copied in smaller towns and even in the diaspora. Mainly Turkish folk music and *özgün müzik* are performed in these venues, which usually display rural Anatolian decorative elements.

Türkü gecesi or türkü akşamı: *"Türkü* night" or *"türkü* evening"; musical evening consisting mainly of Turkish folk music, sometimes also *özgün müzik*, typically performed in a *türkü* bar, but nowadays also occurring in other settings, including more formal concerts.

Uzun hava: Literally "long air"; non-metrical folk song. Used as opposed to *kırık hava.*

Uzun sap: Long neck (*bağlama*).

Yayla or yaylağ: Literally "summer quarters"; mountain meadow, the place where nomadic shepherds and cattlemen and their family dwelled during the summer months to have their livestock pasture. The "winter quarters" were called *kışlağ.*

Zakir: Literally "he who remembers (God)" (Arabic); *bağlama* player during the Alevi *cem.* The *bağlama* is sometimes called *"telli Kuran"* ("stringed Quran").

Zeybek: Symbolic dance from the Aegean Sea region, linked to a culture of resistance against the Ottoman authorities during periods of war or repression. The *zeybeks* and their leaders (*efeler*) belonged to guerrilla troops. The music is in slow or moderate tempo with a rhythm of nine beats.

Zurna: Shawm, double reed instrument with straight conical bore. Forms a fixed duo with *davul* and is played outdoors on traditional festivities in all regions of Turkey.

Appendix 3: Attended Events

Table 1: Overview of the studied musical events (Ghent)

Date	City or town	Location	Short description
23 Oct. 2011	Ghent	Vrijdagmarkt	Cultural festival
2 Dec. 2011	Ghent	Muzikantenhuis	Turkish evening
3 Dec. 2011	Rupelmonde	Salon De Schepper	Circumcision party
15 Jan. 2012	Ghent	Concert hall of De Centrale	*Türkü* night
28 Jan. 2012	Ghent	Concert hall of De Centrale	Open day of intercultural centre
29 Jan. 2012	Ghent	Concert hall of De Centrale	*Türkü* night
10 Feb. 2012	Ghent	Muzikantenhuis	Turkish evening
16 Mar. 2012	Ghent	Venue of Turkish Union of Belgium	Karaoke evening of student club
16 Mar. 2012	Ghent	Muzikantenhuis	Turkish evening
8 Apr. 2012	Nazareth	Ömeroğlu Salon	Wedding party
18 Apr. 2012	Temse	Salon De Rietgors	Suvermez night
30 Apr. 2012	Ghent	Concert hall of De Centrale	*Türkü* night
8 May 2012	Ghent	Reading café of De Centrale	Café concert
18 May 2012	Ghent	Reading café of De Centrale	*Türkü* night
18 May 2012	Ghent	Muzikantenhuis	Jam session
20 May 2012	Ghent	Concert hall of De Centrale	Student festival of world music school
25 May 2012	Ghent	Dance room of De Centrale	*Cem*
27 May 2012	Wachtebeke	Provincial domain Puyenbroeck	Open-air festival (*seyran*)
1 Mar. 2013	Ghent	Music café Mızrap	Official opening of music café
27 Oct. 2013	Ghent	Concert hall of De Centrale	Celebration of 50 years of Turkish migration

Table 2: Overview of the studied musical events (Turkey)

Date (2011)	Province – City/village	Location	Short description[1]
6 June	Izmir – Izmir (city)	*Türkü* bar	*Türkü* night
9 June	Muğla – Milas (town)	Room in the centre	Spending time with a friend
9 June	Muğla – Milas (town)	Courtyard of a hotel	Wedding party
10 June	Muğla – Milas (town)	Alley in the centre	Circumcision party
15 June	Afyon – Emirdağ (town)	Tea house	Spending time with friends
16 June	Afyon – Emirdağ (town)	Restaurant of Teachers' House	Celebration end of school year
17 June	Afyon – Emirdağ – Bağlıca (village)	Trout farm-restaurant	Celebration end of school year + graduation
18 June	Afyon – Emirdağ – Türkmenakören (village)	Courtyards of two houses	Wedding party
19 June	Afyon – Emirdağ – *yayla*	*Yayla*	Visiting old friends
21 June	Kırşehir – Kırşehir (city)	Clubhouse of Fenerbahçe supporters	Musical evening of soccer supporters club
22 June	Kırşehir – Kırşehir (city)	Classroom of folk dance association	Folk dance lesson
22 June	Kırşehir – Kaman (town)	Streets and square	Official opening of cultural association + festival
23 June	Kırşehir – Kırşehir (city)	*Türkü* bar	*Türkü* night
24 June	Kırşehir – Boztepe (town)	Courtyard of house	Wedding party (first day): *kayın*[2]
25 June	Kırşehir – Boztepe + Mucur (town)	Street and courtyards of houses	Wedding party (second day): engagement ceremony, *kayın*, henna night
25 June	Kırşehir – Mucur (town)	Garden of house	Wedding party (second day): *rakı* night
26 June	Kırşehir – Boztepe + Mucur (town)	Street and courtyards of houses	Wedding party (third day): *gelin alma*
26 June	Kırşehir – Çebişler (village)	Street and courtyard of house	Wedding party
26 June	Kırşehir – Tatarilyas (village)	Living room of house	Sharing emotions with family and acquaintances

30 June	Sivas – Sivas (city)	Room of *aşık* and folk dance association	Training of *aşıklık* skills with peers
30 June	Sivas – Sivas (city)	Amphitheatre in city centre	Summer festival
3 July	Sivas – Beypınar (village)	*Cemevi*	Official opening of *cemevi + cem*
3 July	Sivas – Çetinkaya (village)	Festival domain	Summer festival
6 July	Trabzon – Trabzon (city)	Tea garden of Teachers' House	Spending time with friends and colleagues
7 July	Trabzon – Ocaklı – *yayla* (village)	*Yayla*	Summer festival
8 July	Artvin – Şavşat (town)	Private polyvalent room	Spending time with friends and acquaintances

Appendix 4: Visited Institutions and Consulted Informants in Turkey

2011

- Çanakkale: music school. Informant: Akif Mungan (*bağlama* teacher).
- Izmir: Ege University. Informants: Hakan Cevher (Turkish classical music teacher), Abdürrahim Karademir (folk dance teacher), Tarkan Erkan (teacher), Zeynel Demir (*bağlama* teacher), Fatma Reyhan Altınay (teacher), Selim Gülay.
- Muğla-Dibekdere: Dursun Girgin (musician and *muhtar*).
- Muğla: Ibrahim Ethem Yağcı (musician and researcher).
- Emirdağ: Mehmet Özkan (*muhtar*); Halil Rıfat Aydemir, Pınar Halaç (musicians).
- Emirdağ-Karacalar: Aşık Yoksul Derviş.
- Emirdağ-Aşağıpiribeyli: Aşık Bayram Karagöz.
- Kırşehir:
  - o Department of Tourism and Culture. Informants: Ayşegül Kayaoğlu (head of department), Süleyman Can (employee)
  - o Hoy-Dek Folk Dance Association. Informant: Ali Ünsal
  - o Levent Derinyol, Eren Gün, Yüksel Şahin (musicians).
- Sivas:
  - o Department of Tourism and Culture. Informant: Solmaz Kadıoğlu (head of department)
  - o *Cemevi.* Informant: Ali Akyıldız (director)
  - o Şentürk İyidoğan (*bağlama* maker and musician)
  - o Aşık Özlemi (female *aşık*)
  - o Cumhurriyet University – Music Education Faculty. Informant: Zekeriya Kaptan (*bağlama* and choir teacher)
  - o *Aşık* & Folk Dance Association. Informants: *Aşık* Erkani, *Aşık* Kulfani, *Ozan* Efsani.

- Sivas-Ulaş: *Cem & Kültür Evi.* Informant: Ismail Şeker (musician).
- Sivas-Sivrialan: Aşık Veysel museum (birthplace).
- Sivas-Şarkışla: Ahmet Şatıroğlu (musician, son of Aşık Veysel).
- Sivas-Beypınar: *Cemevi.*
- Giresun: Giresun Municipal Conservatory (music school).
- Trabzon: Teachers' House. Informants: Ihsan Eyüboglu, Erol Uzun (musicians).
- Rize: Municipality. Informants: Halil Balcı (employee); Mehmet Güney, Şakir Zurnacı, Resul Karaaslan (musicians).
- Artvin-Şavşat: Ziya Aytekin (musician).
- Ardahan-Çıldır:
  o Ferhat Uzunkaya (researcher)
  o Aşık Mehmet/Erkani, Aşık Israpil/Seyyati.

2012

- Emirdağ: Mehmet Özkan (*muhtar*); Halil Rıfat Aydemir, Pınar Halaç (musicians); Adnan Durmaz (retired teacher).
- Emirdağ-Karacalar: Aşık Yoksul Derviş.
- Emirdağ-Aşağıpiribeyli: Aşık Bayram Karagöz.
- Eskişehir:
  o Halis Erenoğlu (musician)
  o Emirdağ House of Culture
  o Emirdağlılar Foundation.
- Ankara:
  o TRT Radio House
  o TRT General Management. Informants: Kubilay Dökmetaş (head of broadcasting department), Altan Demirel (member of repertoire committee), Sabri Sabuncu (employee).
- Kırşehir:
  o Ayvaz Başaran (*abdal* musician)
  o Municipality.
- Kırşehir-Kaman: Adem Göçer (*abdal* musician).
- Muğla-Dibekdere: Dursun Girgin (musician and *muhtar*).
- Izmir: Ege University. Informants: Abdürrahim Karademir (folk dance teacher), Hale Yamaner Okdan (researcher)

Index

abdal 15, 27, 44, 65–67, 73–74, 90,
121–26, 149–50, 164, 226–27, 231,
235, 245
Aegean Sea Region *61*, 67, 71, 81, 108–9,
112, 117, 122, 127, 151, 244, 249
ağıt 28, 59, 68, 75, 100–101, 232
ağız 60, 77, 80, 84–85, 92, 164
Alevi 27–28, 35, 65–71, 112–17, 121,
127–28, 148, 231–32, 235–36, 242,
245, 248
    cem 27, 35, 63, 68, 96, 101, 112–17,
114, 141, 151, 155, 207, 230–31,
248
    cemevi 27, 101, 112–17, *114*, 116,
145, 207, 231, 233, 248
    cem house *see cemevi*
    music 7, 27, 59, 68–70, 127, 141,
151, *151*, 213, 227, 230
Ali (imam) 68–69, 113–14
amplification 48–49, 66, 78, 123–24, 135,
153, 162, 164, 199, 228, 250
Ankara 12, *63*, 71, 81–82, 84, *86*, 150–51,
152, 169, 227, 250–51
anonymity 83–85, 89–92, 222, 246, 251
arabesk 26, 67, 124, 153, 165
art music *see* classical music
asker düğünü 98, 249
aşık 18, 63–68, 73–74, 84–85, 131–33,
132, 149–50, 223–24, 226, 231, 246,
248
    café 64–65, 102

festival 65, 132, 224
    music 59, *62*, 64, 67–68, 90–91, 132,
155, 222
Aşık Veysel Şatıroğlu 64, 91, *93–94*, 128,
151
Atatürk 1, 54, 75, 79, 114, 133, 138, 222,
239

bağlama 60–63, 68, 91–92, 153, 162, 165,
167, *179–87*, 198–99, 227–28, 239, 245
Balkans 12, *62*, 63, 81–82, 151, 165, 248
Bektashi 63, 65, 68–69, 241
bendir 40, 42, 123, 127, 153
Black Sea Region *62–63*, 65, 85, 91–92,
117–20, 151, *151*, 153, 169, 179–83,
204, 247–48
bozlak 66, 74, 123

Central Anatolia 12, *61–63*, 71, 102–3,
121, 131, *151*, *152*, 153, 167, 169,
226–27, 231
circumcision party 26, 35, 65, 73, 96–98,
108–12, 144–45, 167, 217, 223–27,
231, 247–48
clarinet 73, 104, 134, 136, 153, 164
classical music
    light Turkish 15, 23, 136, 202, 242
    Turkish 15, 26, 56–58, 67, 69, 73, 76,
80–84, 87, *88*, 202
    Western 1, 159, **159**, *160*, 228, 250
commercial music *see* popular music

composition 56, 58, 64, 84, 87, 114, 116, 131, 155, 168, 228, 247
conservatoire, Turkish music 1, 2, 22, 28, 61, 73, 81, 130
in Europe 36
cosmopolitanism 1, 2, 27, 96, 202, 221, 234–35

darbuka 22–23, 40, 42, 73, 104, 122–23, 127, 130, 136–37, 153
davul 65, 73, 100–5, 107–9, 111–12, 117–20, 122–23, 153, 167, 224, 226–27, 231–32
De Centrale (Intercultural Centre) 21–23, 27, 29, 33, 40–48, 52–53, 114–16, 135, 155, 224
dede 35, 52, 68, 113, 115–16, 231, 248
def 28, 73, 123, 153
diaspora 1–5, 25–29, 37–39, 116–17, 128–30, 133, 136–38, 166–68, 202, 218–20, 221–37, 240
didactics 5, 41–44, 115, 236
drone 56–57, 109, 158
düğün see wedding party
düzen see tuning

Eastern Anatolia 12, 33, 105, 127, 139, 151, *151*, 202
education, Turkish folk music 17, 20, 22–23, 29, 41–45, 53, 130–31, 133, 245
elektrosaz 26, 110, 153–54, 157, 164, **164**, 169, 188, 194, 199, 228
Emirdağ 10–12, 14–15, 25, 39, 71–75, 79, 133–37, 151, *152*, 183–88, 227, 236, 245
Emnalar, A. 54, 64, 67–69, 91, 247
engagement ceremony 99, 103, 105–7
Ertaş, Muharrem 66, 91, 131, 247
Ertaş, Neşet 20, 65–67, 90–91, 131, 150, 203, 227, 247
ethnic boundary 13, 29, 137, 226, 234
evening, Turkish *see türkü* night

festival 7, 25–26, 144–45, 167, 249
Gentse Feesten 15–16, *16*, 34, 241
rural 25, 117–21, *118*, *120*, 248
seyran 25, 33, 46, 119–20, *120*
urban 25, 121–26, *123*, *125*, 235

flamenco 126, 129, 165
folk dance 18, 23, 25, 117, 119, 122, 130–31, 133, 151, 224, 231
France 3, 10, 133, 147
function, musical 5, 78, 102, 108, 139–40, 200–20, 226, 229–32, 249, 251

gelin alma 100, 107
Germany 2, 4, 6, 17, 24, 36, 66, 81, 148, 230, 236, 243
Greve, M. 4–5, 157, 236, 240, 242
guitar 17, 26, 36, 40, 49, 110, 119, 124, 153, 162, 165, 198, 227
Gypsy music *see* Roma

halay 105, 110, 119, *120*, 122
Hannerz, U. 30–31, 242
henna night *see kına gecesi*
heterophony 56–57, 156
horon 117–18, *118*
Hussein (imam) 69, 114–16
hybridity 1, 3–5, 14, 26, 29, 92, 125, 156, 159–61, 222, 235, 239

Ibıdıklar (family of musicians) 14–16, *15*, 26, 29, 134, 136–37, *136*, 241
identity 3–5, 68–69, 116, 121, 200–203, 206–7, 210, 213–14, 222, 229–30, 234–36, 239
improvisation 56–58, 64, 66, 75, 78, 92, 97, 100–101, 131–32, 155, 168, 228
Istanbul 5, 12, 48, 82–83, 113, 148, 157, 234

Karahasanoğlu and Skoog 5, 157, 250
kaşık 73, 123, 153
kaval 28, 73, 92, 153
kemençe 91, 118, 153
kına gecesi 28, 74, 85, 99–100, 103, 105, *106*, 107, 148
kırık hava 57–59, 77, 81–82
Kırşehir 65–66, 73–74, 102, 121–23, 130–31, 133–34, 150–51, *152*, 188–94, 227, 247, 250
Kurdish music 27, *151*, 230, 235

lamentation *see ağıt*

284 *Turkish Folk Music between Ghent and Turkey*

life cycle *see* ritual
lullaby *see ninni*

makam 57–58, 61, 76, 78, 242, 246
Markoff, I. 58–60
mehterhane 121–22, 124–26, *125*
Merriam, A. 139, 200, 228, 249
mersiye 59, 69, 114–15
metre 56–60, 70, 75–77, 85, 91–92,
    93–94, 131, 162, 164, 244
    free 57–59, 75, 244
microtonality 55, 57, 85, 87, 90, 92, 153,
    162, 188, 195, 228, 245
migration 1, 2–4, 10–12, 221–22, 236–37
    labour migration 10–11, 16–17
minority, cultural 15, 27, 34, 71, 80, 92,
    96, 125–26, 138, 233, 235, 239
Mızrap (music café) 20, 23–24, 43–44, 48,
    51–52, 51, 244
mobility 29, 227, 233
modality 55–58, 70, 74, *74*, 157, 159–60,
    162, **164**, 170, 198, 228
Mohammad (prophet) 68–69, 113
monophony 56–57, 76, 91, 158
Morocco 10–12
Muzikantenhuis (music café) 20, 23–24,
    33, 38, 40, 43–44, 48–52, 127–30, *129*,
    244
mysticism 19, 63–65, 68–71, 113, 124,
    203–4, 207, 211, 216–17, 230, 241,
    248

nationalism 27, 80, 92, 122, 129, 133,
    137–38, 221, 225, 232, 240, 242
Netherlands, The 3, 10, 16, 29, 36, 110,
    119, 126, 133, 147–48
Nettl, B. 139, 200, 228, 249
ninni 28, 59, 97, 247
nişan töreni see engagement ceremony
Nketia, J. H. K. 6–7
notation 78, 80–92, 228
    transcription 81, 85, 88–90, 170
    use of 42–44, 75–76, 199, 228

ornamentation 43, 55, 58, 60, 77–78, 155,
    158–59, 162, 194, 198
oyun havası (dance tune) 59, 81–82

ozan 44, 63, 65, 91, 131–32
özgün müzik 24, 48, 51, 124, 127–29, 150,
    223, 227, 232, 242

Pir Sultan Abdal 64, 112–13, 248
popular music 1–3, 5, 26–27, 49, 67, 73,
    129, 150, 198, 222, 232
professionalism 2, 27–28, 35–37, 44,
    52, 60, 101, 130, 148–49, 212, 226,
    231–32, 234

rakı night 103, 107, 159–60
Ramadan 101, 223–24, 232, 248, 250
Reinhard, K. 59
Reinhard, U. 6, 58
ritual 96–101, 104, 107, 110–16, 120–21,
    138, 140–42, 208, 217, 224–26,
    230–31, 243
Roma 65–67, 101, 108, 121, 148–49, 226,
    231
    music 22, 27, *151*, 165

semah 59, 69–70, 113, 115–16, 134, 147,
    248
Shiism 27, 65–66, 68, 114, 226, 239, 241
Shiloah and Cohen 228–29
Sivas 64, 112–14, 131–33, 151, *152*,
    204–7, 248
Southeastern Anatolia 74, 151, *151*
standardization 2, 60, 114, 116, 158–59,
    162, 164, **166**, 179, 199, 222–23,
    227–28
Stokes, M. 5, 59–60, 91–92, 157, 200,
    223, 236
Stone, R. 6–7
Sufism *see* mysticism
sünnet düğünü see circumcision party
synthesizer 26, 40, 73, 108, 153, 162, 164,
    167, 183, 227, 250

tavır 43, 60–61, *61–63*, 84–85, 92, 134,
    154, 157, 162, 164, 226, 246
Tını *see* Muzikantenhuis
transnationality 3, 5, 13, 27, 29, 66,
    137–38, 221–22, 224, 231–34, 236–37,
    248
TRT *see* Turkish Radio and Television

tuning 41, 55, 57, 60, 76, 157, 160, 195, 228
Turkish Radio and Television 1, 2, 6, 69, 73, 77–95, 170, 175, 194–99, 222–23, 227, 246–47
Turkmen 65–66, 71, 248
türkü bar 5, 23, 48, 126–30, 225, 227, 232–33, 235, 244
türkü gecesi see türkü night
türkü night 96, 126–30, *127, 129*, 162, 225, 232

ud 26, 73, 92, 136
uzun hava 57–59, 74–75, 77–78, 81–82

value, musical 200–203, 209–10, 218–19, 251
Van Kerckem, K. 13, 249

Van Maanen, H. 200–202, 219, **220**, 229
variation, musical 41, 58, 75, 78

wedding party 14–17, 26–28, 98–100, 102–8, 138, 159–60, 164–65, 167, 188–94, 208, 224–27, 231
women 14, 27–28, 75, 97, 99–101, 103, 109–10, 113–15, 148, 226, 233
world music 38–39, 47, 129, 165

yayla 74, 117, *118*, 120, 233

zakir 63, 68, 70, 113, 115–16, 152, 231, 248
zeybek 7, *61*, 109, 112, 151, 244
zurna 40, 73, 102–5, 107–9, 111–12, 117–20, 122–23, 152–53, 167, 224, 226–27, 231–32